Management
Consulting

Management

Consulting

Delivering an Effective Project

Third Edition

PHILIP WICKHAM
LOUISE WICKHAM

FT Prentice Hall
FINANCIAL TIMES

An imprint of **Pearson Education**

Harlow, England • London • New York • Boston • San Francisco • Toronto • Sydney • Singapore • Hong Kong
Tokyo • Seoul • Taipei • New Delhi • Cape Town • Madrid • Mexico City • Amsterdam • Munich • Paris • Milan

Pearson Education Limited
Edinburgh Gate
Harlow
Essex CM20 2JE
England

and Associated Companies throughout the world

Visit us on the World Wide Web at:
www.pearsoned.co.uk

First published 1999
Second edition published 2004
Third edition published 2008

ISBN: 978-0-273-71184-1

British Library Cataloguing-in-Publication Data
A catalogue record for this book is available from the British Library

10 9 8 7 6 5 4 3 2
11 10 09 08

Typeset in 9.5/12pt Stone Serif by 35
Printed and bound in Great Britain by Ashford Colour Press, Gosport, Hants

The publisher's policy is to use paper manufactured from sustainable forests.

To Ella and Louis

Brief contents

Contents

Supporting resources

Visit **www.pearsoned.co.uk/wickham** to find valuable online resources

For instructors

■ Complete, downloadable Instructor's Manual
■ PowerPoint slides that can be downloaded and used for presentations

For more information please contact your local Pearson Education sales representative or visit **www.pearsoned.co.uk/wickham**

Preface

Consulting is one of the most interesting, exciting and challenging of management roles. For those who can meet its demands, it is one that can bring great financial, professional and intellectual rewards. The skills a consultant develops are highly valuable. Consultancy demands a focus on thorough and insightful analysis, the achieving of well-defined objectives, a concern with utilising resources productively and communicating ideas in a way which influences people. The value of skills like these is not confined just to the narrow delivery of a formal consulting project. They are valuable in management generally. Work in non-profit situations can also benefit from recognition of the benefits a consulting approach can bring. For this reason, a consulting project offers a valuable learning opportunity for students of business and management. It provides a chance to develop skills that will be of use whatever career path is pursued.

The management skills good consultants bring to their projects are rich and varied and draw from a broad range of business disciplines. The consultant must offer an ability to analyse information, to lead and manage projects, often of great complexity, and to build productive relationships with people. The consultant must integrate these abilities into a professional approach to taking advantage of new business opportunities and positively meeting business challenges. This book aims to offer comprehensive support to students who wish to develop these skills through the undertaking of a consulting exercise as part of their learning programme. It will be of value to undergraduates and full-time postgraduates. Its insights and practical advice will also be valuable for post-experience students and students undertaking part-time programmes. The book will also be of use to students undertaking work-based and distance-learning programmes.

Although the book is primarily aimed at students of management, it recognises that students studying many other disciplines face management challenges. It will be of interest to students studying general management and specialist management areas such as marketing, human resource management, operations management and finance. It will also be of interest to students who are studying technical disciplines (such as engineering, computing and information technology) who expect consulting and offering advice to managers to be an important element in their professional life. In addition to those on formal learning programmes, the book will offer insights to practising managers who are eager to learn, particularly those who wish to capitalise on the growing demand for an internal consultancy approach to management tasks in rapidly changing organisations.

Effective consulting, like any form of good management, knits together intellectual understanding and performance abilities. A consulting exercise is most profitable as a learning experience if it does three things. First, if it offers an opportunity to develop a deep conceptual understanding of the critical issues all businesses face in today's increasingly competitive world. Second, if it provides a means of applying that understanding to take advantage of real business situations. Third, and most importantly, if it allows the learning gained to be applied to future management practice.

The first and second editions of *Management Consulting* have occupied an almost unique niche in providing students with the tools to undertake a consulting project, while at the same time providing a framework for new professional practitioners to use. With this in mind, we have again reorganised the material and significantly added to the tools and techniques to make this practical as well as intellectually rigorous. This has been helped in no small measure by the addition of new contributors, most notably Louise Wickham, an experienced consultant with more than 20 years' business experience.

Reflecting the international nature of business in general, and consulting in particular, there is a brand new chapter (Chapter 4) on consulting across borders and cultures by Jeremy Wilcock. Jeremy has nearly 30 years' business experience, all of it with a major British multinational company. He has a Postgraduate Diploma (with Distinction) in Export Marketing and is a long-standing member of the Institute of Export. He has held senior positions in Export Sales and Marketing, International Development, Business Re-engineering, and Strategic Planning. Since 2002 he has been engaged in an academic-related post at the University of Hull Business School, as a Business Development Manager working with the School's corporate partners, and as an Associate Lecturer. Chapter 7 on contracting, influence and team leadership by Kevin Parker is also new. Kevin, after holding senior HR positions in the motor industry, and as a Partner in a large consultancy, is now a Director of an independent consultancy, Socrates Coaching. He works as a 1:1 coach, trainer and consultant in the areas of leadership, performance and teamwork with senior teams in the public and private sector. The chapter on evaluating client capabilities and business opportunities (Chapter 6), contributed by Margaret Dewhurst and Tony Kellett of Boardroom Associates, is also a major rewrite from earlier editions with new techniques. Margaret and Tony are the founders and Directors of Boardroom Associates, a consultancy focused on board level work. Margaret has worked as a consultant for 20 years, mainly in the technology area. Tony has run a number of technology companies, including turn-rounds, taking one from concept to flotation, and has been on many boards.

The other new sections are Chapter 2, which explores in more detail the different types of consulting projects, and Chapter 3, which has more on the selling process of consulting, something that was lacking in earlier editions. Chapter 13 on post project and learning from the project has also been expanded in order to give more insight into consulting from a professional point of view. Chapter 14 on the consulting industry gives students a greater insight if they wish to pursue a career in this industry, which remains a popular destination for graduates. At the end of each chapter is now a short case exercise, many of which are new. Finally, there is a longer case study that runs throughout the book on a major consulting exercise undertaken at the Robinson Mason company. The latter is designed for the student to utilise the knowledge learned in the preceding chapters.

All of these changes are in a large part due to the reviewers of the second edition who gave us many valuable comments and feedback as to how we could improve the text. We would like to thank them for their contributions as well as Jeremy, Kevin, Margaret and Tony for their critical input that was delivered in a prompt and professional manner. Finally, we would like to thank the team at Pearson, particularly Matthew Walker, for all his help and support and without whom this would not be possible.

A live consulting project can be one of the most interesting, challenging and rewarding aspects of a programme of management study. This book aims to help you make the best of it and make the best out of it.

Philip Wickham
Louise Wickham
March 2007

A note on the layout of this book

The management of a consulting project calls on a variety of skills. Effective delivery can be supported by a number of management techniques. This book aims to give an insight into these skills and techniques in a way that makes their use practical and guides practice in using them. Consultants must integrate their skills. The tasks that make up a consulting project cannot be split so that one skill can be used in isolation from the others. People skills must be used to support analysis. Good project management enables relationships to be built. Effective analysis ensures that the project progresses towards delivering the desired outcomes on time and on budget.

A consulting project does not call on skills in a sequential way. One does not follow another. However, a book must, by its very nature, relate them in a linear manner. So there is no one 'right' way to detail the skills and techniques a consultant might use. All that can be hoped is that the organisation of the book is coherent, consistent and logical. We hope this book achieves this. The structure of this text is different to that of the first and second editions. This is based on experience. The revised sequence has been found to be more successful as the basis of a lecture series on management consulting and conducting a project than was the initial structure.

Students who wish to use this book actively to support the consulting exercise will want to work their way through the book in a linear way, especially if it supports a lecture course. To assist this, the book is split into four parts. Part One (Chapters 1–4) is concerned with consulting in its managerial context. It aims to provide foundational ideas that integrate the subject of management consulting into a coherent whole. A central theme of this book is that effective management consulting is based on the integration of three types of skill: analysis skills that enable new opportunities and possibilities to be identified on behalf of the client organisation, project management skills that enable those ideas to be delivered to the client organisation under budget and time constraints, and relationship building skills that sell ideas and provide the leadership that takes the client team forward. Part Two, project definition and analysis (Chapters 5–7), considers the factors that a student should look at to successfully start a project, including vital people and analysis skills. Part Three, undertaking the project (Chapters 8–11), considers the project management and relationship-building skills together as these are not readily separated.

But these skills only work in harmony. The tutor and student will find that they will need to dip in and draw out ideas from different parts at different times if they are actually engaged in a live consulting exercise. The final part of the book

(Chapters 12–14), delivering the product to the client, considers communicating the outcome of the project and learning from the project. It also looks at consulting as a profession and some of its recent developments. Furthermore, it provides a guide to major consulting firms and the career structures they offer. The text contains cross-references to other chapters in which related ideas are covered, or which expand on the original material.

The book aims to be comprehensive and self-contained. A number of pointers are given in the text to the excellent books and journal articles that develop further the ideas presented here. These works are listed in suggestions for further reading. To emphasise their relevance to particular ideas, these are now at the end of individual chapters rather than at the end of the book. The interested student is encouraged to increase his or her understanding by exploring these original works.

An Instructor's Manual and PowerPoint slides to accompany the book are available for lecturers to download from **www.pearsoned.co.uk/wickham**.

Acknowledgements

We would like to thank the following reviewers who contributed to the development of this text:

Naomi Birdthistle, University of Limerick; Keith Harrison, Nottingham University; Caroline Hodgson, Liverpool Hope University; John Kawalek, University of Sheffield; Martin Lindell, Swedish School of Economics, Helsinki; and Uly Ma, London South Bank University.

Publisher's acknowledgements

We are grateful to the following for permission to reproduce copyright material:

Figure 2.2 from The Institute of Risk Management. A Risk Management Standard © AIRMIC, ALARM, IRM 2002; Figure 3.3, Dilbert Cartoon 1998-08-24 Copyright © Scott Adams, Inc./Dist. by UFS, Inc., reproduced by permission; Figure 4.2 from Kotler, Philip; Keller, Kevin Lane, *Marketing Management: Analysis, Planning, Implementation And Control*, 12th Edition, © 2006, p. 680. Reprinted by permission of Pearson Education, Inc., Upper Saddle River, NJ; iSixSigma LLC for Table 5.3, The Cause and Effect Diagram (a.k.a. Fishbone) by Kerri Simon. Copyright © 2000–2007 iSixSigma LLC – all rights reserved; Figure 6.2 adapted with the permission of The Free Press, a Division of Simon & Schuster Adult Publishing Group, from *Competitive Strategy: Techniques for Analyzing Industries and Competitors* by Michael E. Porter. Copyright © 1980, 1998 by The Free Press. All rights reserved; Figure 6.3 from Hax, Arnold C. and Wilde, Dean L., *The Delta Project: Discovering New Sources of Profitability in a Networked Economy*, 2001, Palgrave Macmillan, republished with permission of Palgrave Macmillan; Figure 6.4 reprinted by permission of *Harvard Business Review*. Adapted from Figure 1.1: Translating Vision and Strategy – Four Perspectives from 'Using the balanced scorecard as a strategic management system' by Kaplan, R.S. and Norton, D.P. (Jan–Feb 1996). Copyright © 1996 by the Harvard Business School Publishing Corporation; all rights reserved; Figure 6.6 reprinted by permission of *Harvard Business Review*. Exhibit 1: The Ansoff Matrix from 'Strategies of diversification' by Ansoff, H.I. Issue No. 25(5), Sept/Oct 1957. Copyright © 1957 by the Harvard Business School Publishing Corporation; all rights reserved; Table 9.1, Table 9.2 and Table 9.3 adapted from Hayes, J. and Allinson, C.W. (1994) 'Cognitive style and its relevance for management practice', *British Journal of Management*, 5, 53–71 © Blackwell Publishing; Figure 10.3 reprinted from *Long Range Planning*, Vol. 26, No. 26,

No. 6, P.J. Idenburg, 'Four styles of strategic planning', pp. 132–37, Copyright © 1993 with permission from Elsevier.

PART ONE

Management consulting in context and how it adds value

CHAPTER 1

The nature of management consulting and how it adds value

Learning outcomes

The main learning outcomes from this chapter are to:

- understand the nature of management consulting as a managerial role;
- appreciate the nature of the client–consultant role relationship;
- recognise the responsibilities of the consultant;
- understand what *motivates* a business manager to bring in a consultant;
- recognise the ways in which a consultant can *add value* for a client business;
- understand the things a consultant can *offer* a client business by way of value-creating support.

1.1 What a management consultant does

Management consulting is, as its name suggests, a management *activity*. But it is a special form of management. Many would regard it as one of the most exciting of management challenges. It is certainly one of the most demanding. The upside of this is that it can also be one of the most rewarding – not just financially (though the rewards here can be high indeed for good consultants) but also in terms of task enjoyment, satisfaction with achievements and intellectual stimulation.

A management consultant is rewarded for going into an organisation and undertaking a special project on its behalf. Usually the organisation is a profit-motivated commercial venture. But it does not have to be. It can be an organisation of any type. Consultants are also (and increasingly) called upon to offer their services to non-profit organisations such as charities. Governmental and non-governmental organisations, whether local, national or international, also make frequent calls on the skills of management consultants.

The types of project undertaken by consultants are as varied as management itself. They may involve the proffering of specialist technical expertise, such as the development of information technology systems. Some projects may be 'softer' and aim at generating cultural change within the organisation. In some cases they may have the objective of resolving internal conflicts within the organisation. They may be concerned with helping the organisation build relationships with outside parties. In other instances, they may aim to help the organisation gain some critical resource. Often they will be focused on some specific issue that has been recognised by the organisation's management and has been well defined. In many instances, though, they are of a broad 'business development' nature. The extent to which the client organisation has specific objectives in mind varies greatly. Most projects will involve gathering and analysing information and sharing discoveries with the organisation. Usually the management consulting project is undertaken over a relatively short time scale – say weeks or, at most, a few months. Increasingly, however, projects with a longer time scale (up to a year or more) are in demand.

In short, a management consultant offers his or her management abilities, expertise and insights to the client business in order to *create value for it*. Consulting activity is something that the client business decides to buy in. It represents a *factor* that managers decide they need in order to progress their business and improve its performance. As a factor that is bought in, consulting activity competes with all the other factors a business must buy in if it is to grow: money for investment, people and their skills, raw materials and the equipment necessary to deliver what the business offers. The client will find the service the consultant is offering attractive only if it is something that the business cannot provide for itself. Further, it must be the *best* investment option on offer given all the other things the business could buy in.

This means a consultant must understand a number of things from the outset. Clearly, the consultant must know why what he or she is offering will be of value to the client business. Although important, this is not enough. Consultants must also know why what they are offering represents a good *investment opportunity* for the business given all the other investment opportunities available. This forms the basis of what the consultant can 'sell' to the business. As with any form of selling to organisations, the selling is most effective when the underlying *buying process* is appreciated. 'Organisations' do not buy – individuals within them do. The way in which individuals react, interact and influence each other must be taken into account when delivering a consulting exercise. In short, the consultant must recognise what he or she will enable the business to do in its marketplace, why the business cannot do this for itself and how the individuals who make up the business can unify around the project.

Although management consultancy is seen as a specialist management role, the consultant must have the skills of a general manager. He or she must not only be able to undertake specific (and often technical) projects, he or she must also be able to market what they offer (not forgetting that marketing includes the development of the actual consulting 'product' as well as its promotion), sell the product to clients and manage a relationship with them. This is a challenge. But if it is met effectively the rewards can be great. Consultants often enjoy fast-track careers. Experience in consulting provides such a fast 'learning curve' that they quickly mature as managers and can take on high-level roles, even when quite young. For the ambitious manager, investing in developing the skills that make a consultant effective offers the potential of considerable rewards.

1.2 Consulting and management roles

Given that consulting represents a special form of management, it is necessary to have a preliminary understanding of what management is. The nature of management is subject to a great deal of discussion. A traditional approach defines management in terms of the *functions* the manager undertakes. For example, Henri Fayol, a management thinker of the early twentieth century, decided there were five such basic functions: planning, organising, staffing, directing and controlling.

Planning

Planning is concerned with deciding a future direction for the business and defining the courses of action and projects needed to move the organisation in that direction. Planning varies greatly in its level of formality. A simple project with few tasks and low resource requirements will demand only a minimum of consideration and documentation. A major project with complex, and perhaps risky, outcomes will require a considerable degree of time and effort in its planning. Its implementation will involve complex communication networks drawing together a large number of managers.

Formal planning techniques may be advantageous if project organisation is to be effective. Different businesses differ in their approach to planning and the degree to which it is formalised as a management activity. As well as the nature and complexity of the project and the significance of its outcomes, organisational style, culture and individual management traits will be important determinants in the approach to planning.

Organising

The organising function relates to the overall structuring of the business. Roles, responsibilities and reporting relationships are defined for individuals and sub-groups. In strategic terms this means ensuring that the organisation's structure is appropriate for its strategy and environmental situation. The organisation's structure dictates the way in which it will work and how it will use its capabilities. This is sometimes referred to as the strategy–structure–process fit. This topic is reviewed well by Van de Ven and Drazin (1985).

Staffing

Staffing is the function concerned with making sure that the business has the right people in place. It ensures that its people have the right skills in order to undertake the projects the business needs to carry out to be successful. In modern organisations the staffing function is often integrated into a broader human resource management function. Key elements of the human resource strategy are recruitment and training. Additional elements will include establishing remuneration, career development and staff motivation policies.

Directing

Directing relates to the process of encouraging people to undertake the tasks necessary to deliver the project outcomes the business needs. Originally it referred to the management function of instruction or delegation to subordinates. A modern interpretation would be broader and would include a manager's responsibilities as a leader and motivator of individuals and teams and the creator of a supportive organisational culture.

Controlling

Managers use resources. Resources, be they money, people or productive assets, must be utilised in the best way possible. Controlling is the function that is concerned with making sure that the right resources are in place, that they are being used effectively and that their use is properly accounted for.

Traditionally, controlling was largely about *budgeting*, that is financial control. Now a broader interpretation would regard it as the process of focusing the business towards its goals through the implementation of an appropriate *strategy*. This strategy will direct the utilisation of all the business's resources and the development of its capabilities. A strategic perspective sees resources more broadly than the traditional 'money–labour–machinery' view. Dynamic aspects like organisational knowledge and learning are regarded as resources as well. The consultant engages directly at this resource level.

This traditional approach to the nature of management has been criticised because it offers an idealised image of what the manager actually does. It pictures the manager as 'above' the organisation, coordinating its activities in a detached way, progressing it towards some well-defined, rational end. In fact, most organisations are not like this at all. Managers cannot detach themselves from their organisations; they are very much part of them. The organisation defines the manager as much as the manager defines the organisation. They must work with limited information and make decisions using intuition as much as formal analysis. The ends they work towards may be motivated as much by implicit and emotional drives as explicit and rational ones.

The Canadian management theorist Henry Mintzberg spent a long period observing how managers actually worked. In his groundbreaking 1973 book, *The Nature of Managerial Work*, he suggested that a more productive approach was to look at the *roles* managers actually undertake rather than the *functions* they are supposed to undertake. He suggested that there are ten such roles, which fall into three groups: *interpersonal* roles, *informational* roles and *decisional* roles.

Interpersonal roles relate to the ways in which managers interact with other organisational members. It is through interpersonal roles that managers draw their power and authority. The three key interpersonal roles are the figurehead, the leader and the liaison.

The figurehead

The figurehead role is the one in which the manager represents his or her organisation, or the part of it for which he or she is responsible, in a formal manner. This role draws on the responsibilities defined in a job description, though traditional activities, informal elements and unwritten expectations may also play an important part in characterising the figurehead role. The figurehead role is very important for entrepreneurs and the manager of a small business.

The leader

The leader role refers to the manager's interaction with subordinates. It is the role the manager is playing when he or she is delegating tasks, motivating people to undertake these tasks and supporting them in achieving them. Leadership is different to authority. Authority arises from a position within an organisational hierarchy. This position makes leadership possible, but it does not guarantee it.

The liaison

Many managers have a responsibility for representing the business to the outside world. Sales people, procurement managers and finance specialists in particular have important responsibilities in this way. The liaison role is the one in which managers interact with people from other organisations. The critical responsibility is one of gaining some resource for the business such as, for the management roles noted, customer goodwill, essential productive factors or investment capital.

Managers must make decisions on behalf of their organisations. Indeed it might be argued that decision-making is a manager's fundamental responsibility. To do so they must make use of available information on both the internal state of the business and what is happening in its environment. *Informational roles* are concerned with obtaining and manipulating the information the business needs. The three critical informational roles are the monitor, the disseminator and the spokesperson.

The monitor

The monitor role is that which leads the manager to identify and acquire information on behalf of the organisation. It may also involve the processing and storage of that information so that it is readily available for use by decision-makers. Analysis is a critical task for the monitor. The production of sales statistics, accounts and market intelligence are important tasks for the monitor.

The disseminator

Managers do not work in isolation. Information must be shared with others in the organisation. The disseminator role is concerned with making sure that available information is passed on within the organisation to information processors and decision-makers. Dissemination occurs through a variety of means. Reports, meetings and presentations represent formal means of dissemination. Unofficial 'grapevines' are often a very influential way of disseminating information informally. Monitors may also take on disseminator roles, but this is far from inevitable, especially in larger organisations.

The spokesperson

The spokesperson is also involved in disseminating information, but to the outside world rather than internally. Important spokesperson roles are taken on by sales and marketing staff, who tell customers about what the company has on offer, purchasing managers, who let suppliers know what the company needs, and financial managers, who let investors know about the company's status and prospects.

The third class of roles, *decisional roles,* are involved in identifying a future direction for the organisation, defining the projects needed in order to get it there and dealing with the crises that tend to knock it off the path it must follow while getting there.

The entrepreneur

The entrepreneur role is concerned with shaping and making decisions that lead the organisation forward in a significant way. Mintzberg uses the term entrepreneurial in a broader sense than it is used in traditional management theory. In Mintzberg's sense, the entrepreneur need not be an owner or founder of the organisation. Any manager can take on the entrepreneurial role, not just those who set up and own businesses. An entrepreneurial decision is one that aims to exploit an opportunity or address a threat. Such a decision may be significant, but it is not usually pressing at the time. It encompasses the activities of conventional entrepreneurs and what have come to be known as *intrapreneurs*, managers who take an entrepreneurial approach within an established business.

The entrepreneurial role demands that information be taken from those undertaking the informational roles and then used to identify new opportunities and new ways of doing things. To make entrepreneurial decisions really happen will demand effective use of the interpersonal roles. The entrepreneurial decision-maker takes resources and makes good use of them, even if it means he or she may be exposed to risk. Critically, the entrepreneurial role is concerned with driving change. The organisation is not the same after the entrepreneurial decision-maker has finished with it.

The disturbance handler

Organisations tend to establish and then follow set patterns of behaviour. They find their own ways of doing things and stick to them. This is known as organisational inertia. A fixed pattern of working will produce satisfactory results provided that there is no change in either the organisation's internal state or its external condition. If change does occur, the organisation's way of doing things may no longer produce the desired results. Such a change is known as a disturbance.

Disturbances can arise from internal events such as intergroup conflicts or the loss of a critical person from the organisation. External disturbances usually result from the organisation losing access to an essential resource. This might be loss in sales income from an important customer or group of customers. The cause of this may be a customer moving to a competitor or going out of business. The loss of an important input from a supplier also represents a disturbance. Disturbances can also arise if an investor loses faith in the business and pulls out investment capital. This can be critical for fast-growing entrepreneurial businesses.

The opportunities and threats the entrepreneurial decision-maker addresses are long term. Disturbances, on the other hand, demand immediate attention. The business will suffer a reduced performance or even fail if they are not dealt with promptly. A disturbance is often referred to as a management crisis. Organisational inertia conditions management's response to a crisis. Often, the first reaction of managers when faced with a crisis is to try to replace the missing resource and so keep the organisation in its original state. Maintaining the status quo when the organisation has been knocked off track by a disturbance is the responsibility of the disturbance handler.

The kinds of project the disturbance handler undertakes will depend on the type of disturbance affecting the organisation. Disturbance handlers may attempt to resolve intergroup conflicts. If a critical resource such as a customer, supplier or investor is lost, they will lead the search for a suitable replacement.

Disturbance handling is not a continuous role. It comes into play only when a crisis happens. Some managers may be predisposed to deal with certain crises as a consequence of their roles: sales managers, for example, will be in the front line if an important customer is lost; purchasing managers will lead the way in finding a new supplier. If the crisis is significant enough, conventional relationships can be driven into a state of flux. Recrimination and organisational politics can arise. Eventually new roles and even new leaders may emerge. Leaders often come to the fore in a crisis. Sometimes the projects undertaken to deal with disturbances will be successful. The organisation may be able to return to its original state. Often, though, the crisis will be too great and the organisation's ability to respond too limited. In this case the organisation will need to make functional and structural changes in order to survive in the changed circumstances it faces.

The resource allocator

Businesses consume resources. They do so in order to pursue the opportunities that present themselves. These resources are valuable and must be used in the best way possible if the business is to be successful. Few businesses face a simple yes or no answer when considering future possibilities. It is not the cost of investing in a project that matters so much as its opportunity cost: the returns that might have been gained if the resources invested in the project had been invested elsewhere.

Managers must decide which of the opportunities that offer themselves is the best one at a particular time. In practice this means that managers must decide how to allocate the resources they have to hand across a variety of projects. This consideration resolves itself into a series of immediate and practical tasks. For example, should the business invest in that advertising campaign or would the money be better spent on a new sales representative? Should export efforts be directed at the Far East or are the developing economies of central Europe likely to offer a better return? Should investment be directed at a new product, or might it be more profitable to acquire that competitor? It is questions like these that managers must address every day. In doing so they are taking on the resource allocator role. As with the entrepreneurial role, the resource allocator is dependent on the informational role in order to make good decisions about where resources are best placed.

The negotiator

People come together and work in organisations because value can be created by differentiating and coordinating tasks. The extra value created must, however, be shared both within organisations and between the different organisations that come into contact with each other. Individuals and organisations must be active in advocating their right to a particular share of resources available. This advocacy is reflected in the negotiator role. Sometimes this role is concerned with sharing resources with outside organisations. The sales manager will negotiate with customers. The purchasing manager will negotiate with suppliers. Finance managers will negotiate with investors and lenders. Sometimes it will be concerned with the internal allocation of resources. Personnel managers will negotiate remuneration packages with employees. Managers will negotiate with resource allocators in order to gain a budget for investment in the projects they wish to see happen.

Not all negotiations are so formal. Many negotiations take on an informal character. They may manifest themselves as unofficial 'understandings' between managers about how resources will be shared. Organisational politics is often both a consequence of, and limited by, unofficially negotiated outcomes. It should not be thought that all negotiations are a 'zero-sum' game: that if one party wins, the other must lose. Effective negotiators look for win–win solutions. Nor is effective negotiation about taking a stance and holding to it. It is more about identifying what is wanted out of a situation and then being flexible in finding ways to achieve what is wanted.

Any one management role will have a profile that combines some or even all of these ten pure roles in a particular way. The way in which these roles define the profile of management responsibilities within the organisation will depend on a range of factors. The organisation's size will be a critical determinant. The bigger the business and the more managers it employs, the greater will be the latitude for managers to specialise. In a small business, a single entrepreneur may take on most, if not all, the roles at some time or other. In a large multinational corporation, managers may be in a position where their roles will be more narrowly defined.

The complexity of the organisation and its environment will also be important. Complexity refers to the amount of information managers must process before making a decision. If complexity is high, informational roles will be important and it may be necessary to have managers dedicated to these roles. A fast-growing organisation undergoing rapid change may present a special leadership challenge and demand that particular attention be paid to interpersonal roles. The profile of management roles will reflect the organisation, the stage in its evolution and its environmental situation.

1.3   The client–consultant interaction

The consultant *is* a manager. We must understand the nature of the consultant's tasks in terms of them being *management* tasks. Like any manager, the consultant will at times take on many if not all of the ten roles defined by Mintzberg. The consultant's role parallels and integrates with that of managers within the client organisation. It is through the interaction of these roles that the client–consultant relationship is built.

The managers who make up organisations work in a network of relationships. These relationships exist between managers working within a particular organisation and between the managers in different organisations who come into contact with each other. The consultant who moves into an organisation must define the relationship he or she wishes to create with the managers who already work in the client business, and, often, with some of those in other organisations with which the client comes into contact. Two considerations will determine what sort of relationship this will be. These are:

■ the nature and structure of management roles in the client organisation; and

■ the objectives of the consulting exercise.

Every organisation is different and so is every manager. However, it is possible to see consistent patterns in the way in which managerial roles take shape. Different organisations will require a different profile of management roles. But every organisation will demand that managers carry out the interpersonal, informational and decisional roles in a way that is right for the business. These roles must be carried out with the correct degree of competence and in balance with each other.

The motivation to call in a consultant (a topic discussed fully in Chapter 2) arises because managers have identified a project that they think will benefit the organisation but they recognise that they are not in a position to deliver it themselves. The reason for their inability to deliver may be articulated in the form of resource or skill gaps. In entering to fill these gaps the consultant is offering to complement and develop the role profile within the organisation.

The managerial roles described by Henry Mintzberg provide a clue to the kind of interaction that will take place between the consultant and the client organisation's management team. We can use a visual metaphor to picture the ways in which a consultant can interact with and develop the business management role profile.

Think of the role profile as a triangle, with each apex representing one of the groups of roles. This is illustrated in Figure 1.1.

Using this simple diagram we can create a visual depiction of the five primary types of consultant–management role interaction: supplementing, complementing, differentiating, integrating and enhancing.

Supplementing

Supplementing involves the consultant adding to the existing skill profile to increase its capability but not alter its overall shape. The consultant is an additional resource who takes on a project that could well have been taken on by an existing manager had time been available. An example might be a business with a local sales base using a consultant with sales experience to test the possibility of expanding into a new area. Had a sales manager from within the company been available then he or she would have done the job in exactly the same way. In principle, the consultant could be recruited into the organisation and there would be little change in the way in which he or she operates and interacts with the rest of the organisation.

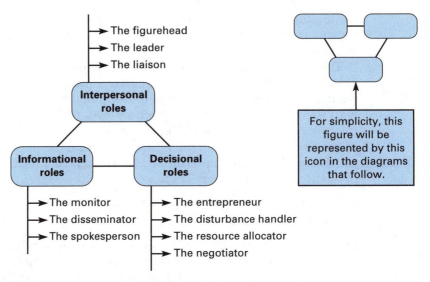

Figure 1.1 The managerial role profile

This type of consulting role offers a way of enabling the business to manage demand fluctuations in a low-risk way. The consultant allows the business to add and subtract human resources in a flexible manner. The consultant is neutral in development terms and does not aim to make any fundamental changes in the organisation. We can picture the supplementing role as a simple addition to the existing role profile (*see* Figure 1.2).

Complementing

Complementing occurs when the organisation notices a gap in its profile of management roles and asks the consultant to fill that role. This may require the consultant to specialise in any one of the basic role types.

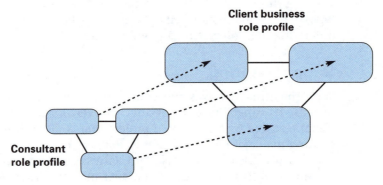

Supplementing involves the consultant simply adding to the role profile already present in the client business.

Figure 1.2 The consultant–manager role supplementing interaction

For example, a consultant may be required to complement the organisation's liaison role and develop the way it represents itself to the outside world. Projects that enhance the business's marketing approach or develop presentations to financial backers are important examples. Consultants can play an important role in supporting existing managers to improve leadership, through, say, the development of a unifying organisational mission.

A wide range of projects can involve the consultant complementing the informational role. Important examples might include marketing research and the setting up of management information systems. These projects will make demands on both the monitoring and disseminating aspects of the informational role. The consultant may also be active in supporting the spokesperson role. Developing communications aimed at customers and investors is the task of the public relations expert. Lobbyists may be employed to communicate and influence decision-makers in government.

The consultant can contribute to the decisional role in a variety of ways. Speculative business development projects, which explore a range of possibilities for the business in the future, complement the *entrepreneurial role*. A consultant may be called in as a *disturbance handler* to help the business's management deal with a crisis. The setting up of budgeting management control systems is an example of the consultant complementing the work of the *resource allocator*. Some consultants specialise in *negotiating* and can contribute to the way in which the business approaches important customers, suppliers or investors. The complementing role can be pictured as the consultant filling in a gap in the management's existing role profile. Figure 1.3 shows how this may be illustrated.

Differentiating

The overall profile of management roles will depend on a number of factors. The size of the organisation will be critical. The larger the business, the greater the latitude for allowing managers to specialise their roles. One aspect of the process of organisational growth will be an increasing tendency towards role specialisation.

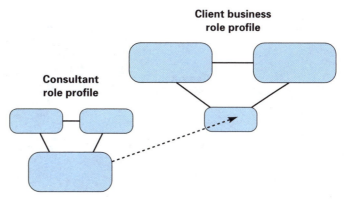

Complementing involves the consultant bringing along a role specialism to complement a weakness in the client business role profile.

Figure 1.3 The consultant–manager role complementing interaction

For example, a small business will tend to have a leading entrepreneur (perhaps with a high level of ownership) undertaking the decisional and the spokesperson roles. He or she may also have responsibility for the informational roles. As the business grows the entrepreneur can allow other managers to take on more responsibility. A sales and marketing function may emerge to take on the spokesperson roles and promote the product to customers. A management information system can be set up to monitor financial data and so supplement the informational role. The entrepreneur can also delegate certain areas of decision-making to subordinate managers.

This process of role differentiation is critical if the organisation is to grow successfully. It is only through such specialisation that the business can not only grow but also improve its performance as it grows. However, such differentiation is not always easy. Managers (not least successful entrepreneurs) often resist giving away areas of responsibility. They would rather use the organisation's growth to 'build their empire'. This can result in the manager having too large an area of responsibility, too much information to analyse and not enough time. Invariably, the quality of decision-making suffers.

Consultants can help facilitate the process of role differentiation. At one level this involves designing appropriate organisation structures, defining managerial responsibilities and setting up communication systems. But this is just the 'hardware' of the organisation. Managers must feel comfortable with their new responsibilities, be motivated to work within them and interact positively with colleagues. Changing the 'software' is a change management process calling upon a specialist type of consulting. This type of role differentiation can be illustrated as in Figure 1.4.

Integrating

Mature organisations are characterised by well-defined organisation structure and role responsibilities. These become established and are subject to organisational inertia. They may persist even when they are no longer appropriate. If the business's environment and competitive situation change then an evolution in the way the

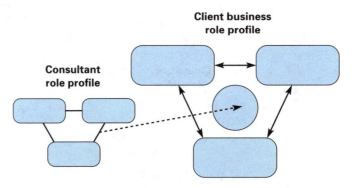

Differentiating involves the consultant helping the client business to differentiate its management roles and allow managers to specialise.

Figure 1.4 The consultant–manager role differentiating interaction

business does things may be called for. If environmental change is particularly fast, the occasional revolution may be called for. Such changes demand that the old role profile be broken down and a new profile allowed to emerge. The new roles may combine or integrate a number of aspects of the old roles.

An important recent trend in organisational change has been the shift from vertically ordered functions to horizontally ordered teams. Traditional departments such as marketing, finance, operations and the like have been supplemented, or even replaced, by small, multidisciplinary teams. The focus shifts to the team undertaking specific tasks rather than the department fulfilling fixed roles. This allows a more flexible response to the shifting needs of the marketplace.

This process makes a number of demands on managers. Of course, team working must be made effective (a topic discussed in Chapter 7), but there are more subtle demands as well. The hierarchical department offers a traditional path for promotion in the organisation. If it goes, managers may see no clear way for advancing and may become demotivated. If the team structure is combined with traditional functions (a structure known as a matrix organisation), managers may become disorientated at having two bosses (the team leader and the departmental manager). Such 'challenges' to the departmental manager's authority may also be a recipe for political infighting.

As with differentiating, the consultant called in to integrate roles into a new, more flexible structure must address both hardware and software issues. A new structure must be invented and the change management issues needed to motivate managers to work within it must be addressed. Role integrating may be illustrated as in Figure 1.5.

Enhancing

Enhancing is the most general type of role development process. It demands not so much that the role profile of the organisation be changed but that the manager's overall level of performance be improved. There are a variety of ways this might be achieved. Training of individual managers is usually an important part. This

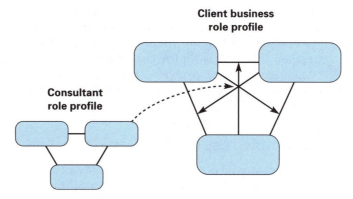

Integrating involves the consultant helping the client business to reorganise its management roles and build a new set of manager relationships and responsibilities.

Figure 1.5 The consultant–manager role integrating interaction

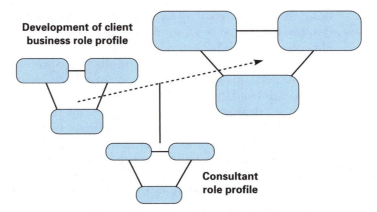

Development of client
business role profile

Consultant
role profile

Enhancing involves the consultant helping the client
management team improve the effectiveness
of their overall management role profile.

Figure 1.6 The consultant–manager role enhancing interaction

training may be directed towards improving technical and functional skills or may develop interpersonal skills such as motivation and leadership. Training may be supplemented through structural changes such as improved communication systems and attention to overall strategic understanding. The process of role enhancement is illustrated in Figure 1.6.

1.4 The responsibilities of the management consultant

All managers have responsibilities. They have responsibilities both to organisations and to the individuals who work in them. At one level, organisations are collections of individuals, so it is individual managers who must take on responsibilities on behalf of the organisations they work for. The consultant is in a special position. He or she must take on the responsibilities of being a manager, not just for the organisation they work for but also for the organisation they work with. It has been suggested (by Archie Carroll in an article in 1979) that managerial and organisational responsibilities operate at four levels. These may be referred to as the economic, the legal, the moral and the discretionary.

Economic responsibilities

The fundamental economic responsibility of the manager is to act in a way which is consistent with the long-term health of their business, and maximise its value for its investors. This is not to suggest that the manager, like the economist's perfect entrepreneur, simply tries to maximise short-term profits. Real-world managers do not have the information to behave like this. Short-term profits to investors may be diverted in order to fund reinvestment projects aimed to achieve growth and so deliver more profits in the future. Potential profits may be compromised if other responsibilities are given priority. An area of economics called *agency theory* suggests that the interests of managers and investors differ and that, under certain circumstances, managers will act in their own best interests. Given these constraints, it may still be properly said that the consultant's economic responsibility is to advocate only projects which genuinely seem, in light of the information available, to be in the best interests of the business as a whole, given its stated strategic objectives and the concerns of the stakeholders who have an interest in it.

Legal responsibilities

All businesses have a responsibility to operate within the rule of law. Laws provide the official 'rules of the game' through which businesses interact with each other. Legal systems around the world differ, but generally have two codes: the *criminal*, which the state takes responsibility for implementing, and the *civil*, in which the responsibility for initiating proceedings lies with individuals. Business activity is subject to both codes. Nowadays, most governments try to minimise the impact of legislation on business. In that legal restrictions impede business activity, they are seen as an evil, albeit a necessary one. Consideration of the impact of a new law on business is, these days, usually taken into account in the legislative process. This means that the laws that remain are usually there for a good reason.

The consultant has a legal responsibility to ensure that the activities of the organisation he or she is working for, and any activities he or she may advocate on its behalf, are legitimate in light of the criminal and civil laws to which the business is subject. The exact nature of this legal responsibility, and the extent to which the consultant may face recrimination if it is breached, will depend on the law involved, the consultant's contractual obligations and the degree of culpability for outcomes. Ensuring that this condition is met, especially when the business is operating in a highly technical area, or in a part of the world with a different legal system, can be quite challenging. In this case, taking legal advice from experts (not least about one's own responsibilities) may be an important part of the consulting exercise.

Moral responsibilities

Moral responsibilities go one step beyond legal ones. The societies in which businesses operate function on the basis of a whole complex of rules, norms and expectations. Some of these rules are written down in the form of laws or contractual agreements (which are often subject to civil law). But many are unwritten. They may not even be spoken. They are merely an understanding about what is 'right' and what is 'wrong'. They are expectations about how people should behave towards each other. These rules may not even be noticed – until they are broken!

Though it is not always made explicit, every society, and to some extent every distinct grouping within a society, has its own code of morality. These codes often relate to the way in which stakeholders will be treated, above and beyond simple contractual rights. For example, most managers feel a higher degree of responsibility to employees than their contracts of employment dictate. This can manifest itself in many ways. Losing people is painful: a business may retain people who are not absolutely necessary. Entrepreneurs who own their business may allow family members a greater performance latitude than non-family members.

Many cultures have their own distinct rule systems. In displaced ethnic groups, networking may be supported by moral expectations about the responsibilities of members of the community towards each other. Edicts on the way in which debt is structured are common, as are rules about reciprocity of favours. Recognising such moral codes is an important aspect of the consultant's job. The consultant must recognise that he or she is as subject to these moral responsibilities as to the legal ones. Moral responsibilities are not merely 'nice to have'. Ignoring them will limit the effectiveness of the consulting exercise. Outcomes which go against the moral expectations of the client will, at best, not be implemented. Outright rejection can often occur.

Discretionary responsibilities

Discretionary responsibilities are those the consultant decides to take on as part of a personal moral order. They are not responsibilities the industry would normally be expected to observe. Discretionary responsibilities usually relate to a refusal to work in certain project areas, or to work towards project outcomes of which the consultant does not approve. This may mean avoiding certain industry sectors or types of project. Typically, such discretionary responsibilities arise as a result of the consultant's personal concerns about a range of domestic political issues, the environment or business activity in the developing world.

Although this may mean that the consultant must occasionally turn down valuable projects, it can also be a means of differentiation from the values other (perhaps competing) consultants advocate. Discretionary values may make a consultant more attractive to certain individuals and organisations. There is nothing inconsistent in using discretionary responsibilities as a means of gaining an edge in the marketplace. Where discretionary values offer an edge they may eventually set the standard for consulting as a whole.

1.5   Types of client

In a 1997 paper, Edgar Schein suggested that process consulting can be enhanced by an appreciation of the different types of client involved. He suggested that the consultant interacts with a number of individuals within the client organisation and that the concept of the individual client may be problematic. Rather, the consultant interacts with a network of individuals who play subtly different roles. Schein proposed six such client types.

Contact clients

The contact client is the person, or persons, who first approach the consultant and propose the consultant addresses a problem or issue on behalf of the organisation. The contact client may or may not be involved in the final project engagement. Sometimes contact clients are themselves from outside the organisation, for example other consultants, business advisers or venture capitalists.

Intermediate clients

Intermediate clients are members of the organisation who become involved in the consulting project. They will work with the consultant and provide information. They will sit in on meetings and influence the way the project unfolds. Intermediate clients may be the actual recipients of the final report.

Primary clients

The primary client is the person or persons who have identified the problem or issue the consultant has been called in to address and who are most immediately affected by it. It is they who will be willing to pay in order to have the issue resolved.

Unwitting clients

Unwitting clients are members of the organisation who will be affected by the intervention of the consultant. They do not initiate the project and have no direct or formal control over it. They are not aware that they will be affected by the project.

Indirect clients

Indirect clients are members of the organisation who will be affected by the intervention of the consultant and who are aware that they will be affected. However, the consultant is not aware that the project will have an impact on them. Indirect clients may feel either positive or negative about the consultant's intervention. They can be very influential behind the scenes and, unbeknown to the consultant, can facilitate or hinder the progress of the project.

Ultimate clients

Ultimate clients are the total community that will be affected by the consultant's intervention. This will include members of the organisation and, possibly, members of the organisations which come into contact with the client organisation. The ultimate client group forms the universe of whose interests the consultant must take account when progressing the project.

1.6   Modes of consulting

All managers have their own approach to the tasks they face and the way they deal with people. This is an important factor in determining the manager's style. A critical element here is the perception the manager has about his or her fundamental role in the organisation. Consulting is also characterised by different approaches which reflect fundamental assumptions about the role of the consultant. These are referred to as *modes*. In his 1987 book *Process Consultation*, Edgar Schein characterised three basic modes based on the relationship between the consultant and client: the expert, the doctor–patient and the process consulting modes.

The expert mode

In the expert mode the client identifies a particular problem with the business, analyses the problem and articulates it to the consultant. The consultant then uses his or her expertise to identify a solution to the problem. This form of consulting is often found in areas where the consultant has a specialist knowledge which the client organisation recognises that it lacks.

The doctor–patient mode

The doctor–patient mode is also characterised by the consultant acting as an expert. In this mode, however, the consultant also takes responsibility for diagnosing the problem in the first place. The client may just express an opinion that the business 'could be better' in some way or that 'something is not quite right'. Again, the consultant is expected to contribute specialist knowledge and insights to the business.

The process consulting mode

Both the expert mode and the doctor–patient mode demand that the consultant, an outsider, offers a solution – a prescription – to address the problems that the business faces. Process consulting takes a different stance. It is based on the premise that the only people who can, ultimately, help the business are the people who make it up. The consultant, as an outsider, cannot impose a solution on the organisation. What the consultant can do, however, is assist those who make up the organisation with the process of recognising problems and then discovering the solutions to them. The consultant is not so much an expert, more a facilitator of change.

Schein makes a strong case of the process mode. This is for good reasons. Consultants can recommend better ways of doing things but these will become reality only if the people who make up the organisation feel that they have ownership of the new approach, that they have had a part in creating it and that it will work for them. A process approach to consulting helps ensure that the client organisation feels it is coming up with its own solutions to its own problems and so solutions which are right for its business. A note of caution is in order though. Consultants do bring along expertise and should not be frightened to recognise that they are doing so. Further, the client will often expect the consultant to show evidence of expertise and to 'take charge' of the issues the business faces. 'After all,' it is often heard said, 'that's what they are being paid for!' An over-reliance on a process approach can sometimes leave clients feeling that they have done all the work themselves. Indeed, by the very nature of the process mode, the more proficient the consultant is in using it, the greater the risk that the client will feel that the consultant has not made a 'real' contribution. Rather than advocate one mode as right in all circumstances the effective consultant recognises the advantages of flexibility. He or she learns when, and under what circumstances, to adopt each mode.

The decision to use a consultant

Why should a business manager ask the advice of an independent consultant? The decision is a significant one for a number of reasons. There may be an immediate financial cost. Leading management consulting firms have daily rates that are well into four figures. Even if the consulting is 'free' because it is being undertaken through an undergraduate consulting team, or the cost is being borne by a small business support agency, there may still be significant indirect costs. The consultant team may need money from the client to undertake marketing research, for example.

There will also be a cost due to the need to dedicate management time to the consulting exercise. If a consulting project is to be successful, the consultant team must be supported in their activities. They will need briefing sessions and regular review meetings. The management time that must be dedicated to this is valuable, especially in a small business. Also, the activities of consultants can be upsetting to the business as a whole. Consultants will disrupt a manager's routines. If not managed effectively their involvement can raise suspicions and lead to political infighting between managers. The cost of a consultant to the client must be thought of not just in terms of direct cost (amount of money paid) but also opportunity cost, what is missed because the money could have been spent elsewhere.

The decision to call in consultants is like the decision to buy anything else for the business. It happens after a consideration of the costs and benefits involved and a conclusion that the benefits outweigh the costs. This is not a one-off decision. It is something that the client business constantly assesses. Maintaining the client's confidence and the belief that the consultancy exercise has something of value to offer is a critical responsibility for the consultant.

This presents a particular challenge for *management* consultants. Consultants who work in highly technical areas such as computing and engineering clearly offer the business an expertise the business itself does not have. That they offer something different and valuable is evident. However, every business, without fail, will have *management* expertise. And the chances are (or at least the business will *feel*) that this expertise is greater than that offered by outsiders who have no knowledge of the business, its customers and its markets. In any case, even if the business recognises the need for additional management resources, why should consultants be used? Why not just employ more managers?

In short, the management consultant must constantly ask three fundamental questions:

1 What can I offer the client business that will enhance its performance and help it achieve its objectives?

2 Why will my contribution be more valuable than that which existing managers, and potential recruits, can contribute?

3 How can I communicate to the client business that what I offer is valuable?

Answering these three questions involves the application of analytical, project management and relationship-building skills. This chapter aims to set the scene for discussion of how these skills may be developed and applied by considering what a management consultant has to offer the client business. The actual outputs of a consulting exercise centre on providing one or more of six things: information, specialist expertise, a new perspective on problems, support for internal arguments, support in gaining a critical resource and the creation of organisational change. Each of these will now be examined in depth.

1.8   Provision of information

Managers make decisions. If those decisions are to be good ones, they must be based on a full and proper understanding of the business and its situation. Information is needed if decision-making is to be effective.

Some areas of information that are critical to a business include:

- the business's customers: their needs and buying behaviour;
- the business's products: their design, technology and development;
- the markets in which the business operates: their size, growth and dynamics;
- outside organisations (including suppliers) that can offer support: who they are, what they offer and how they can be contacted;
- the business's competitors: who they are, their strengths and the threat they pose.

Information is valuable to a business. As a result it has a cost. Information is a resource that must be managed. Much information has a direct cost – that obtained from market researchers, for example – while if there is no direct cost there may be a hidden cost in the management time and effort in gathering information. Even if managers are willing to face this cost they can do so only if they know what information is available, where it is stored and how it can be accessed. There is no guarantee they can do this. The consultant can offer the small business manager a service in providing him or her with information that can help the business. However, this is only the start of the consultant's service. Decisions are not made on the basis of hard data alone – those data must first be processed and interpreted. The consultant can add value by analysing and presenting information in a way that enables the business manager to make effective decisions from it. To do this requires the analysis skills that will be considered in Part Two of this book.

1.9   Provision of specialist expertise

Some managers, especially those running small businesses, must be generalists. The demands of managing a small business are such that managers cannot afford to specialise in a narrow area of management such as marketing, operations or finance. They must do all these things at once. This means that at times they will seek the advice of people with specialist knowledge.

Some important areas of management that can benefit from the insights and ideas of a specialist are:

- business strategy: its development, evaluation and planning;

- marketing strategy development: defining a successful marketing mix;

- marketing research studies: utilising sophisticated research methodologies;

- promotional campaign development: how to ensure that promotional drives are well designed and cost effective;

- new product development programmes: converting customer needs into a successful product offering;

- developing proposals for financial support: identifying and approaching backers and making a good case for their support;

- information systems development: enabling managers to get the information they need to make decisions;

- planning exporting and international marketing: providing the business with a valuable route to growth.

Projects such as these benefit from the application of technical knowledge and an ability to use specialist analysis techniques. Rather than have to learn these themselves managers will often call upon the support of consultants. The key to successful consulting in this area is not to make decisions on behalf of the manager but to *help* the manager in making their own. It is their business, they have a detailed knowledge of what it is about and know what it aims to achieve. This knowledge of the business is much greater than any the consultant can develop in the short time he or she will be working with the business. The consultant adds value by bringing along a 'tool-kit' of conceptual frameworks and idea-generating models that can be used to make sense of the information and knowledge the manager already has. This then enables the manager to make better decisions. The management of projects involving the provision of specialist expertise will be discussed further in Chapter 2.

1.10   Provision of a new perspective

Managers are not decision-making automata. They are human beings who must analyse complex environments, use well-developed but necessarily limited cognitive skills and then make decisions in the face of uncertainty. Managers use 'cognitive maps', 'mindsets' or 'dominant logics' through which they see their managerial world. These act to focus the manager's attention on certain aspects of their environment, select particular facts as relevant, link causes to effects and then suggest courses of action. Such cognitive schema are not rational decision-making devices. They manifest themselves as the manager's interests, priorities, prejudices and judgement. Cognitive schema become established and resist change. They determine the way managers see their organisations and competitors. They have a bearing on the way joint ventures are managed, for example. Interested students are referred to the articles by Caloris, Johnson and Sarnin (1994), Daniels, Johnson and de Chernatony (1994) and Prahalad and Bettis (1986) for illuminating discussions of these issues. In a study of what he refers to as 'groupthink', Irvin L. Janis (1982) examined in great depth decisions by US Presidents and close advisory groups that led to far-reaching policy errors in international affairs (such as the Bay of Pigs invasion of Cuba and the escalation of the Korean War). He concluded that seven defects in decision-making can arise when a group becomes over-coherent and begins to share expectations and norms:

1 The group's considerations are limited to a narrow range of options – possibilities outside this set are rejected out of hand or not considered at all.

2 The initial objectives to be fulfilled by the course of action are not reviewed or challenged.

3 Newly discovered risks are not used to challenge the initially preferred course of action.

4 Courses of action initially rejected by the group are not reconsidered in the light of new information.

5 The experience and expertise of external experts are not sought or considered.

6 When new information comes to light, the group emphasises and prioritises information that backs its initial hypotheses and ignores information that contradicts them – this is sometimes referred to as a 'myside bias'.

7 The group spends little time considering how bureaucratic inertia or organisational resistance might inhibit the implementation of chosen policies.

While Janis's examples are drawn from political decision-making, their relevance to organisational decision-making in general is not in doubt. The effective consultant should be aware of these factors and be prepared to challenge group thinking. In simple terms, managers, and close managerial groups, limit their problem-solving ability because they often get too close to an issue. They see it only in terms of their existing expectations, understanding and 'way of doing things'. The consultant can add value by helping the manager to step back from a problem, to see it in a different way and to see new means to its solution. Indeed, the consultant should ultimately aim to help managers see 'problems' really as opportunities to do things differently and perhaps better.

To do this the consultant may simply offer a fresh mind to an issue. Better still, the consultant can contribute some conceptual frameworks that open up thinking and aid the development of the manager's cognitive schema. Consultants can also offer support in helping individuals and groups become more innovative in their thinking by using the creativity techniques described in Chapter 9.

1.11 Provision of support for internal arguments

Managers do not always agree with each other. Disagreements arise over a wide range of issues. Conflicts of opinion take a variety of forms. They range from open, honest exploration of different options to often quite nefarious political intriguing. They can be seen as a refreshing opening of possibilities or they may lead to smouldering resentment. A manager may be tempted to use a consultant not so much to provide an impartial view but to back up his or her position in a debate. A consultant's opinion is of clear value here. It can be presented as 'independent' and as coming from an 'expert'. How should a consultant react to being used in this way?

The first thing to note is that the existence of different perspectives and a tolerance of dissent that allows them to be expressed is a healthy thing. Managers should be paid to think and express themselves and must be free to do so. In a competitive environment (in which ideas compete for resources) they should also be free to marshal whatever resources they can to make their case. This may include external consultants. A consultant must recognise that he or she is not employed by a company in the abstract but rather by *individuals* within a company. The decision to use consultants is made by a group or 'decision-making unit' within the business. (This idea is covered in detail in Chapter 10.) The consultant is responsible for delivering findings and advice to individuals, and must be sensitive to the interests of those individuals and what their objectives are. This may involve supporting them in internal debates. However, the consultant must be careful.

If the consultant is too obviously in the camp of a particular manager, his or her impartiality will be impaired. Other management groups may become suspicious and will find grounds on which to reject the consultant's advice. If the consultant is seen to be twisting facts to fit a particular position, his or her credibility will be damaged. At a minimum the consultant will lose the support and goodwill of other managers. This can make the consultant's job difficult and uncomfortable. So being called upon to support a particular position, especially when it is contentious, demands sensitive management on the part of the consultant.

A few useful ground rules are as follows:

■ Understand the 'politics' of the consulting exercise.

■ Be sensitive to who is supporting different positions in the organisation.

■ Recognise who will benefit and who will lose from the different options under discussion.

■ Make sure the objectives of the consulting exercise are clear and in the open.

■ Make sure any information used can be legitimated and any analysis undertaken justified.

■ Build rapport with the client (a skill discussed in Chapter 7) and be honest with the client about the strengths and weaknesses of his or her argument.

■ Introduce and explore options which reconcile different positions in a win–win way.

■ Provide the client manager with information and insights but allow him or her to make a particular case within the business – don't be tempted to advocate it on his or her behalf.

■ If put in a position where credibility might be lost, remind the manager that a loss of impartiality and credibility will defeat the point of using independent consultants in the first place!

1.12   Provision of support for gaining a critical resource

An organisation must attract resources in order to survive. One of the manager's most critical functions is attracting resources on behalf of the firm. Some important resources for the business include:

- the goodwill of customers;
- capital from investors;
- capital from government support agencies;
- people with particular skills and knowledge;
- specialist materials, equipment and services.

The consultant can offer the client business valuable support in gaining these resources. Key tasks involve identifying who can supply the particular resources, how they might be contacted and the issues involved in working with them. The consultant can be particularly valuable by working with the client and developing a communication strategy, which helps the business be successful in its approach to suppliers of critical resources.

Gaining the goodwill of customers is the function of marketing in its broadest sense. The consultant can assist in the developing of marketing plans, communication strategies and promotional campaigns. There are a number of support programmes provided by government and non-governmental organisations to businesses, especially small businesses. They take a variety of forms and change regularly. They often demand that a specific, well-organised proposal be made. The consultant can be of great value in structuring a proposal and advising on how it might be delivered.

People, especially those with special knowledge and skills, are a critical – if not *the* critical – resource for businesses. Consultants can add much value by advising a business on its people requirements, developing an understanding of the market for such people and developing advertisements to attract them. The consultant may also advise on the interview and selection procedures. A business may have identified suppliers of the materials and services it needs to undertake its activities. It is increasingly recognised that a business can improve its performance by actively *reverse marketing* itself to suppliers. This ensures that suppliers are aware of the business's needs and are responsive to them. It may, for example, encourage suppliers to innovate and make their offerings more suited to the buyer's requirements. This demands communication with both existing and potential suppliers, a process a consultant can assist greatly.

Many businesses will benefit from further cash injection by investors. Different stages of growth create different capital requirements. An important, and exciting, type of consulting activity is the assistance given in helping businesses gain the support of investors such as banks and venture capitalists. This involves developing a picture of the potential of the firm and why it might offer an exciting investment opportunity, identifying suitable investment organisations, preparing a business plan and perhaps even formally presenting it. The different types of output consulting projects aim to acquire are not mutually exclusive. A consulting exercise may combine elements from a number of them. Each project should be considered on its own merit: how it adds value for the client and helps his or her business achieve its objectives.

1.13   Facilitating organisational change

All organisations are undergoing change all the time. Sometimes this is a 'natural' response to the internal dynamics of organisational growth. At other times it may be in response to an external impetus or shock that forces the organisation to modify the way in which it does things. All of the types of project above may, if they are to be implemented successfully, demand some degree of change in the structures and operating practices of the business. They may also demand that managers change their roles and responsibilities.

Change usually meets resistance. Managers, like most human beings, tend to be conservative when it comes to altering the way things are done. This is only to be expected. Although change may offer new possibilities, it also presents uncertainties. It is only natural that a manager tries to hold on to what he or she knows to be reliable and rewarding. How can he or she be certain that a different future will offer the satisfactions achieved at present? Are the changes in his or her best interest? Even if change *seems* to offer the possibility of greater satisfaction, what are the risks? What happens if the manager is dissatisfied with the outcomes? What 'insurance' against unwanted consequences can he or she call on? It is concerns such as these which can lead to distrust of consultants operating in a business. The effective management of organisational change demands that these questions be addressed. Sometimes organisations call for change as the primary goal of the consulting exercise. In response to this, *change management* has developed as a specialist consulting area. More often, though, change management is required as a subsidiary area in order to effect the implementation of more specific organisational projects, such as business expansion or structural reorganisation. Whatever the motive and source of the change, the effective consultant must be aware of the human dimensions to the change he or she is advocating and be competent in addressing the issues it creates.

Team discussion points

1 Do the external and the internal consultant add value in different ways?

2 How might the client/employer's expectations of how they add value differ?

3 How might specialisation of roles within the consulting team influence the way in which it might add value for the client?

4 Consider the way in which your team is adding value for your client based on the five platforms for value addition discussed above.

Summary of key ideas

- Consulting is a special type of management activity.

- The consultant can be understood to provide ten types of managerial role to the client business. These are placed into three groups:
  - the interpersonal (featuring the roles of the figurehead, the liaison and the leader);
  - the informational (featuring the roles of the monitor, the disseminator and the spokesperson); and
  - the decisional (featuring the roles of the entrepreneur, the disturbance handler, the resource allocator and the negotiator).

- The consultant must integrate these roles with those already operating in the client business. This can happen in one of five ways:
  - supplementary (adding extra skills to those already present);
  - complementary (adding a missing role);
  - differentiating (helping managers distinguish roles among themselves);
  - integrating (helping managers build a new order of roles and individual responsibilities);
  - enhancing (helping managers make their existing roles more effective).

- The consultant must operate with four levels of managerial responsibility. These are:
  - economic (a responsibility to ensure that the projects advocated are in the best interests of the client business);
  - legal (a responsibility to ensure that projects operate within the law);
  - moral (a responsibility to ensure that project outcomes meet with the moral and ethical expectations of the client); and
  - discretionary (the right of the consultant to select or reject projects on the basis of personal ethical considerations).

- Consultants must be able to do something for a business that it is unable to do for itself.

- This must genuinely offer new value to the client business.

- Important areas of value addition include the provision of:
  - information;
  - specialist expertise;
  - a new and innovative perspective;
  - support for internal arguments;
  - support in gaining critical resources such as capital, people or productive factors;
  - driving organisational change.

- Many consulting projects involve a combination of a number of these elements.

- The consultant must constantly communicate to the client the new value he or she is creating through these outputs.

Key reading

Canback, S. (1999) 'The logic of management consulting', *Journal of Management Consulting*, 10 (3), 190–220.

Gallessich, J. (1985) 'Towards a meta-theory of consultation', *Counselling Psychologist*, 13 (3), 336–54.

Further reading

Bell, C.R. and Nadler, L. (1979) *Clients and Consultants*. Houston, TX: Gulf Publishing.

Blake, R.R. and Mouton, J.S. (1976) *Consultation*. Reading, MA: Addison-Wesley.

Caloris, R., Johnson, G. and Sarnin, P. (1994) 'CEO's cognitive maps and the scope of the organisation', *Strategic Management Journal*, 15, 437–57.

Carroll, A. (1979) 'A three-dimensional model of corporate performance', *Academy of Management Review*, 4 (4), 497–505.

Daniels, K., Johnson, G. and de Chernatony, L. (1994) 'Differences in managerial cognitions of competition', *British Journal of Management*, 5 Special Issue, S21–S29.

Dawes, P.L., Dowling, G.R. and Patterson, P.G. (1993) 'Determinants of pre-purchase search effort for management consulting services', *Journal of Business-to-Business Marketing*, 1 (1), 31–61.

Drucker, P.F. (1954) *The Practice of Management*. New York: Harper & Row.

Exton, W. (1982) 'Ethical and moral considerations and the principle of excellence in management consulting', *Journal of Business Ethics*, 1 (3), 211–18.

Golembiewski, R.T. (ed.) (1993) *Handbook of Organizational Consultation*. New York: Marcell Decker.

Janis, I.L. (1982) *Groupthink*. Boston, MA: Houghton Mifflin Company.

Kumar, V. and Simon, A. (2000) 'Strategic capabilities which lead to management consulting success in Australia', *Management Decision*, 38 (1/2), 24–33.

Lundberg, C.C. (1997) 'Towards a general model of consultancy', *Journal of Organizational Change Management*, 10 (3), 193–201.

Lundberg, C.C. and Finney, M. (1987) 'Emerging models of consultancy', *Consultation*, 6 (1).

Mintzberg, H. (1973) *The Nature of Managerial Work*. New York: Harper & Row.

Mintzberg, H. (1975) 'The manager's job: folklore and fact', *Harvard Business Review*, July–August, 49–61.

Patterson, P.G. (2000) 'A contingency approach to modelling satisfaction with management consulting services', *Journal of Service Research*, 3 (2), 138–52.

Prahalad, C.K. and Bettis, R.A. (1986) 'The dominant logic: A new linkage between diversity and performance', *Strategic Management Journal*, 7 (6), 485–501.

Schein, E.H. (1985) *Organizational Culture and Leadership*. San Francisco: Jossey-Bass.

Schein, E.H. (1987) *Process Consultation*, Vol. II. Reading, MA: Addison-Wesley.

Schein, E.H. (1988) *Process Consultation*, Vol. I (revised edn). Reading, MA: Addison-Wesley.

Schein, E.H. (1997) 'The concept of "client" from a process consultation perspective: A guide for change agents', *Journal of Organizational Change Management*, 10 (3), 202–16.

Van de Ven, A.H. and Drazin, R. (1985) 'The concept of fit in contingency theory', *Research of Organizational Behaviour*, 7, 333–65.

Natural Beauty Ltd

Natural Beauty Ltd is a business which manufactures and markets a range of premium-priced toiletries and beauty products with a 'no *animal* testing – natural ingredients' positioning. Distribution is direct to the customer via catalogue ordering. The business was started some eight years ago and after enjoying early success now employs 11 people. It recognises its success and is ambitious for growth. Maggie, a member of the firm's 'commercial team' (the business is run on a co-operative basis and prefers not to define formal management roles), has approached an undergraduate consulting team to assist the business and help it formulate its expansion plans.

During an introductory meeting with the consulting team, Maggie explains that the business feels it has a worthwhile product with good potential in the marketplace. There is a general feeling, however, that the present approach of the business – direct marketing in the UK – is largely saturated: there is no room for further growth. If the business is to grow further it must take a different approach. There is a lot of debate within the commercial team as to the best way forward. Two options are emerging from the discussions.

The first is a move from direct marketing into retailing in the UK, possibly on a franchise basis. The second option is to expand the direct marketing approach into Continental and Eastern Europe. Maggie admits to preferring this option. Despite the fact it will mean finding partners in Europe to act as agents, she feels it is the lower-risk option. She asks the consulting team to evaluate both options on behalf of the business and make a recommendation as to the best way forward.

Q1 Which of the outputs discussed in this chapter might be involved in the final consulting project that can add value for Maggie and Natural Beauty Ltd?

Q2 Consider the nature of the consultant–client interaction for the project.

Q3 What are the costs, both direct and opportunity, that the client might face in taking on a consultant?

CHAPTER 2

Consulting: the wider context and consulting process

The learning outcomes from this chapter are to:

- recognise the types of project consultants are called upon to undertake within the business environment;
- appreciate the ways in which those projects add value;
- recognise the sequence of activities that characterise the typical consulting project;
- appreciate the management issues that each of these stages presents to the consultant;
- understand how the challenges of each stage may be approached to ensure the success of the consulting project.

2.1 Management consulting: core processes of a business

The discussion about the management role of consultants and the ways in which they add value (Chapter 1) makes it clear that the challenges consultants face are as wide as management itself. However, when consultants are called in to undertake work on behalf of a business, it is with a specific project in mind. Management consulting looks at the core processes of a firm including strategy, sales and marketing, business development and finance (*see* Figure 2.1). For many, this would be the classic view of consulting. It is in this manner that the large, well-known firms such as McKinsey operate.

Business planning

One of the broadest project types is working with a firm on its growth strategy, sometimes referred to as 'business planning' or 'business development'. A project of this type is a great opportunity. It offers the consultant a broad remit to

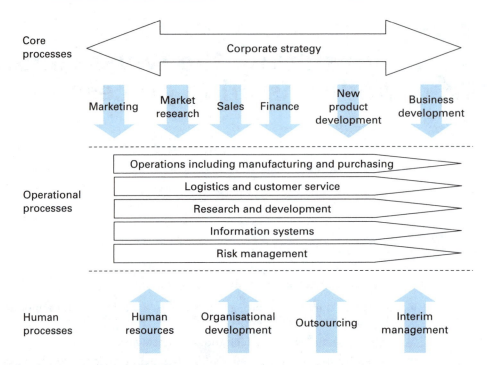

Figure 2.1 Firm's main processes

contribute to the development of the business. However, some care is called for in interpretation. The first task the consultant faces is to establish exactly what the client wants from a 'business development' project. Sometimes the client has something specific in mind, but often not. Common outcomes desired from such assignments include:

- growth of the business within its core markets by capitalising on market growth or market share increase;
- expansion of the business into new market sectors;
- development of new products;
- increasing profits through cost-reduction programmes;
- internal structural reorganisations.

The client may simply state that he or she wants to 'grow the business'. If this is so then the consultant will need to step back, evaluate the possible options for growth and propose the best path to the client. At this stage many 'strategy' projects (another term used by consultants for these wide-ranging briefs) resolve themselves into one or more of the project types listed above. The effective consultant can use the project proposal to establish exactly what the client wants and to manage his or her expectations about what can realistically be achieved.

Marketing research

Marketing research is the process through which managers discover the nature of the competitive environment in which they are operating. The objective of marketing research is to obtain information that managers can use to support their decision-making. Information reduces risk and enables managers to dedicate valuable resources in a more reliable way. Marketing research falls into two types, based on the sort of questions it aims to answer and the source of the answers. First there is *primary research*, that is information collected for the specific project. This is further subdivided as follows:

- *Quantitative research* provides answers to questions when those answers need to be expressed in statistical or numerical form. It aims to answer the 'how much, how often and how many' questions that managers pose.

- *Qualitative research* provides answers to questions that do not demand a quantified answer. It provides the insights that answer managers' 'who, what and why' questions.

Secondary research is based on information that has been collated earlier for reasons other than the project at hand. It takes the form of existing reports, articles and commentaries that just prove to be relevant to the project. These approaches to answering managers' questions about business opportunities are reviewed more fully in Chapter 6.

Marketing research takes a number of forms. At one level it is market 'intelligence': an ongoing review of articles, reports and customer gossip about a market. At another level it might be a cognitive study aimed at consolidating the experience of a group of managers and insights into their working environment. Ultimately, it can demand the use of complex statistical techniques or sophisticated psychometric methodologies to develop a complete picture of how customers see and buy a product category and the details of their expenditure. At this level marketing research demands a high degree of expertise on the part of the researcher. Good consultants recognise their limitations. They know when it is time to call in the expert marketing researcher. This does not mean they cannot add value for the client. A consultant is in a better position to develop a brief for a professional marketing research exercise and can help the client understand what the results mean. For this reason, consultants often subcontract marketing research when necessary.

Marketing

Marketing research is a powerful approach to identifying business opportunities. Exploiting them, though, requires a *marketing strategy* and a *marketing plan*. A marketing strategy defines the approach the business will take in order to get the customers' attention and – critically – get them to spend their money on the business's products or services. The marketing mix dictates the key elements of a marketing strategy. The marketing strategy will be built on the answers to the following questions:

- What products do customers want from a sector's producers?
- In what way are competitors failing to provide these products?
- What price are customers expecting or willing to pay?
- What channels are available for getting the product to the customer?
- Who might be the partners in the distribution process?

- How might they be approached?
- In what ways can customers be informed that the product is available?
- How can the customers' interest be stimulated through promotion?

In developing a marketing strategy the consultant is answering these questions. Often, getting the answers will demand the contribution of experts such as marketing researchers and advertising specialists. If this is the case the consultant can be involved in a number of ways. He or she might simply be asked to highlight these needs so that the client can pick up the project. Alternatively, he or she may be invited in to support the client in working with such experts. In some cases, the client may give the consultant complete control and have him or her subcontract work with specialists as an integral part of the consulting project. Implementing a marketing strategy (i.e. a marketing plan) involves a range of activities. The implementation can resolve itself into the product development, promotional and sales activity projects detailed below. Clearly, an effective, well-presented marketing strategy project creates follow-up opportunities for the consultant.

The key part of the marketing plan is the promotional campaign. This is any programme of activities dedicated to informing customers about a product, stimulating their interest and encouraging purchase. Examples include advertising and public relations campaigns, web marketing, sales drives, direct mailings, exhibitions and in-store demonstrations. Though each of these approaches is different, the consultant faces a common profile of tasks when developing such campaigns. The key questions the client will be asking will be:

- What methods will prove to be cost effective?
- What will be the mechanics of running the campaign?
- How can it be monitored?

The consultant must develop an understanding of how much it will cost, using each technique available, to contact a potential customer, the impact each is likely to have on the potential customer, the likelihood that they will make a purchase, how much they will spend if they do and over what period. A comparison of the techniques can then be made which, in light of the client's promotional objectives and available budget, provides the basis for designing an effective promotional plan.

Sales

For many businesses, especially small and medium-sized ones, the sales team is the primary promotional tool. Expenditure on sales force activity is one of the most important investments the firm will make. Detailed and thoughtful planning of sales force activity is a process which offers real returns. This is an area in which the consultant can offer valuable support. Some of the key issues that might be addressed include the following.

Overall organisation of the team

How should the team be organised? For what should individual salespeople have responsibility? Options include a geographic area, a group of customers or a product category. The answer will depend on the size of the team, the type and range of products sold and the nature and size of customers.

Sales team training

What skills do the sales team need in order to be effective? How might they be encouraged to focus on customer service rather than 'short-term' sales? How might they become more active in obtaining market intelligence while out selling? Might the sales team use their knowledge of customers to contribute more directly to new product development?

Sales team motivation

Most salespeople are motivated by a combination of fixed salary and a performance-based bonus. This bonus element is critical in directing and motivating the sales team. Some important issues to be addressed when designing the bonus scheme include:

- What level of expenditure do managers wish to invest in the bonus scheme?
- How can the bonus be used to align the thrust of the sales with the firm's overall strategic objectives?
- Will the sales team find the scheme transparent and easy to understand?
- Will it be seen as 'fair'?
- Does it leave latitude for managers to deal with contingencies and conflicts?
- How will the bonus scheme fit with the organisation's broader motivational and development strategy?

Planning sales campaigns

A sales campaign is a plan detailing how the sales team will operate. It may reflect ongoing activity or it may be a short-term period of special activity to support, say, a new product launch, the firm's entry into a new geographic area or a move into a new customer sector. The important decision elements of a sales campaign include:

- Which members of the sales force will be involved?
- What products will be given priority?
- Which customers will be targeted?
- In what geographic area?
- The sales literature that will be used.
- The special prices and deals that can be used to motivate purchase.
- Bonuses and rewards for sales performance.
- Other marketing and PR activity that will support the sales drive.

The decision about each of these elements will affect not only the cost of the promotion but also its overall success. Insights may be gained from both the qualitative management experience and quantitative management science methods. Clearly, there is an opportunity for the consultant to add considerable value here.

New product development

It is a business's products (which can include services as well as tangible products) that the customer ultimately buys. They are the basis on which a business is built. A well-designed product that addresses the customer's needs in an effective manner is only part of a business success story: but it is an *essential* part. New product development represents a complex project that draws in most, if not all, of the firm's functions. Research and development, marketing and sales, production, purchasing and human resources will all be called upon to make a contribution. New product development is often undertaken by interdisciplinary teams, which cut across departmental boundaries. The consultant can offer support to the new product development programme in a number of ways. The most important include:

- ensuring the firm's new product development process is as efficient as possible (set against benchmarks of other leading companies);
- understanding the customer's needs through market research;
- technical advice on product development;
- identifying and contacting suppliers of critical components;
- development of marketing and PR campaigns to support the launch;
- developing promotion campaigns to get distributors on board;
- financial planning and evaluation of the return on new product investment.

In a broader sense, the consultant may be invited in to facilitate change management programmes designed to integrate the new product development team and enhance its performance.

Finance

Businesses often need injections of capital. New start-ups and high-growth businesses in particular need funds – in addition to those provided by customers – in order to ensure they reach their potential. Investment capital can be obtained from a number of sources. Banks and venture capital companies are important to new and high-growth businesses. Government grants may be available to small businesses in some areas. More mature firms can obtain funds from stock market flotations. Consultants are often called in to offer advice in four critical areas:

- evaluation of the business's investment needs;
- identification of funding providers and how they might be contacted;
- developing an understanding of the criteria employed by funding providers and how these might be addressed;
- developing communications with funding providers, particularly in relation to proposals and business plans.

Though general in form, these project areas will vary in their details according to the business and the fund provider it is approaching. Potential investors such as venture capitalists also use consultants to conduct 'commercial due diligence' on a proposed purchase. Here the consultant's specialist knowledge of the market sector will help the potential buyer to answer some of their key questions:

- What is the market situation for this company, i.e. what are the growth prospects?
- What is the competitive arena in which the company finds itself and how is this likely to change?
- Are the forecasts for sales and profits realistic?

2.2 'Hard' side consulting: operational processes of a business

Whilst it is evident that a successful business needs good core processes, it also requires well-run operational processes (*see* Figure 2.1). Products or services need to be delivered correctly and on time to the customers in order for the business to remain competitive. As business becomes more complex in terms of manufacturing and distribution, there are more areas where the process may fail or be suboptimal. This is where consultants have helped businesses for a long time, starting with the first consultancy, Arthur D. Little, in the late nineteenth century. His mission was to help firms to benefit from the new technologies available to the businesses of the time, notably the railway for transport and the telegraph for communication. While new technologies, particularly computers, continue to change the way firms can operate, consultants can look at the operational processes of a business and recommend (and often implement) better ways of working.

Operations management

Consulting in the area of operations management often involves large complex assignments engaging a variety of disciplines including manufacturing, logistics (distribution of products or services), purchasing (the buying in of raw materials and services) and customer service. Consultants can help answer the following questions that a business may pose:

- Where in the manufacturing process do most of my products fail (or are rejected on quality grounds, i.e quality bottlenecks) and how can I rectify it?
- Can my manufacturing process be ordered in a better way to improve productivity (i.e. more products delivered quicker or at lower cost)?
- Why are some of my manufacturing lines more efficient than others and can I raise all of them to the standard of the best?
- Is there a more cost-effective way to deliver products to customers?
- Is there a way in which I can buy my raw materials more cost effectively and reduce waste?
- How can I improve customer service, so customer retention is increased?

Answers to the above offer a platform for very tangible consulting projects where outputs can be measured: the percentage of products rejected on quality grounds or the number of customers retained over a defined period. It is not surprising that many of today's popular consulting tools, such as Six Sigma's DMAIC process (see Chapter 5) have been developed from operations management projects.

Information technology management

Managers need information if they are to make good decisions. They need information on both the business's external situation – its competitive environment –
and its internal state. Information is, as Paul Tom points out in his 1987 book, a
corporate resource. Management information systems aim to collect and organise
such information and present it to managers in a usable form. Nowadays, management information systems are based on computer technology. They therefore
require a good deal of technical expertise to implement. However, even the non-
technical consultant can add value, particularly in developing an understanding
of the information needs of the business, the way in which information flows
around the organisation and the competitive advantage that might be gained
through investment in information technology. Management information is not
just about managers *having* information; it is about them *using* it effectively. Such
a consulting exercise provides a sound basis on which to progress the technical
implementation and helps ensure that it will be rewarding.

One example of the above is customer relationship management or CRM systems. Firms that have a large number of customers are looking for ways to improve
the relationship that they have with individual customers. Tesco in the UK, for
example, with its Clubcard system, has been very successful in identifying customer
trends from the data they collect every time one of the Clubcard holders makes
a purchase. It helps them decide on the range of products to be stocked in an
individual store, for instance. It also enables them to send out targeted mailings
to customers based on historic purchases, for example those who have bought
dog food in the past could be sent a voucher for a new range of treats for dogs.
Many believe this is a much more cost-effective way to target potential customers
than the traditional methods of, say, TV or press advertising. Consultants have an
important role here as they can:

■ Look at the process by which data is collected and analysed, as this is critical to
  make it useful.

■ Interpret the findings of the analysis and recommend how the data should be
  used for targeting.

■ Look at measures to evaluate how well the CRM system is performing in terms
  of increased sales and profits.

Technical

A great deal of consulting activity involves the application of specialist technical
expertise. Even within technologically orientated organisations it is important to
draw a distinction between consulting that aims to contribute to technical know-
how, expertise and outputs and management consulting that aims to facilitate
managerial structures that enhance such activity. Design is of increasing importance to businesses. *Exogenous* technological advances – those that a group of firms
share rather than being the property of a single firm – mean that few businesses
have access to a unique technology that makes a core product different to its competitors. In many categories most offerings from different firms perform in pretty
much the same way (think of mid-price cars, airlines and personal computers!).
To ensure differentiation from competitors – ensuring the buyer feels the product

is different in a substantive way – means that producers must turn to aesthetic and emotional benefits rather than core performance benefits. Those with an expertise in the arts, media and design are in a position to add value directly by providing technical support to such projects. Specialist consulting agencies exist to undertake this. Typical projects include product and packaging design, the development of communication strategies (increasingly via the Internet) and general advertising.

However, the general management consultant, who does not have such technical knowledge, should never be intimidated by the technical nature of the task in hand. General consultants can still add value by refining and clarifying what managers want from creative consulting. They can facilitate the development of managerial processes and structures that make best use of the opportunities creative design offers. More immediately, they can help managers develop specific and clear-sighted briefings for creative designers. A major boost to technical consulting in science and engineering has been the rapid growth in science parks, often associated with universities, that aim to provide a commercial conduit between the university's fundamental – 'blue-sky' – research and the application of that technology to practical products. Many major advances in medicine, electronics, chemical engineering and information technology have arisen through this route. An interesting example is the firm set up by three mathematicians based at the Massachusetts Institute of Technology – Adi Shamir, Ron Rivest and Leonard Adleman – to promote a cryptographic encryption key based on prime numbers known as RSA. Their work started in number theory, which is concerned with a most abstract and ostensively, at least, practical area of mathematics. However, it was found that their mathematical algorithm could be used to provide a high degree of security for credit card transactions on the Internet, an application of enormous commercial value.

The importance of the distinction between providing direct technical assistance and the provision of managerial advice in how to make best use of technology applies as much to consulting in science and engineering as it does to consulting in the creative arts. Technical innovations do not promote themselves. The experts who develop ideas are not usually equipped with the managerial skills necessary to set up firms to produce and promote them effectively in a competitive marketplace. Often venture capitalists and other financial backers will wish to see a high degree of managerial expertise complementing the technical ability of the innovation team. Consultants have a clear role to play here.

Risk management

While firms take the health and safety of their workers very seriously, in today's world there are many other risks that have be managed. The Institute of Risk Management has defined four main areas: financial, strategic, operational and hazard (*see* Figure 2.2).

Companies providing a public service (e.g. transport, leisure facilities, retail outlets or products consumed by the public) also have to consider risks to their customers either from accidents or, increasingly, from deliberate sabotage. A consultant can help a firm assess the likelihood of certain events happening and put in place contingency plans to deal with them. For publicly quoted companies (those whose shares are traded on the stock exchange), there are risks associated with 'corporate

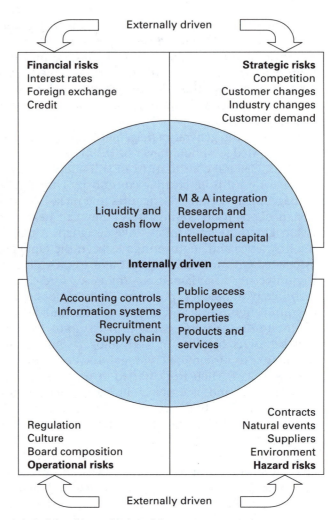

Figure 2.2 Examples of the drivers for key risks

Source: The Institute of Risk Management. A Risk Management Standard © AIRMIC, ALARM, IRM 2002. Reproduced with permission.

governance', i.e. the way in which the firm operates and specifically how it reports information to its shareholders. There have been many high-profile cases recently, most notably Enron in the US, that have highlighted the issues associated with poor (or indeed illegal) corporate governance. Consultants can help firms either prior to a flotation (launching of shares on the stock exchange) or when the rules change (i.e. post-Enron) to ensure they have the appropriate systems in place.

2.3 'Soft' side consulting: human processes of a business

Whilst both the core and operational processes are key in the functioning of a well-run business, most firms rely heavily on their human capital. In terms of consulting, this has often been regarded as the most difficult to quantify in terms of benefits to an organisation. However, that does not mean that it is not important and a good consultant in this area can be highly effective if the major issues of a company are around the actions of its people. In today's complex organisations, dysfunctional teams at any level can be highly destructive. The best consultants in any field are also able to understand the human dynamics of a project. This is discussed further in Chapter 7.

Human resources

People, it is often said, are a business's most important resource. Attracting the right sort of people to contribute to the business is certainly an important challenge managers must address, especially those in high-growth businesses. A consultant can be of value in this area in several ways. Important contributions to recruitment projects might include:

- assessing the firm's human resource requirement and identifying skill and knowledge gaps, both currently and predicting for the future;
- creating advertisements (with insights into both message and medium) to attract the right people;
- developing assessment criteria, interview procedures and, possibly, psychometric testing of candidates;
- advice on the reimbursement packages new recruits will expect.

Successful recruitment can demand a degree of specialist knowledge. As a result it is often an area in which dedicated consultants operate. Staff retention is equally important and consultants can advise firms on their human resources policies in terms of remuneration packages (pay, pensions, holiday and sickness benefits and other 'perks' such as company cars).

Organisational development

This is a long and established area for consulting, having begun in the early part of the twentieth century with advocates attempting to define the 'best' way to organise a workforce, just as machines could be ordered in the mass production era. Over the next hundred years, the ideas evolved as the notion that there was one optimal way to organise a firm was shown to be wrong. The situation that a firm found itself in was more relevant in determining its organisational structure. Consultants can help firms on many levels. They can work with individuals as a personal coach to improve their ways of working and motivation levels. They can work with groups to improve their collective performance and productivity. They can also look at the whole organisation to advise on its structure, discuss the organisational culture and its leadership styles. In all of these it is the very fact that consultants are outsiders – that they are deemed to be 'neutral' – that enables them to address issues which a boss or colleague may feel unable to do.

Organisational development projects can often arise when the firm is facing another issue. For example, many successful entrepreneurs want to sell their business but they are not only the owner but also the leader of the firm. The existing management team operates with a very strong leader whose opinions are of major importance. When that leader decides to leave, the team can lack this strong focus and may find it difficult to carry on operating in the same way. Here a consultant can help the team assess their strengths and weaknesses and identify solutions to the problem. Perhaps they need another strong leader/owner or one of them could 'step' up to the post of leader: it would depend on the personalities involved and a good consultant would recognise these.

Interim management

Interim management is the temporary appointment of a manager by a firm for a fixed period. They can either undertake a change programme or project, or take on a specified role that hitherto had been filled by a permanent employee. It is estimated that there are 5000 interim managers active in the UK alone. How does an interim manager differ from a management consultant? It is somethimes difficult to differentiate between these two roles, as the lines can be blurred and the task the same. A consultant usually, though, is an 'outsider' making recommendations to an organisation's management team whereas an interim manager has explicit responsibility to deliver as an employee would do. Firms would use interim managers for temporarily vacant positions either because a restructuring of the organisation has caused a gap or someone has left and a permanent replacement has not been found. They may also have the short-term requirement for a position relating to an internal project that cannot be filled by their existing personnel. Many management consultants are also interim managers and vice versa, as they need similar skills.

Outsourcing

This is a rapidly developing area for many businesses, where processes that traditionally have been done by the company themselves are given to another organisation to carry out. In 2005, the outsourcing market in Europe accounted for €12.9 billion (*source*: feaco.org/content/content2.php?CatID=148&NewsID=406, consulted 21 August 2007) and represented 21 per cent of the total market for consulting. Worldwide, Kennedy Information estimates consulting services to the outsourcing business to be worth $4.8 billion alone (*source*: consultingcentral.com/downloads/BPO-Transformation-Summary.pdf?C=HCuB13rUGHX0c8Za, consulted 21 August 2007). There are two main areas: ITO, or information technology outsourcing, and BPO, or business process outsourcing. The former became popular as information technology became more complex and the degree of skill required favoured specialists such as IBM. They would effectively take over and run the IT processes of a company. Many believe that this has now reached its peak as the latest figures from TPI show a decline in revenues for ITO in the third quarter of 2006 (*source*: tpi.net/pdf/index/3Q06%20TPI%20Index%20Presentation.pdf, consulted 21 August 2007).

By contrast, revenues in BPO are still growing strongly, up 10 per cent year on year in the third quarter of 2006 (*source*: ibid). Business process outsourcing covers all the areas outside IT. The most common example is customer care centres that are often run by specialist call centre companies: Indian firms in particular have been successful in attracting a lot of this business due to their lower costs. However, many other business processes are now regularly conducted by third parties. These include many finance functions such as accounts, customer billing and cash management; human resource functions, e.g. management of employee records and recruitment, and procurement or purchasing of goods and services. All are specialist functions and for many firms it is more cost effective for someone else to do them. Consultants working for outsourcing companies can offer added value by advising their clients on the best ways to carry out the processes based on their experience.

2.4 Consulting to the non-profit and public sectors

In Europe, consulting to the non-profit and government sectors accounted for nearly 17 per cent of the total in 2004 (*source*: feaco.mayflowerserver.de/images/downloads/Anlagen/FeacoSurvey_2004_FINAL.pdf, consulted 21 August 2007) but more importantly it was one of the fastest growing segments, up 21 per cent on the previous year. Whilst a proportion of this is government spending on large IT projects, a significant amount comes from the non-profit sector: largely charities that rely on public donations. They provide goods and services that our society believe should be provided without making a profit, for example care of historical buildings and landscapes or the provision of housing for low-income people. Although they do not make a profit, the non-profit organisation does operate in the business world and so faces many similar challenges. So a consultant in the non-profit sector may find the actual work the same as in the profit sector, for example identification of a strategy or delivery of a marketing plan. However, there are a few specialist areas that a consultant may get involved with. The first is fund-raising, which is where many of these organisations derive their income. Another may be the management of endowments and legacies that can critically affect the ability of the non-profit organisation to operate.

Consulting to the public sector or government organisations again has many similarities to the private (or profit) sector. The government is a major employer, particularly in healthcare, so many of the human consulting projects described in the section above are applicable. In addition, public sector projects such as urban regeneration also require the type of consulting skills described in the section above on operational processes. The main difference between consulting in the profit sector and for government is the financial aspect. As the key objectives of a public project do not include a profit target, the cost of managing a project can sometimes be difficult to handle. This is due to getting a balance between achieving the government's policy aims and getting the best value by keeping costs to a minimum.

2.5 Overview of the consulting process

A *process* is a sequence of events directed towards achieving some overall outcome. When we recognise a process we recognise the interconnectedness and interrelatedness of independent actions. It is not just *what* we do that matters. It is the *order* in which we do things. A consulting project will be successful only if the right actions are carried out in the right order. A client will not accept a solution to a problem he or she does not yet recognise exists. It is premature to decide on the best options for a business if no analysis of what that business is about has been carried out. It is no good presenting the customer with a bill if he or she has not received any advice yet!

Most consulting projects go through nine stages. The process starts with an initial contact between the consultant and the client. This is followed by recognition that the consultant can help the business in some way and a project is initiated. In the third stage the consultant will suggest further investigation into and analysis of the issues facing the client's business before proposing a set of formal objectives that both should work towards. Fourth, the consultant will then document those objectives in a formal proposal. This constitutes the 'contract' between the consultant and client. The fifth stage requires developing a project charter that supports this contract. The development of the project can only be undertaken on the basis of a sound understanding of the business and its context. The sixth stage of the project involves undertaking this analysis. This stage never really ends, as further analysis may be required as the project progresses, even in the final follow-up stage.

The seventh stage is the implementation of the project. This stage will demand further information gathering, evaluation of the business issues, analysis and evaluation of options and formulation of recommendations. When this is complete, the eighth stage involves communicating those findings and recommendations back to the client in some way. This communication will aim to encourage and facilitate implementation. In the final stage, the consultant may maintain contact with the client if this can in some way benefit one or preferably both parties. This process is illustrated in Figure 2.3. Every consulting project is different. The

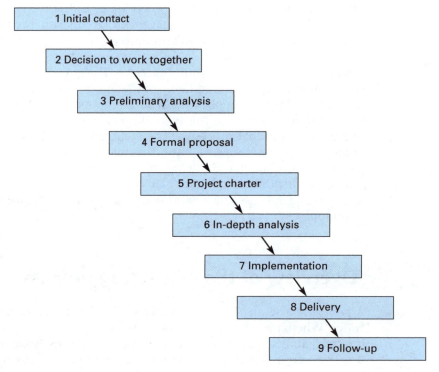

Figure 2.3 Consulting process

nine stages of different consulting exercises will vary in length and complexity. The consultant's approach to each stage will differ depending on the nature of the consulting project and the client with whom he or she is working. This said, every successful consulting project achieves its aims because the consultant has managed each stage effectively. We will now examine each stage in detail.

2.6   Initial contact and initiating the project

Consultants meet with potential clients in a great number of forums. In principle, there are four mechanisms by which the consultant and client meet and decide they should work together.

- The consultant and client meet in an impromptu way.
- The consultant proposes his or her services to a client.
- The client seeks out the services of a particular consultant.
- A third party brings the consultant and client together.

Project initiation may occur with both consultant and client sharing a clear understanding of what the client wants. Quite often, though, the client is unclear as to specific objectives. He or she may just feel that things could be better with the business. In this case, the consultant must be adept at probing the client and getting him or her to reveal something about the business. Such probing must be undertaken with subtlety if it is not to be seen as obvious and invasive. This demands effective use of the questioning techniques detailed in Section 7.6. Business networks bring many people together seeking ways to help each other. This is often an important forum for consultants to make contact and present what they have to offer. Business networks exist in and between business sectors. They may be stimulated by professional bodies, which will set up conferences and seminars. An example is the *Marketing Network* associated with the Chartered Institute of Marketing.

Consultants, like any other business service providers, are responsible for promoting the service they offer to their customers. This may be through professional bodies that offer some endorsement for the service on offer and support its promotion. Consultants can also promote themselves via advertising, particularly in specialist industry publications. Direct marketing to potential clients may also be a useful tool. Clients may sometimes approach a consultant in search of advice. This may be in response to the consultant's promotional activities or be a result of recommendations from another satisfied customer. The decision to work together is a significant one for both the client and the consultant. The client is making the decision to invest in his or her business through buying the insights and advice of an outside expert. The consultant is deciding to offer his or her expertise to the client. This demands a considerable commitment and means the consultant cannot pursue other projects. Taking on a particular project represents an *opportunity cost* to the consultant.

Both client and consultant must be clear on exactly what is being initiated. It could be the entire project. It is more likely, though, that it is actually an invitation by the client to the consultant to make a *formal proposal* for the project (stage 4 of the process). This will certainly be the case if the consultant is being invited to make a proposal or pitch in competition with other consultants. Even if no competition is involved and the client is inviting the consultant to move straight on to the full project, an interim proposal is still a good idea. As discussed below, it is an effective means of managing the client's expectations about the project's outcomes. The actual initiation of the project can take a variety of forms. The degree of formality that the initiation takes is particularly important. It may be a simple verbal agreement to go ahead. It may take the form of an informal note or letter. In other cases the project may be initiated by a formal and detailed contract. The formality of the initiation will reflect the interests of both client and consultant. A number of factors will affect this, the most important of which are as follows.

How well the consultant and client know each other

If the consultant and client know each other very well, the project can be initiated with a low degree of formality. If there is a good deal of trust between both parties to the exercise then both will rely on the fact that the details of the project can be adjusted through mutual agreement as understanding develops.

Expectations from the project

The agreement to initiate the project will reflect the expectations of the client as to the outcomes of the project. If those expectations have been thoroughly thought through by the client and have been well defined, the client may use the initiation of the project as an opportunity to articulate those outcomes and communicate them to the consultant. In this case the initiation may take a more formal guise.

Level of resources committed to the project by the client

The more the client is likely to invest in the consulting exercise (by way of money, people and time), the more likely it is that he or she will want to document the decision in some way and to formalise the initiation.

Investment by the consultant in making the formal proposal

As noted below, preparing the formal proposal demands time, energy and possibly direct expenditure on the part of the consultant. How much commitment is made here will depend on the nature (and value) of the project, the need to collect information, the level of detail in the proposal and the mechanism of delivering it to the client. A great deal of preparation may be needed, especially if the pitch for the project is a competitive one. In this case, the consultant may require the client to offer a degree of commitment to undertaking the project and to make this commitment explicit in the terms of the proposal.

The need to communicate within the client business

If the client business is quite large, a manager in the middle of the organisational hierarchy may initiate the consulting exercise. If so, such a person may want to record the decision to initiate a consulting exercise. He or she may need to do so in order to inform superiors and to comply with internal decision-control procedures.

The need to inform third parties

The delivery of the exercise may be of interest to a number of people outside the client organisation. Often institutional investors such as banks and venture capitalists will demand the opinions of outside experts before committing capital. If the business is the subject of a possible acquisition, the acquirer may require that a consultant evaluate the business. In these cases the initiation may be formalised so as to keep the third party informed.

2.7 Preliminary analysis of the issues and defining objectives

The consultant must make a decision about what can be achieved by the consulting exercise. It is this that will be offered to the client in the formal proposal. This decision must be based on an understanding of the business and its situation. Background research and an evaluation of the business will be called for. This stage calls on the analytical approaches discussed in Chapter 6.

There are three key questions to be answered by this preliminary analysis:

1 What are the major opportunities and issues the business faces?
2 What prevents the business capitalising on the opportunity or dealing with the issues?
3 How can the consultant's service help the business overcome this block?

The formal proposal will be made around the answers to these questions.

It should not be forgotten that this is a *preliminary* analysis. Any analysis demands an investment of time and effort (and possibly direct expenditure) in developing an understanding. This investment must be of the right order for the project. On the one hand, it should be sufficient so that a proposal can be made which is relevant, meaningful and, critically, attractive to the client. If the consultant is in a competitive situation, then investing in this understanding may offer good dividends. On the other hand, the investment should not be too high in relation to the final scope of the project. Clients rarely pay the consultant for making the initial proposal. The costing of this preliminary evaluation must, ultimately, be included in the overall bill for the exercise. If the pitch is competitive, the consultant will not see any return on the investment if the proposal is not successful.

A simple test can be applied before a consultant dedicates resources to gaining new information at this stage. This is to ask how the information will be used. If it is needed to develop an understanding of how the client *potentially* may be helped, it may be useful. If it will be used only for *delivering* that help, it can safely be left until a commitment has been made to the full project. A management project of any significance should be defined around its *objectives*; that is, what it aims to achieve. Objectives provide a means of communicating the reason the project exists, provide a common focal point for all involved and act as an indication of what level of investment is appropriate, given the options available for other projects.

Defining proper objectives is a very important part of the project. A critical element in the success of the consulting exercise is that its objectives are well defined and understood by all involved. It is the objectives of the project that the client is 'buying'. At this stage it should be noted that objectives represent the link between where the business is now and where it might be with the consultant's help. It is also useful to note that objectives are different from *outcomes*. An objective is what the consulting project will achieve. An outcome is what the business will be able to do as a result of the consulting exercise.

2.8 Pitching the project: the formal proposal and project charter

The formal proposal is a pivotal point in the consulting exercise. It represents the consultant's statement of what he or she can achieve on behalf of the client business. The proposal defines what the client will be paying for. Investing time and effort in the preparation and communication of a good proposal always pays dividends. A full exploration of the details to be included in and the structuring and writing of a formal proposal is given in Chapter 3. An important point to be made at this stage is that the proposal operates at a number of levels.

The key functions of the proposal are as follows. The proposal:

- provides a concise and efficient means of communicating the objectives of the project to the client;
- guides analysis and ensures that investment in information gathering is at an appropriate level;
- gives the consulting team a common focus when differentiating tasks and organising the project delivery;
- provides a fixed point of reference which can be referred back to if it is felt the project is drifting;
- can be used to manage the expectations of the client.

This last point is very important. If properly written and presented, the proposal prevents expectations of the outcomes becoming unrealistic. This can easily happen and if expectations get too high, even a good project will disappoint the client. The project charter is discussed in more detail in Section 5.4. This provides the key document for the project and the 'ground rules' for the team. The project charter is a very useful document, not just for the client but for the consulting team as well. It acts as an anchor for the project and manages the expectations of both parties. It is often kept to one page and is always agreed by the project team at the start. It can change only if all members of the team agree and they have very strong reasons for changing it.

2.9   Project progression and follow-up

Progression represents the actual undertaking of the project. At this stage the consultant applies his or her insights, expertise and knowledge to create a new understanding for the client. Every consulting project has its own character but also includes some essential activities, which are common to most projects. The important ones are as follows.

Information gathering

An understanding of the business and its context must be developed. Information is needed to understand the opportunities and issues the business faces and its capabilities in relation to them. Information gathering is an ongoing activity that is assisted by the techniques discussed in Chapter 6. A crucial point that will be developed in this discussion is that the need for information must always be challenged in relation to its cost and the objectives of the project.

Analysis and interpretation

Information on its own is of little use. It is the *sense* that the consultant can make of it that is valuable for the client. The consultant must interpret the information and create a new perspective from it. Developing this new perspective can be aided by the creative approaches described in Chapter 9 and the auditing techniques in Chapter 6. Analysis does not occur in isolation from information gathering: it is iterative with it. Information prompts analysis and analysis highlights information gaps.

Interaction with the client business

The consultant team, or a representative of it, will usually maintain contact with a manager, or managers, in the client business. This may be driven by the need to keep the client informed of the progression of the project. It may also be a consequence of the need to obtain further information about the business. Contact can be through meetings, telephone calls, written and electronic communications. Whatever the motivation, or the means, interacting with the client is an opportunity not just to give and obtain information but also to build a relationship with the client, which can lead to a more effective project. Approaches to building this relationship are discussed in Chapter 7.

Project management and monitoring

The project proposal and charter commit the consultant to three things. These are a set of *agreed objectives* that will be delivered at a *specified time* for a *given budget*. Slippage in any one of these aspects can lead to unsatisfactory outcomes for the client, the consultant or both. Monitoring is the activity dedicated to ensuring that the project is progressing in a satisfactory manner. It will involve ensuring that key events are happening on time and that expenditure is in line with that anticipated. Effective monitoring procedures ensure that if slippage does occur, remedial action can be taken to get the project back on track.

Keeping records

Effective consultants invest time in keeping a good record of the progression of a project. As a minimum, this will be a file of important documents and notes on communications. A project log such as that discussed in Section 11.7 may supplement this. It may involve more formal records such as plans and budgets. Keeping records is good practice for several reasons. It enables progression of the project to be monitored. Queries may be resolved quickly by reference back to communications. Most important, though, is the fact that a good set of records allows the consultant to reflect on the project, learn from the experience in an active way and so enhance performance in the future.

Consulting is an activity that can build value through interaction with the client. The benefits of the exercise are delivered over time, especially if a process consulting approach is taken. Even so, the client will see the final communication of the results of the consulting exercise as an important event. This is often seen as the delivery of the actual consulting 'product' – the tangible item the client has actually paid for. There are a variety of reasons why the client and consultant might want to keep in touch after the formal outputs of the project have been delivered. Some of the more important are as follows.

Advice on implementation

The final report will make a series of recommendations to the client. It is usually up to the client to put those recommendations into practice. However, the client may feel the need to call further upon the skills and insights of the consultant for clarification of points in the final report and for guidance on how implementation might be effected. An agreement to support the client in this way may be a feature of the project proposal.

Preparing ground for new project

Even if the consultant has not made an explicit agreement to support the client after the final report has been delivered, it may be judicious to do so. If the client is satisfied with the outputs of the project then there is the possibility that the client and consultant may both gain by working together on a future project.

Seeking an endorsement

A consultant builds his or her career on reputation. If a project has been undertaken well, that is something the consultant might use in the future. The endorsement of a satisfied client, a statement that he or she has benefited from the advice of the consultant, can be very valuable, particularly if the client represents a well-known business that is challenging in the demands it makes on its suppliers.

Of course, confidentiality is important. Some circumspection may be needed in referring to a particular project. But this is an issue that can usually be resolved.

Project review and evaluation

As noted in the point about record keeping, effective consultants engage in active learning. They are always alert to the possibility of improving their performance. This demands that they learn from their experiences. Reviewing how the project went, in terms of both positives to be repeated and negatives to learn from, is an important part of this. The views of the client may be sought, either through informal discussion or by means of a more formal questionnaire.

Networking

The consultant may seek to maintain a relationship with the client merely to build his or her presence in the business network. The benefits may not be immediately clear, but awareness of the consultant and what he or she can offer is built. There is always the possibility that new business will emerge if the client recommends the consultant to a contact.

Team discussion points

1   Chapter 1 discussed the mechanisms by which consultants can create value for their clients. In summary, these were:

- the provision of information;
- the provision of specialist expertise;
- the provision of a new perspective;
- the provision of support for internal arguments;
- the provision of support in gaining a critical resource;
- the creation of organisational change.

Each member of the team should select one of the project types listed in this chapter. Using the framework in Chapter 1, each team member should prepare and deliver a short (one-page) presentation detailing how each means of value creation can support the project type selected and ensure that its outcomes will be satisfactory for the client.

2   Most consulting teams differentiate individual roles within the team. In this way they get the best out of a team effort. The exact profile of roles varies. Often the following roles make an appearance:

- a team coordinator;
- an information gatherer;
- an information analyser;
- a report writer;
- a report presenter;
- a client contactor;
- a team counsellor.

These roles are discussed more fully in Section 11.1.

Discuss, as a group, how each role might contribute to each stage of the consulting process. You may care to set up a grid summarising your ideas (stages vertically and roles horizontally). Retain this for planning individual involvement in the project when the project charter is developed.

Summary of key ideas

Consultants take on a variety of projects on behalf of their clients. They can be split into those looking at the core processes of a firm, those dealing with the operational processes and, finally, those dealing with the human processes. Many that would be considered typical 'management consulting' are those involved with the core processes such as strategy or business development, marketing and sales. Operations management and IT management are examples of areas where consultants are used to improve the firm's performance. Human resource and organisational consulting has traditionally been strong but related areas of interim management and outsourcing are now providing the growth in this type of consulting.

A consulting exercise is a project that moves through a number of distinct stages. The key stages are:

■ Initiation: the consultant and client meet and decide to work together.

■ Preliminary analysis: development of an understanding of what the consultant can do for the client.

■ Formal proposal: a statement by the consultant to the client of what the project will achieve for the business.

■ Progression of project: actual undertaking of the project.

■ Delivery of results: communicating the findings to the client.

■ Following up: post-delivery activities.

Different projects move through these stages in different ways but each represents a distinct management challenge that can be met by using analysis, project management and relationship-building skills.

Key reading

Biswas, S. and Twitchell, D. (2002) *Management Consulting: A Complete Guide to the Industry*. New York: John Wiley and Sons Inc (Chapters 1–4).

Block, P. (2000) *Flawless Consulting: A Guide to Getting Your Expertise Used*. San Francisco, CA: Jossey-Bass/Pfeiffer (Chapter 3).

Further reading

Coster, R.A. and Dalton, D.R. (1993) 'Management consulting: Planning, entry and performance', *Journal of Counseling and Development*, 72 (2), 191–8.

Czerniawska, F. and May, P. (2006) *Management Consulting in Practice*. London: Kogan Page.

Czerniawska, F. and Toppin, G. (2005) *Business Consulting: A Guide to How It Works and How to Make It Work*. London: Economist Books.

Floyd, C. (1997) *Managing Technology for Corporate Success*. Aldershot: Gower.

Kakabadse, A., Ludlow, R. and Vinnicombe, S. (2005) *Working in Organizations*. London: Penguin.

Lippitt, G. and Lippitt, R. (1994) *The Consulting Process in Action*. Chichester, West Sussex: Pfeiffer Wiley.

Robbins, S.P. (2004) *Essentials of Organizational Behaviour* (8th edn). Upper Saddle River, NJ: Prentice-Hall.

Sturdy, A. (1997) 'The consultancy process – an insecure business', *Journal of Management Studies*, 34 (3), 389–413.

Tom, P.L. (1987) *Managing Information as a Corporate Resource*. Glenview, IL: Scott, Foresman and Co.

Case exercise

Southern Food Services

Southern Food Services (SFS) is a medium-sized, publicly quoted company based in the UK and with the majority of its sales there. It makes ready meals and other chilled food products, for example desserts. It supplies the UK and Irish supermarket trade with products under their brand (known as 'own-label' products). It also sells products through the supermarkets under its own brands such as 'Quikcook ready meals' and 'Mrs Beeton's sponge puddings', known as branded products.

The last few years have been difficult ones for SFS: their overall sales are declining and so too are their profits. Their share price has halved in the last year after a series of profit warnings (notification to the City and their investors that profits will be below expectations). Their Chief Executive, Tom Ferguson, is a worried man: both for the company and his job! He sees no alternative but to get some outside help and calls you in as a consultant to advise on what he should do.

At the first meeting, Tom tells you what he thinks are the problems facing SFS:

- Sales are growing strongly in the own-label sector (over 10 per cent a year) but we are making no profit in this sector.

- Sales in the branded sector are falling by over 15 per cent a year but we are making a profit here, even if that too is falling.

- The factories are not at full capacity due to the falling sales, particularly in the higher volume branded sector where machinery and labour is often idle.

- A lot of stock is wasted as they are often delivered late to the customer and thus rejected for having too short a shelf life.

- The IT systems are old and it is difficult to communicate customer orders quick enough in order to manufacture on time.

- Raw material costs including energy are rising faster than the price increases we are able to pass on to our customers.

- My management team is dysfunctional: most meetings end up with lots of arguments and no agreements!

- The Chairman of the Board is new and is seeking to assert his authority by undermining me and my efforts to improve the company's position.

- The shares are poorly rated and we have high levels of debt which makes it difficult to make the necessary investment to update IT systems, for example.

- Our organisational structure is too complex and it is therefore difficult to make decisions: more critically, we do not present a united front to our powerful customers.

- Our products are suffering from the current trends in healthy eating.

Q1 From the long list of problems above, consider some of the consulting projects that might help the company.

Q2 Take one of the above and consider the stages that you might go through using the consulting process outlined above.

Q3 Consider what questions you would ask Tom to try to understand what the critical issues are, as you cannot solve everything at once!

CHAPTER 3

The skills of the consultant and the project proposal

Learning outcomes

The learning outcomes from this chapter are to:

- appreciate the skills effective management consultants bring to the job; and in particular:
  - recognise the importance of the *project management skills* necessary to keep the consulting project on schedule and on budget;
  - recognise the importance of the *analysis skills* needed to understand the client business, identify the opportunities it faces and develop strategies to exploit them;
  - recognise the importance of the *relationship-building skills* needed to relate ideas, to positively influence decision-makers and to make the project happen in real organisations;
- understand the selling process of a consulting project;
- recognise the key elements of the project proposal and how they may be articulated in order to have an impact and to influence the recipient.

3.1 The effective consultant's skill profile

Consulting represents a particularly challenging management task for a number of reasons. First, the consultant is not working within his or her 'own' organisation. He or she is, in the first stages of the consulting exercise at least, an 'outsider'. In some ways this offers advantages. It may allow the consultant to ask questions and make recommendations that an 'insider' feels they cannot. Managers within a business tend to adopt the organisation's way of seeing things – a kind of 'groupthink', which limits the way both problems and opportunities are seen. A consultant may view things in a different way. He or she might well see opportunities in a fresher, more responsive way. As the consultant ultimately leaves the organisation, he or she can afford a more dispassionate approach. Painful 'home truths' may be recognised more readily (or at least not denied!) by the consultant. For this reason, the consultant will be in a stronger position to advocate difficult courses than someone who does not wish to compromise an open-ended and long-term position within the business.

However, being an outsider presents some challenges. It means that the consultant must actively build relationships and create a sense of trust. Established managers can often take these for granted. Consultants may formally be employed by an organisation, but often they must operate some distance from it. The employing organisation offers support in a variety of ways but the consultant is 'out on his or her own' in a way the conventional manager is not. The consultant must be both self-supporting and self-starting. The consultant is often involved in projects that are 'strategic'. Strategic projects have significant consequences and affect the future of the whole business. They can cut across the interests of the managers of established parts or functions within the business. Managers may resist what they see as interference in 'their' areas and challenges to 'their' interests. (These issues are explored at length in the studies by Guth and MacMillan (1986) and Wooldridge and Floyd (1990).) Managing such projects demands an ability to deal with such organisational politics in a firm, sensitive and responsible way. All managers must offer a value-adding service to their organisations. However, a consultant is able to offer a service in a way that is *explicit*. What a consultant offers is subject to scrutiny which is much more intense and continuous than the scrutiny to which an established manager is exposed. An effective (and politically astute) consultant must be willing to let the client management take credit for successes while often being prepared to take the blame for mistakes.

In order to meet the challenge of managing the consulting project the consultant must develop a skill profile that allows him or her to call upon abilities in three key areas:

- an ability to manage the consulting exercise as a *formal project*;
- an ability to manage the *analytical skills* necessary to gain an understanding of the client business and the possibilities it faces;
- an ability to *communicate ideas* and *positively influence* others.

These three areas represent distinct types of management skill. Learning and using them can be supported by a variety of concepts and techniques. These concepts and techniques are drawn from a wide range of management disciplines and traditions. However, it should not be forgotten that the effective consultant could not only call upon skills in each of these areas but also integrate them into a seamless whole of management practice. We can picture these three skill areas working together as illustrated in Figure 3.1.

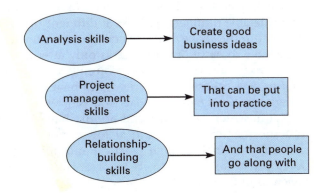

Figure 3.1 The skills of the consultant

The next three sections provide an overview of these consulting skill areas. These reviews are an introduction. They will leave unanswered many questions about the type of challenges these skills can be used to address, how the skills may be developed and how they can be used. It will be the task of the following sections in this book to explore these questions in depth.

3.2   Project management skills

A consulting exercise is a self-contained project within a business environment. The best results are achieved if the consulting exercise is managed as such. Important project management skills include the following.

An ability to define objectives and outcomes

An objective states what the project is going to achieve for the client. However, not every statement is a good objective. A stated objective must be subject to a critical review. Is it well defined? Will the organisation know when it has achieved the objective? Is the objective achievable, given the external market conditions that face the business? Is it realistic, given the business's internal resources? How is the objective to be phrased? Will those who will play a part in achieving it readily and clearly understand it? Is the objective one that all involved in the business can commit to? If not, why not? How will this matter? These questions will be explored fully in Chapter 5.

An ability to develop formal plans

A plan is a course of action specified in order to achieve a certain objective. Critical aspects of planning include defining tasks, ordering them and understanding the resource implications of the task sequence; in particular, identifying who will be responsible for carrying out the tasks and the financial implications of their activities. A plan must be properly articulated and communicated if it is to work. A variety of project planning techniques are discussed in Chapter 11.

An ability to sequence and prioritise tasks

Even a simple plan will demand that different people carry out a number – often a considerable number – of tasks at different times. Those tasks must be coordinated within the shape of the overall project. Timetabling will be important. It will be possible to carry out some tasks only after others have been carried out first. Some tasks may be performed alongside each other. Some tasks must be given priority over others if resources are to be used effectively. Prioritisation must be undertaken both *by* individuals and *between* individuals on the project team. A project in which task order and priority have been well defined will be delivered in a shorter time period and at lower cost than one where they have not. A number of formal (though practical and quite easy to use) methods have been developed to assist managers in organising complex task sequences. These are reviewed in Chapter 11.

An ability to manage the financial resources that are to be invested in the consulting project

All management activity demands that money be spent. As a minimum, managers and other workers must be paid for their work. The purchase of external goods (market research, for example) may also be required. With some projects capital expenditure may be expected. For example, the consultant may take responsibility for the purchase of a major piece of equipment or building or investment in an expensive promotional campaign. Keeping track of that expenditure is a critical management responsibility. Profiles of expected expenditure – budgets – must be set before the project starts so that the resource requirements may be understood. These budgets must be managed. Actual expenditure must be monitored against anticipated expenditure. A project, no matter how good its outcomes, runs the risk of disappointing the client if it turns out to be more expensive than anticipated.

Most consulting projects undertaken by students do not demand the management of large financial sums. However, clients have been known to make money available to the student team, especially if a project is going well and they are keen to expand its possibilities. It is far from uncommon for a client who is pleased with the outcomes of a consulting exercise to ask members of the student team who have delivered it to come in on a full-time basis and implement its recommendations. For these reasons developing an awareness of budget management issues and recognising the skills necessary for managing them are valuable parts of the consulting learning experience. An effective approach to managing the budget for a consulting project is discussed in Section 11.3.

An ability to recognise the human expertise necessary to deliver the project

A particularly important aspect of recognising the human expertise necessary to deliver a project is to understand how the various members of the consulting team can specialise their roles. It is often said that people are a business's greatest asset. After all, it is only people who can make one business different from another. Consultants must work as part of a team. At any one time professional consultants will be members of at least two teams: one based with their own employing business and one at the client business. Student consultants are also likely to be members of a team made up of other students. This team will be an adjunct to the management team at the client business. Productive team working is crucial for consulting success. (This issue is discussed in detail in Chapter 7.) One area where team working and project management skills meet is in deciding who will do what. Not every member of the team can or should attempt to undertake every task. It is unlikely, given people's individual preferences, that they would wish to. A lot of value can be created by differentiation activities and allowing an individual in the team an opportunity to specialise his or her contribution. The range of individual roles in the project is considered in Section 11.1.

An ability to manage personal time

Time is the most precious of resources. We never seem to have enough of it. All managers must learn to use their time well. This is no less so for the student consultant. The consulting exercise will not be the only thing on the agenda. Other courses must be attended, tutorials prepared for and examinations revised for. A little time for a social life would also be nice! The management of personal time is an important aspect of project management. Time management skills are discussed in detail in Chapter 11. They are worth investing in. Not only do they allow time to be used productively, they also mean that last-minute panics are avoided. This reduces stress. Relaxed management is more effective, engenders confidence, and makes learning easier and much more enjoyable.

3.3   Analysis skills

A consulting exercise must do something for the client business. It must offer the business the chance of moving from where it is 'now' to somewhere 'new and better'. This demands both an analysis of the business's current situation and an analysis of the opportunities open to it. Analysis involves taking information about the business and its situation and processing that information so that effective decisions may be made from it. The management consultant's analysis skills may be considered at two levels. At one level there are skills that enable information in general to be manipulated and used. These are skills which all people use all the time. However, a consultant must hone them to a high level. At a more technical level there are skills that facilitate the analysis of business activity. Consultants must be specialists in understanding a business, its strengths and weaknesses, its situation and the opportunities and threats it presents. To do so requires the application of more specific concepts and techniques. General analysis skills are often subsumed into management 'intuition'. They are just what experienced managers do on the basis of what they know. Just because they are not necessarily explicit does not mean they are not important. In fact, this is evidence of *deep learning* (a technique that can be mastered). General analysis skills include the following.

An ability to identify what information is available in a particular situation

Decision-makers demand information. The more information that is taken into account, the more confidence there can be in the decision made. A good decision-maker is active in auditing the information that is available to be used in a decision-making situation. In many cases this will involve background research and reviews of published information. However, at an immediate level it will demand effective questioning of those with experience of the business and its situation to get them to share the information they have (and which they may not even know they have!). This process involves both problem definition and questioning skills. Problem definition is reviewed in Chapter 5. Questioning skills are critical to communication and are considered in Section 7.6.

An ability to identify what information is needed in a particular situation

Often in a decision-making situation it is not a lack of information that presents a problem. Quite the reverse in fact: it is that too much is available. The consultant always walks a tightrope between not gaining enough information and so making uninformed decisions and having so much that focused decision-making is impaired – between what two of the founders of modern systems thinking, Kast and Rosenzweig (1985), have called 'extinction by instinct' and 'paralysis by analysis'. Anne Langley explores the practical implications of this issue in a 1995 paper. Having identified what information is available in a situation a consultant must decide which information is pertinent to the decision in hand. The information that is needed to make the decision an effective one must be distinguished from that which is merely a distraction. The balance will lie in the nature of the decision, its significance to the consulting project and the business, and the type of information available.

An ability to process that information to identify the important relationships within it

Information on its own is not much use. It must be processed in order to identify the important relationships within it. Critically, what the information is really saying about the business and the opportunities open to it must be revealed. For instance, consumer demand figures suggest a market is growing. Does this present an opportunity for your client's business? Or does it just make life easier for competitors? Will it attract new ones into your client's market? For example, a report in the *Financial Times* suggests an important competitor of your client is failing. Does this suggest an easier time for your client or does it herald a tougher time for your client's sector as a whole? An innovative product of the client business is making a real impact in the market. Good. But will it lead to cash flow problems? Drawing conclusions such as these demands an understanding of patterns of relationships and causal linkages that connect businesses, their customers and their environments. Creative approaches to analysis are discussed in Chapter 9.

An ability to draw meaning from that information and use it to support decision-making

Once connections have been made and conclusions drawn it is necessary to identify the impact of those conclusions on the courses of action open to the client business and their significance to the consulting project. This processing of information has both 'private' and 'public' aspects. The private aspect involves a detached and reflective consideration of what the information means and what, in consequence, is the best option for the business. The public aspect demands using information to make the case for a particular course of action, to advocate particular options, to convince others of the correctness of that course and to meet objections. These two aspects do, of course, go hand in hand. The 'intuitive' side of analysis is often supplemented by the use of formal techniques that can help business decision-making. Some of the more important consulting analysis skills are in the areas dealt with in the following sections.

An ability to recognise the business's profile of strengths, weaknesses and capabilities

All businesses are different. They develop strengths that allow them to deliver certain sorts of value to particular customers in a special and valuable way.

They have weaknesses that leave them open to attack by competitors. A variety of conceptual frameworks can be used to guide the exploration of a firm's strengths, capabilities and weaknesses.

An ability to recognise the opportunities and challenges the environment offers the business

A business's environment presents a constantly shifting kaleidoscope of possibilities. Some offer new opportunities to serve customers better and so grow and develop the business. Others expose weaknesses that at best leave the business in a position where it will fail to reach its potential and at worst will cause its decline. An ability to evaluate the opportunities and threats its markets offer the business is a fundamental prerequisite to devising rewarding consulting projects and defining their objectives.

An ability to assess the business's financial situation

Financial performance is not the only measure of a business's success. But it is fundamental. It is only through a sound financial performance that a business can reward its stakeholders. An analysis of a company's financial situation offers a route to understanding its performance in its marketplace, the risks to which it is exposed and the resources it has available to invest in the future. Financial analysis is easiest and most rewarding when undertaken with the guidance of formal ratio methods. All of these methods of analysis will be considered in detail in Chapter 6.

An ability to evaluate the business's markets and how they are developing

A market is the total of demand for a particular good or service. A particular business gains sales through having a share of that market. The growth of the business will be sensitive to the development of its markets. If the market is growing, new business opportunities may present themselves. But new competitors may be attracted to them as well. If the market is in decline, business pressures may be building. If the market is fragmenting, new niches may be opening up and innovation may be rewarded. An analysis of trends in the business's markets, combined with a consideration of the firm's capabilities, can be used to define consulting project outcomes that make a real contribution to the business's development. The techniques that can be used to explore market conditions and the opportunities they present will be considered in Chapter 6.

An ability to assess the business's internal conditions

A business is able to exploit market opportunities only if it has the internal conditions that allow it to meet them head-on. The business must have internal conditions that are flexible and responsive to new possibilities and have the resources needed to innovate in an appropriate way. The business must have the capacity to grow in response to those possibilities or be able to get hold of the resources it will need to invest in growth. These resources include human skills as well as productive capacity.

An ability to analyse the way in which decision-making occurs within the business

Understanding the possibilities open to a business and devising ways in which those possibilities can be exploited is only the first half of the consultant's responsibilities. If the consultant is to offer real value to a business, he or she must also help the business make those possibilities a reality. One of the few, perhaps the only, unquestionable truths about organisational life is that businesses rarely recognise good ideas instantly and pursue them without question. Usually a consultant must convince the client business that what he or she is suggesting is a real opportunity. To do this an effective consultant must understand decision-making in the business and use this knowledge to his or her advantage. This demands knowing who is involved in the decision-making process and the roles different individuals play. It also means a sensitivity to who will gain (and who might lose) if particular ideas are put into practice. The consultant must be aware that not all objections are purely rational. Analysing the decision-making processes in the client business is a first stage in building relationships with individuals in the business. Models that assist in this analysis are discussed in Chapters 6 and 9.

3.4   Relationship-building skills

Analysis skills offer an insight into where the client business might go. Project management skills offer an ability to deliver the project necessary to move the business forward. However, these skills are of only very limited use if the client firm's management and influential outsiders cannot be convinced that this is the right way to go and that they should give their support to the project and the direction it offers. Gaining this support demands relationship-building skills. Critical relationship-building skills include the following.

An ability to build rapport and trust with the client

Rapport is hard to define – but it is easy to recognise. Two people have a rapport when they communicate with ease and work together effectively. It is clear that they have a trust in each other and a commitment to each other. Rapport is not confined to face-to-face communication. It is a feature of all communication. Rapport can be built through written and verbal communications as well. It is not just subject to what is said. How things are said matters as well. Rapport is very important in 'lubricating' the consultant's activities within the organisation. Developing rapport demands practice. It is a skill that can be developed through active learning. Guidance and some hints on how to build rapport are given in Chapter 7.

An ability to question effectively

Questioning is one of the fundamental communication skills. Questioning is not only a way to get information (though this is important). It is also a way to build rapport and to control the direction of a conversation. Effective questioning skills are an important plank in any manager's leadership strategy. They are especially important for the consultant. Questioning is so important that it is discussed in a separate section (7.6).

An ability to communicate ideas succinctly and precisely

A consultant brings a special level of expertise to a business. He or she must offer something the business cannot offer itself. This may mean that the consultant is working in an area with a high technical content, for example finance or marketing. Areas such as these and many others have a language all of their own. The consultant must be cautious about using this language directly to the client. After all, the client is not interested in the consultant's knowledge of a technical area but in his or her ability to use that knowledge in a way that creates value for the business. A consultant has most impact when he or she talks the same language as the client. Ideas must be related in a way that is succinct and precise and uses no more technical jargon than the client is comfortable with. Converting technical ideas into plain language is not always easy. But it is important and is a skill of its own which can be developed with practice.

An ability to negotiate objectives and outcomes

A consulting project must have definite objectives and outcomes. The value the project is expected to deliver to the client business must be explicit. However, the consultant and the client do not always agree, in the first instance at least, on what those outcomes should be. The client may not have a clear idea of what is wanted for the business. If he or she does have a definite idea it may be beyond the scope of what the consultant is in a position to offer realistically. It may be that the consultant is not convinced that what the client is demanding as an outcome is absolutely right for the business. Such disagreements can often occur with student consulting projects where the client's expectations are very high and there is a need to reconcile commercial with educational outcomes.

Whatever the source of any disagreement, the project outcomes must be defined and agreed by consultant and client. This is a process of negotiation that results in the formal project brief. The need to negotiate is not an admission that there is necessarily a conflict between the client and the consultant. Rather, it is a recognition that the consultancy exercise will work best when both client and consultant have clear expectations as to what will result from the consulting exercise and what the responsibility of both parties will be in achieving them. The consultant must be aware that disappointment in consultancy (for both client and consultant team) results more from unclear expectations than from poor outcomes. Ways to approach negotiating the outcomes of the project are considered in Chapter 5.

An ability to convince through verbal, written and visual mediums

In business, having good ideas is not enough. Ideas must be used to encourage people to follow them as courses of action. They must be used to encourage the business's managers to implement plans and its backers to make supportive investment decisions. Ideas must be communicated in a way that convinces people that they are good and are worth implementing. This conviction comes as much from the 'how' of communication as from the 'what', that is, from the form of the communication as well as its content. Conviction results if ideas are communicated in a manner that is appropriate to the audience; for example, if the communication uses the right language, is of the right length and adopts a proper style. This applies to communication in any situation and whether the medium is verbal, visual or written.

An ability to use information to make a case for a particular course of action

Of course, ideas must have some substance if they are to deliver real value. Communication of ideas must be backed up with information. This includes both facts and interpretation of facts. The logic of that interpretation must be clear. Different people in the client business will seek and will be convinced by different corroborating information, at different levels and presented in different ways. Some information will be included in an initial communication. Other parts may be kept back as a response to questions and challenges. Knowing when to use particular information, and how to use it to convince, is an important communication skill for the consultant, especially as a consultant's ideas are likely to be under close scrutiny by the client business, certainly more so than those of internal managers. Convincing with information and well-structured, well-communicated arguments is a theme developed in Chapter 12.

An ability to develop selling strategies

Effective selling calls for a definite, well developed and quite well understood set of skills. Selling of goods and services is a specialist management activity. However, all managers are involved in selling their ideas all the time. Consultants must certainly sell their ideas. But they must also sell themselves and their own organisations as *providers* of ideas. This is a particular challenge for consultants involved in general management rather than some specialist area. A business may readily accept that it lacks technical knowledge in product development, information technology or finance. However, few businesses will readily admit to being deficient in general management skills. The consultant can draw on a variety of formal selling skills. These must be used appropriately though. Consultancy, as a 'product', does not usually respond to a 'hard sell' approach. Rather, a formal selling approach should be used as the tactic in a well-thought-through selling strategy. This strategy should aim to communicate what the consultant can genuinely offer the client and be used to build a long-term, mutually rewarding relationship.

An ability to work effectively as a member of a team

Many consulting tasks (especially those of major significance) require a team effort. As a minimum they will demand that the consultant and client work together. Usually they will involve an extended management team in the client business. Often the consulting task will have significant resource implications and will be complex to deliver. The scope of its demands will go beyond the capabilities of one individual, certainly in time and perhaps in technical knowledge. Delivering the project will require the consultant to work as part of a team. Good team working is essential for business success and not just in consulting. It is a skill in itself. It demands many things. It requires, for example, a careful definition of individual roles in relation to the team as a whole. It also requires well-honed interpersonal, motivation and conflict-resolution skills. Most of all, perhaps, it demands a willingness to align the interests of the individuals who make up the team with the overall task the team must address. This requires an ability to advocate individual interests and yet, when necessary, to compromise individual concerns for the interests of the group as a whole.

If the team is to develop a productive coherence through which its members can make individual contributions, it must be actively managed. Chapter 7 considers the issues involved in and the skills needed for team working. These will be considered with the support of conceptual thinking about the dynamics of team working.

An ability to demonstrate leadership

Leadership is an ability to focus and direct the individuals in an organisation in a way that brings the whole organisation benefits. Leadership is perhaps the most valuable commodity a senior manager can offer his or her organisation. Leadership draws together a variety of relationship skills – not least articulation of vision, motivation and communication – into a coherent behavioural strategy. It should not be thought that a consulting team can have only one, permanent leader and that the remainder of the team must be followers. Such an assumption lies behind many intragroup conflicts. Leadership is not an inherent and fixed property of an individual. It is situational; that is, it arises out of the conditions of a particular situation in which people interact in a particular way. Leadership may shift between members as the project evolves and the situation changes. The individual who shows leadership for the team may not be the same person who shows leadership towards the client business or towards people from outside the team offering support to the project. In professional consulting, as in business generally, leadership up the formal reporting hierarchy, from subordinate to superior, may be as important as traditional leadership down it.

A consulting project is one of the best opportunities a student will be given to recognise the nature and value of leadership, and to develop leadership skills. The nature of leadership skills important for the consultant is discussed in Chapter 7. The project management, analysis and relationship skill areas do not work in isolation. They must operate in conjunction and in balance with each other. Relationship building must be based on a proficient analysis of the business and the people in it. Project management must be aimed at delivering negotiated outcomes. Good project management skills offer a base on which can be built a trust that outcomes will be delivered.

3.5 The consulting selling process

There are many consultants, often with similar skills. So how does a firm choose to use one consultant over another? Personal experience is a very strong motivator:

people feel more comfortable with those they have worked with before or are recommended by someone they trust. However, there are times when the potential buyer of consulting does not personally know who can help: then they must look for information on who might help them. As with buying any service, the potential buyer of consulting has some common criteria:

- Have I heard of this company (i.e. a 'brand' that I trust)?
- Do they offer the service I require?
- Are their rates competitive?
- Do they have testimonials from other satisfied customers?
- Are they efficient at handling my initial enquiry?
- Do I trust and empathise with the representative(s) of the company who I meet, i.e. do they speak the same language and understand my issues?

From a consultant's point of view, they need to ensure that any potential clients are not only aware of them but also have a good (if second-hand) opinion of them. This means that they have to effectively market themselves, just like any business. This demands a marketing strategy and an action plan, detailing the activities that they will undertake. Figure 3.2 shows the process that an effective consultant goes through to achieve a sale.

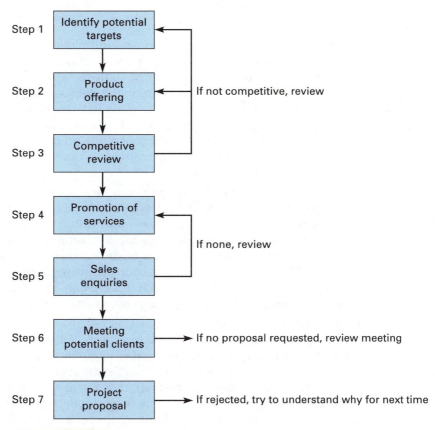

Figure 3.2 The selling process

Step 1: Identify potential targets

Depending on the size of the consulting firm, i.e. the number of consultants they have and the skills of those people, the targets could be defined as follows:

- All those from one type of industry, e.g. food and drink, or a sector within an industry, e.g. frozen food.
- Firms of a certain size (turnover between £50 and £100 million or those with profits in excess of £50 million, for example).
- In geographical terms by region (Europe, for example), country or even area within a country, e.g. north-west England.
- With personal contacts of consulting firm's members: these could be former colleagues or those that they have worked with in a consulting capacity.
- All those requiring a particular product or service, for example cost reduction in factories.

When the consultant has identified the firms they wish to target, they need to think about the key people within their target companies. It might be assumed that this is obvious but, in selling consultancy, there are complex relationships that must be understood to identify who will ensure a consulting project goes ahead. Heiman, Sanchez and Tuleja (2004), in their book *The New Strategic Selling*, have identified four types of 'buyers' who are all-important when consultants are considering selling their services:

- *Economic buyer* – this is the person who ultimately approves the funds for the project to go ahead. They could be the Chief Executive or the Finance Director or, for more complex organisations, someone else, for example the head of a department that will benefit from the consulting project. They have the right to veto a project when everyone else has agreed. They can also be a strong ally in accepting an unpopular consulting assignment, for example large-scale change programmes. While many consulting projects have been sold just with the approval of the economic buyer, they are never as well implemented unless the other buyers are considered.
- *User buyer* – these will be the ones who are directly affected by the consulting project. They may have to devote time to the project in addition to their 'day' job. The outcome of the project may influence their future job or career. Critically their input can 'make or break' a project and determine whether a consulting firm is able to get repeat business. Also in the sale process, they can be valuable sources of information for the proposal to make it as 'sellable' as possible. They do not, however, sign the cheque, so while concentrating solely on this group can yield a creditable proposal, it will not get the funds approved.
- *Technical buyer* – these are specialists within the firm who will 'vet' any consulting proposals, for example the head of IT will be the technical buyer for a new customer relationship management system. They can judge whether the proposal is feasible given the company's current position. So while they cannot give a final 'yes' (like the user buyer), they are in a position to reject a proposal on technical grounds. Again they may be a good source of information for the proposal but consultants need to maintain their impartiality, especially if they are advocating a radical solution.

■ *Coach* – this is your 'friendly face' in the target company (occasionally they may be outside the target firm but would have a close professional relationship with it). They can find you the other buyers within the organisation and make introductions. They can also help you if you are having problems getting the information you need from user and technical buyers. What they cannot do is complete the sale for you. However, not having a coach makes the process much harder and the success rate lower.

Step 2: Product offering

The next stage is to understand what will be offered to potential clients. These could range from very specific products, for example offering commercial due diligence to venture capitalists interested in investing in new technology firms, to more general ones which rely on the skills of the consultants themselves, for example organisational development. David Maister's chapter on 'The Anatomy of a Consulting Firm' in Fombrun and Nevins (2004) argues that the structure and management of consulting firms is determined by two key factors: the degree of customisation in the firm's work activities and the extent of face-to-face interaction with the client. So a consulting firm has to think about whether it is going to offer mainly a standardised process, where all potential clients get an 'off the peg' solution or a customised one which is bespoke. Both have their advantages: the first is easy to administer and less highly skilled staff are needed. The latter attracts higher fee rates and the work is more intellectually rewarding for the consultant. The reality is that few firms can offer both with credibility, just as designer labels struggle to be aspirational and mass market. The other variable is the extent to which a consultant is involved with the client and this is explored further in Chapter 8.

Step 3: Competitive review

The key is for the consultant to be able to offer something that differentiates themselves as far as possible from their competitors. So, as with any good marketing strategy, they need to understand their competitors' services. They can then compare themselves and ensure that what they offer is competitive. Given that personal relationships are often important in selling a consultancy, you may want to look for 'gaps' where your competitors are not operating. This may be because they think those customers are too small for them or that they are not natural buyers of consulting, for example other professional services such as lawyers or accountants.

Step 4: Promotion of services

Consultants must then tell their potential customers what they have to offer. All the standard promotional techniques can be used: face-to-face meetings, mailings, advertisements and links to the website. However, as consultants' key benefit are their personal skills, public relation events, such as speaking at business conferences and other meetings where potential clients may attend, also offer a useful tool. Perhaps the most powerful promotional tool a consultant has is their previous work for a client. This 'repeat business' is highly sought after as it is relatively cheap to acquire and the likelihood of success should be greater as the consultant knows the buyers better.

Step 5: Sales enquiries

This should elicit sales enquiries, if the steps above are correctly carried out, i.e. the correct target audience has been identified, with the right product offering and correctly promoted. There are broadly two types of sales enquiries. The first is where the client has worked with the consultant before and the consultant has had an active role in getting the enquiry. For example, at the end of a business strategy project, there may be new opportunities for the consultant to help the firm implement it. This could include developing a marketing strategy or new product development. Obviously the consultant has to have the right skills to be able to offer these additional services but provided the first project went well, they have a good chance of succeeding. The second type is where the client has not worked with the consulting firm. This can either be as a result of a formal competitive tender process (often used by the public sector as a way of achieving best value) or an invitation to make a proposal following an informal meeting (business presentation, for example, discussed above). The former will be a definite brief and a consultant can decide whether they wish to join the competitive bidding process, where chances of success are lower than the latter type of invitation to make a proposal. Turning down the latter would only be done in extreme circumstances when there were no resources available or the consultant felt the proposal was beyond their scope of expertise. If this is the case, then the consultant may want to review their promotional activities, as they are obviously giving out the wrong message!

Step 6: Meeting potential clients

The next stage – meeting with the client to discuss the project – is sometimes the hardest as it relies on listening carefully to the potential client's issues and the reason for their sales call. An effective consultant will *not* go into a sales meeting with the aim to sell a specific project, even if it is a formal tender. If they do so, it will be at their peril! This is one of the biggest mistakes a consultant can make and the most disastrous as it could lead either to the project proposal being rejected by the client or if in the event the project does go ahead, it does not deliver what the client wants. It may take quite a few meetings and a lot of preparation before the consultant is clear about what exactly the client needs to address their issue. Here the consultant should not be afraid to ask, even simple, questions. Trying to look clever but not understanding what the client is saying can be fatal! A client should not expect that the consultant knows everything about their business.

Neil Rackham, in his book *Spin®-Selling* (1995), identifies four stages in a sales meeting: preliminaries, investigating, demonstrating capability and obtaining commitment. Preliminaries are critical because many potential clients will make up their mind in the first few minutes of meeting as to their opinion of the consultant. The next stage should involve uncovering the client's needs through investigation, i.e. asking the right questions. In a complex sale such as a consultancy project this may involve two stages. The first elicits 'implied needs' that need to be gently tested. For example, the client may believe that the reason for their low sales is that they are targeting the wrong sort of customers. Questions such as 'How are your competitors doing?' or 'Who are your *right* customers?' may show that in fact their products are in a poor competitive position. So the 'explicit need' has been identified. The next stage in a successful call is demonstrating your capability. This does not mean that you come up with a solution there and then but show the potential client that you have worked in this area before. Finally, you need to obtain commitment. This is usually in the form of preparing a proposal.

Step 7: Project proposal

The final step in the selling process is the project proposal, which is discussed in more detail in the sections below. A good proposal will be the result of a consultant really understanding the client's needs and having gone through the selling process properly. A poor proposal can be the result of the selling process going wrong, particularly the last stage when the consultant meets with the potential client.

3.6   The function of the project proposal

The project proposal is a short, straightforward document. It has two simple aims. These are to state what the consulting exercise aims to achieve and to get the client to commit to it. Despite its brevity the project proposal is very important. It is the pivot about which the whole project revolves. A good proposal gets the project off to a good start. A weak one will hinder the project from the outset. The proposal is a statement to the client of what the project is about and what it will do for the business. The proposal is what the client is *buying* from the consultant. It needs to present what the consultant has to offer in a positive light. It has to make the consultant's offering appear as an attractive investment given all the other things the business has an opportunity to invest in. If the consultant's pitch is a competitive one, the proposal has to present the consultant as the best available.

A further and equally important function of the proposal is to manage the client's *expectations*. An individual's satisfaction with a product or service is not usually based on the absolute utility of what he or she receives. More often it is based on outcomes relative to expectations. If expectations are met or exceeded, then satisfaction will occur. If expectations are not met, disappointment will inevitably result. If the client recognises the proposal as what he or she is buying then it is against this that the final project delivery will be compared. Some managers have an unrealistic idea of what a consultant is capable of, or at least capable of given the resources the manager is able to invest in the consulting project, both in terms of the money the client is putting forward and the time and capabilities of the consultant. If this is so then the manager is likely to be dissatisfied with the results of a consulting exercise *even if, in absolute terms, that project is a good one*. However, a manager who has doubts about the ability of a consultant to offer anything of value may well be pleasantly satisfied with the results of a quite mediocre project. (Though, of course, such a manager may resist using a consultant in the first place!)

The proposal must serve a twofold function. On the one hand, it must 'sell' what the consultant has to offer. On the other, it must manage the expectations of the client manager so that he or she does not make an unreasonable demand on the consultant given the resources that are available. The project proposal demands a balanced approach from the consultant. The temptation to 'get a sale' by offering a lot must be tempered by a care not to raise the client's expectations so high that they cannot be met. There are a few simple rules that will allow this balance to be struck. First, understand what the client would *really* like for his or her business. Do not fall into the trap of assuming that he or she will want what the 'textbooks' suggest they *should* have, or that they must take what you think is best for them. Managers often reject the obvious answers for very good reasons. Second, enquire into, and gain a thorough understanding of, the extent to which the client expects the consulting exercise to contribute to the overall goal for the business. It is particularly important to ensure that the client makes the distinction between the consulting project offering a *means* to achieve the business's goals and its actually *implementing* them: between the consultant pointing out a *direction* for the business and actually *taking* it there. This is an issue about which the consultant and client can easily develop different expectations.

Developing this understanding of the client's needs and expectations must take place at the preliminary analysis stage of the project. It is best done through a personal meeting between the manager and the consulting team or a representative of it. At this stage the objective of the meeting should be to gather information about the business and what might be done for it. It is not a time to start negotiating on outcomes. It is better to wait until the written proposal has been presented before starting negotiating on precisely what can and cannot be achieved. The proposal helps here. It provides something tangible around which discussions can centre. The initial proposal can always be modified in light of further discussion. How to approach these negotiations will be dealt with fully in Chapter 5. If the proposal is modified, however, do produce a written version so that finalised aims, objectives and outcomes are clear to all and can be referred back to.

3.7   What to include in the proposal and an example

The proposal needs to be succinct and must make an impact. It must speak for itself; you cannot rely on having an opportunity to explain it in person. Typically it will be one to two pages long. If it is longer than this it will risk losing its impact. If the proper groundwork has been done, then it will really be the confirmation of a project. As with any business communication, the proposal should always be approached with a fresh mind. There are always new ways of doing things to be discovered. However, there are some key elements which, when included in the proposal, do add to its impact and help it communicate effectively within the constraints described above. These will now be described in detail.

A title

All that is necessary is a short title for the project, perhaps the client company's name and a brief descriptive phrase. This provides a reference for the project in the future and helps locate it in the minds of all involved.

Client's requirements

This should be a brief statement about the company, the opportunities or issues it faces and the scope of the project. The scope may be drawn from the types of consulting project described in Chapter 2. The background statement should aim to convey the fact that the consultant understands the key issue or issues and is committed to addressing them. It should not be a complete description of the business and its situation. This would be far too long and as the client possesses this information they would not be interested.

Overall aim

This is a statement of what the project aims to achieve, in broad terms. This might be thought of as the mission for the project from which definite objectives might be drawn.

Objectives

This is a list of the detailed objectives for the project. Objectives should be active; they are statements of what the project will do. A good way of starting the list is to use the phrase:

This consulting exercise aims to . . .

Outcomes

Outcomes are subtly different from objectives. They are a statement of what the business *will be able to do* as a result of receiving the consulting exercise and the delivery of its objectives. Again, they should be active. A good way of starting the list is to use the phrase:

As a result of this consulting exercise the business will be able to . . .

Both objectives and outcomes are best summarised in the form of a bullet-point list. Objectives and outcomes should be complete in themselves. Do not be tempted to expand on them or qualify them with subsidiary paragraphs. If the consulting exercise is long and complex it may be proper to develop interim objectives and outcomes for the intermediate stages of the project. The development and articulation of good objectives and outcomes is discussed in Chapter 5.

Our approach

This section provides an opportunity for the consulting group to describe how it will address the exercise. It should highlight the approach in broad terms. It might detail activities such as market research, analysis and guidance with implementation. It should not give a detailed exposition of the methodologies that might be adopted. This section is an opportunity for the consulting team to indicate what it has to offer. The emphasis should be on why what the group can offer is different or special. It is a further opportunity to manage the client's expectations and in particular to emphasise the distinction between developing a plan for the business and actually implementing it.

Time plan

The time plan is an indication of when the outcomes of the exercise will be delivered and identifies important milestones *en route*. Milestones are key events along the way to the final delivery and might include things like meetings with the client and information providers, interim reports and presentations. The amounts of detail in the time plan will reflect the length and complexity of the project.

Key personnel

This is perhaps the most important section after detailing your approach. Consulting is about paying for people's skills and knowledge. It is also useful to describe, briefly, what will be the individual roles of the consultants in the team. The client may not meet all of these people but it adds weight to the proposal if you can demonstrate the breadth of experience you have in your organisation. The information you give about each person should be relevant to the project and ideally list similar projects that they have worked on. Be realistic and honest, putting down lots of names may impress but if you know that they will have little or no contact with the project, then the client may feel you are deceiving them.

Costings

Costings are statements of how much the project will cost the client. Important elements are the consultant's fees, the consultant's expenses (often just a *pro rata* cost on top of fees) and any direct expenditure needed. Direct expenditure might be needed for buying market research or undertaking surveys.

What not to include in the proposal

It is as important to know what *not* to include in the project proposal as to know what to put in. A lot of background on the business does not usually help. It 'pads out' the proposal, making it longer than it need be. It tells the client things he or she already knows and runs the risk of losing his or her interest before the important aspects of the proposal are reached. The temptation to discuss the methodology that will be adopted should also be avoided. The formal business analysis techniques used by the consultant in developing an understanding of the business and how it might be moved forward are the consultant's concern – not the client's! A simple analogy with the repairing of your car makes the point. If you take your car to the garage for repair, you are not particularly interested in what tools the mechanic will use. Management consulting is the same. The consultant is an expert who is brought in because he or she knows how to call upon a range of tools to deal with business issues. There is no reason to reveal those tools to the client before the project starts. Exhibit 3.1 presents an example of a project proposal along the lines discussed in this chapter.

Exhibit 3.1 Consulting proposal

Greyline Printers: support for a business expansion programme

Your requirements

Greyline Printers is a small but ambitious and fast growing firm offering a range of printing and reprographic services. The consulting team has been invited to work with the senior management team and explore the opportunities for growth the business might successfully capitalise upon, given the business's current resources.

Overall aim

The main aim of the consulting project is to give Greyline Printers a clear sense of direction for the way in which the business might be expanded into new market sectors.

Objectives

The consulting project aims to:

- evaluate the market context of Greyline Printers;
- identify high-growth customer segments;
- develop an understanding of what those customers require from a good print and reprographics supplier – in terms of both products and service support;
- identify major competitors of the business;
- evaluate what those competitors offer and identify how Greyline Printers might develop a competitive edge;
- summarise the findings in the form of a brief for the business's sales team;
- make recommendations on a PR campaign to increase awareness of the company and its products among target customers.

Outcomes

As a result of this consulting exercise Greyline Printers will be able to:

- develop an understanding of the market sectors that are most attractive for new business development;
- dedicate valuable resources towards the exploitation of those market sectors;
- position itself in a way which is competitive given the current profile of competitors.

In particular the business will be able to:

- refine its product range and service offering to increase competitiveness;
- initiate a sales campaign dedicated to gaining new customers in those sectors;
- support sales activity with a well-focused PR campaign.

Our approach

Our approach will emphasise the importance of reliable information to the decision-makers of Greyline Printers. Secondary marketing research will be used to establish a picture of the dynamics of the print and reprographics market and the competitive situation. Building on this, primary market research will be used to investigate customer needs and expectations. The findings will be used to give a clear direction for new product development. Market intelligence will be summarised in a form that makes it accessible to the sales team. A review of publications that reach important customers will be undertaken. This will be used to develop for Greyline Printers an awareness-building communication plan.

▶

Time plan

Key events in the project will be as follows:

October 2007:	Initial meeting with client to discuss requirements.
November 2007:	Initial proposal presented to client and reviewed.
November 2007:	Final proposal based on review: agreement to go ahead.
December 2007:	Progression of project. Further meetings with client (three expected over period).
January 2008:	Secondary marketing research.
February 2008:	Primary research with buyers.
April 2008:	Preparation of final report. Sales brief and PR plan appended.
May 2008	Final presentation of findings.

Key personnel

There will be three consultants involved in this project. Mr A will lead the project and ensure that the work is completed to your satisfaction. He has 20 years' experience in this field and worked on similar projects for Xerox and Canon. He will be assisted by Mrs B, an experienced consultant in the area of marketing within the communication industries, having previously worked for Hewlett Packard as their marketing manager. She will be responsible for the majority of the work outlined above and be your main point of contact on a day-to-day basis. Finally Miss C, an analyst in our specialist Communications practice will conduct the market research described above. She is a recent MBA graduate and has worked with Mr A on the project for Xerox and recently completed a market research study for IBM.

Costings

There are two elements to this proposal. The first is the fees charged based on the estimated time spent by our consultants:

Mr A	5 days @ £2,000	£10,000
Mrs B	30 days @ £1,000	£30,000
Miss C	20 days @ £500	£10,000
Total		£50,000

The second is our expenses. These will be charged at cost; however, we estimate that they will be around 10 per cent of our fees. If this figure is likely to be significantly higher then we will inform you in advance.

Team discussion points

1 You have undertaken a consulting exercise with a local travel firm. The firm is very pleased with the outcomes of the project and by way of thanks offers your group a free holiday together. Consider this holiday as a project. What project management, analysis and relationship-building skills must the group use if you are to make the holiday enjoyable for all?

Hint

Consider the various stages of the 'project':

- deciding where to go, when to go and how long to stay;
- deciding what needs to be taken and packing your luggage;
- travelling to your destination;
- enjoying the activities available on the holiday;
- returning home.

What skills will be called on at each stage?

2 You have decided to set up a company with some of your fellow students that will offer consulting services to local businesses who rely on the student trade. Go through the selling process described above to identify your targets, products you will offer and your promotional ideas to get sales enquiries.

 ## Summary of key ideas

The effective consultant offers the client firm a way to add value that it cannot do on its own (*see* Figure 3.3). To do this the consultant must call on three areas of management skill:

- *analysis skills* – an ability to know where to go and how to get there;
- *relationship-building skills* – an ability to take people along with you;
- *project management skills* – an ability to make it happen!

These are general management skills. Consulting presents a steep learning curve. This means it is a challenge. However, the rewards are high. An effective consultant can expect to take on highly responsible roles at an early stage in his or her career.

The sales process of a consulting project has to be structured to be effective. Potential target companies, their buyers and product offerings should be looked at first. Then a check for competitiveness is required, followed by a promotional plan. This should lead to sales enquiries, sales meetings and the invitation to write a proposal.

The project proposal is a critical part of the consulting project. It does two things:

- It sells what the consultant has to offer.
- It can be used to manage the client's expectations about the outcomes of the consulting exercise.

Figure 3.3 The consultant must always convince the client that the service on offer is of real value!

Source: Copyright © Scott Adams, Inc./Dist by UFS, Inc. Reproduced by permission.

The proposal should be a short, impactful document. The key elements to include are:

1 a title;
2 a brief statement of the client's requirements;
3 an overall aim for the consulting project;
4 a list of specific objectives – what the project aims to do;
5 a list of specific outcomes – what the business will be able to do as a result of the project;
6 a statement about your approach to the project – how you intend to tackle the project and why this will be effective.

If appropriate, the following may be added:

7 a time plan detailing key events; and
8 details of key personnel;
9 a costing for the project, detailing fees and expenditure.

Key reading

Fombrun, C.J. and Nevins, M.D. (2004) *The Advice Business: Essential Tools and Models for Management Consulting*. Upper Saddle River, NJ: Pearson Prentice Hall (Chapters 2 and 9).

Markham, C. (2004) *The Top Consultant: Developing Your Skills for Greater Effectiveness* (4th edn). London: Kogan Page Ltd (Chapters 4 and 5).

Further reading

Creplet, F., Dupouet, O., Kern, F., Mehmanpazir, B. and Munier, F. (2001) 'Consultants and experts in management consulting firms', *Research Policy*, 30 (9), 1517–35.

Guth, W.D. and MacMillan, I.C. (1986) 'Strategy implementation versus middle management self-interest', *Strategic Management Journal*, 7, 313–27.

Heiman, S.E., Sanchez D. and Tuleja, T. (2004) *The New Strategic Selling* (3rd edn). London: Kogan Page.

Kast, F.G. and Rosenzweig, J.G. (1985) *Organization and Management* (4th edn). New York: McGraw-Hill.

Langley, A. (1995) 'Between "paralysis by analysis" and "extinction by instinct"', *Sloan Management Review*, Spring, 63–76.

Rackham, N. (1995) *Spin®-Selling*. Aldershot, Hampshire: Gower.

Schaffer, R.H. (1997) 'Looking at the 5 fatal flaws of management consulting', *Journal for Quality and Participation*, 20 (3), 44–50.

Simon, A. and Kumar, V. (2001) 'Client's views on strategic capabilities which lead to management consulting success', *Management Decision*, 39 (5), 362–72.

Wooldridge, W. and Floyd, S.W. (1990) 'The strategy process, middle management involvement and organisational performance', *Strategic Management Journal*, 11, 231–41.

Young, J. and Jinloo, L. (1998) 'Factors influencing the success of management consulting projects', *International Journal of Project Management*, 16 (2), 67–72.

Case exercise

Golden Star

Golden Star is a manufacturer of prams (baby/child carriages) and has been in business for over 100 years. They are a family run firm and are proud of their traditional products, which have been used and trusted by many generations of parents. Endorsed by royalty and many famous people, they are the by-word for security for the child. They currently sell over 80 per cent of their output to the large retailers in Europe. The brand 'Golden Star' is universally recognised; however, their newer models have not been as successful as their traditional ones. There is one big problem: their turnover is £10 million per annum but they are making a £2 million loss. The directors are all family members, and shareholders. They want to capitalise their assets and sell the company to a venture capitalist. However, they need to improve the performance of the company in the short term to make the company more attractive and secure a higher price. They have a loyal, highly skilled workforce that is willing to work flexibly to secure the future of the business.

Mr X, the Managing Director and majority shareholder, has called you to a meeting, as a good friend of his has recommended you. He believes that the loss is a short-term issue associated with not producing enough stock to sell (the products are still largely handmade) and being forced to accept lower margins by the large retailers. He therefore wants you to look at his production to find ways of making it more efficient and also look for alternative channels for selling, for example selling direct to the public via the web.

Q1 What are the questions you would ask Mr X to challenge some of his assumptions and uncover his 'explicit needs'?

Q2 Based on the evidence above, what other issues do you think Golden Star faces and what type of consulting project (from Chapter 2) might be used?

Q3 Assuming that Mr X is correct in his assumption that they need to look for alternative sales channels, prepare a proposal on how you might help him as a consultant.

Consulting across borders and cultures

Jeremy Wilcock

Learning outcomes

The learning outcomes from this chapter are to:

■ appreciate the additional challenges and complexities implied by operating internationally both for the client and the consultant;

■ have an awareness of the specific areas where consultant input will benefit the company;

■ understand how consultant expertise can add value;

■ understand how the consultant/client relationship can best be managed.

4.1 The great wide world

Given the increasing international aspect of business today, it is important that, as a consultant, you are aware of the issues that face your client. This can be in terms of either their export plans or the wider international marketing strategies that they wish to adopt. Further, many firms now routinely operate multinational teams where potentially sensitive cultural issues may arise in the course of a consulting project. Looking first at exporting: 'whoever said "exporting is fun" had obviously never actually done any. There are many words that might describe exporting, but "fun" would not be the most obvious one. "Frustrating" would be in there somewhere, as would "complicated", "confusing", "unpredictable", and even "infuriating"' (Sherlock, 2006).

The sheer number of companies either exporting or marketing their brands on a global basis testifies to the appeal of operating outside the home market. Successful brands such as Chanel, Gucci, BMW, Nescafé, Colgate, Heineken, Dettol and Nike to name but a few would never have developed to the extent they have if their owners had opted for the safety and security of the domestic market alone. The attraction of 'going abroad' is obvious: access to larger markets, seeking opportunities for growth if the home market is mature or in economic recession, enjoying economies of scale through increased production volumes, or gaining first mover advantage over a competitor by launching ahead of them in unexploited markets.

Yet for the unwary there are more pitfalls than prizes, and a manager contemplating overseas activity will require a far wider range of knowledge than if the company were simply to remain domestic. Which country to enter? What are the political, economic, social, technological, environmental and legal issues? How will culture impact on the marketing programme? Can the domestic brand name be used, or does the trademark belong to someone else? Is the brand name offensive or comic in the local language? What level of presence should be established? Would a local partner be more appropriate, and if so – who? Does the product need to be modified or reformulated? How will the products reach the end-user? How can planning and forecasting be conducted with any degree of confidence? Most important – how will payment be made?

None of these issues need deter the company. Rather, they need to ensure their managers are fully equipped and prepared so that decisions can be taken confidently, as the result of good information. The role of the consultant is to facilitate the provision of such knowledge. No manager, however competent, will be able to deal successfully with these issues without expert assistance.

4.2   Factors encouraging international operation

When helping a client with their overall strategy, a consultant needs to consider the firm's desire to expand internationally. The principal economic factors behind international trade by firms fall under three main headings. First, due to the non-availability or difficulty of producing an item in one country, the need will be met by importing from elsewhere. The first exports from the British Isles some two thousand years ago are said to have been Cornish tin ore exploited by the Phoenicians and transported to their Mediterranean homeland. Similarly, nowadays commodities such as citrus fruit, coffee, tobacco and oil are imported by countries unable to source them in their home market.

Second, there is the argument mooted by David Ricardo's theory of the law of comparative costs. This holds that countries will gain from international trade if each country exports a commodity in which its costs of production are comparatively lower, and imports a commodity in which its costs are comparatively higher (Katrak, 1971). In other words, each producer will stand to gain if they offer for exchange a commodity in the production of which they enjoy a comparative advantage.

Third, and most appropriate to the overall thrust of this chapter, there is the opportunity for differentiated products. There are sound commercial reasons for seeking to develop a presence outside the domestic market. The most compelling of these will clearly be the potential for significantly increased turnover and profit through offering goods and services to a substantially greater number of customers. Yet who will be these customers? To date, they have managed quite happily without the company's offering. They may have different tastes and requirements, and may live in countries that are difficult to access. They may not respond as readily to the company's promotional message as do its domestic consumers. Nor may they have the same levels of affluence or discretionary spending. Consequently, while the prospect may be very simple, the reality may prove more challenging.

Together with increased volume would come other benefits – the achievement of economies of scale, increased plant throughput, or better utilisation of company resources such as procurement, R&D, packaging development and graphic design, the cost of all of which would be spread over a significantly larger output. Similarly, the company's leverage with its suppliers and agencies would be enhanced due to its greater buying and negotiating power.

A company operating internationally should also be able to spread any risk by virtue of the fact that it is not confined simply to one country, where the economy may go into recession or the market and product life cycles may have matured. Potential peaks and troughs of seasonal demand may also be offset due to the company being in a wider number of markets. Further, increased and more efficient factory utilisation should be able to deliver greater security of employment, enhanced workforce morale and new training and skilling opportunities. Operating internationally will also boost the company's image and increase its exposure. It will develop global brands, market more competitive products, which reflect overseas market requirements and legal issues, and potentially improve the rate of its technological development through the need to respond to world market opportunities. In theory, a higher calibre of management may be able to be recruited, due to the greater challenges presented, the prospect of increased job satisfaction, and the sheer appeal and excitement of working in an international environment with customers of differing cultures.

What may be an opportunity for one company, however, may be a threat for another. In this context, it is intriguing to consider a North American perspective. Smaller nations such as the UK, the Netherlands or France, which have a long history of maritime trading and interaction with differing cultures through their colonial history, have for years viewed the wider world as an opportunity and have successfully established global brands. Yet the North American attitude may be more sceptical. In his book *Marketing Management* (2000) Professor Philip Kotler writes, 'most companies would prefer to remain domestic if their domestic market were large enough. Managers would not need to learn other languages and laws, deal with volatile currencies, face political and legal uncertainties, or redesign their products to suit different customer needs and expectations. Business would be easier and safer.'

Kotler then goes on to cite what he considers to be the key challenges in marketing internationally: huge foreign debts accumulated by countries such as Indonesia and Mexico; unstable regimes which expose foreign firms to the risks of expropriation, nationalisation, and limits on profit repatriation; foreign exchange problems which may decrease the value of a country's currency; host country government regulations which may include the requirement for majority ownership by a local partner; tariffs and 'invisible' trade barriers; corruption and the expectation of bribes (prohibited under US law); technological pirating and copying, an example being the production of low-cost generic pharmaceuticals once the patent has expired; the potentially high cost of product and communication adaptation; and the 'moving target' threat implied by changes to the country's national boundaries. Taken together, these might represent a powerful argument for isolationism, yet the skill will lie in appreciating that certainly there are likely risks, but that the company is properly informed about the nature of such risks, and can therefore plan how to address them, including developing contingency plans. A consultant will have a key role in facilitating such thinking.

Even the seasoned international operator will be contending with these risks and concerns on a daily basis. Payment involves a longer period of credit, possibly 90 or even 180 days. An extreme case would be Syria in the 1970s, when an import licence would not be issued unless the exporter granted 365 days' credit. Clearly the need for extended credit poses cash flow problems, especially at times of high interest rates in the supplier country, and it may be necessary to engage a factoring company to carry the credit risk at a discounted price.

As identified by Kotler, interest and exchange rates pose further threats, as do economic 'boom and bust' cycles. Hedging against exchange rate movement, keeping abreast of expert financial opinion, and maintaining close awareness of the eco-political environment in the country of destination will be important disciplines for the company to follow in such circumstances. Buyers may default, import duties may be increased without warning, price controls may be introduced, new packaging and labelling laws may be announced – all of these have to be taken in the company's stride as the realities of operating across frontiers. The challenge is to manage them, so that the potential gains can be achieved despite the obvious risks.

4.3   Researching and selecting overseas markets

Deciding which countries to enter will be a critical decision for the company. If it makes the wrong choice it will be confronted with two sets of costs: the expense, distraction and complexity of failure, as well as the opportunity cost of missing the chance to enter a market where its offerings might have proved more successful (Bradley, 2002). Consequently, accurate information, the systematic screening of several countries according to clearly defined criteria, and the ability to take a dispassionate and objective decision as to which to enter and in what sequence will be important considerations. It is here that an independent consultant can add significant value. But these will merely identify what are *prima facie* the best opportunities: the next step will be to conduct market research inside the countries themselves to ascertain whether the company's offerings will be attractive to potential customers, and whether an appropriate revenue and profit flow can be enjoyed as a result.

For small and medium enterprises, overseas market entry may simply be reactive, such as receiving an unexpected order or enquiry. Alternatively, they may plan to venture abroad, but in a low risk manner. Johanson and Vahlne (1977) suggest three sets of criteria for such an approach: (i) low 'psychic' distance, or low uncertainty about the country and the difficulty of obtaining information about it (psychic distance is taken to mean differences in language, culture, political system, level of education or level of industrial development), (ii) low 'cultural' distance, in other words, low perceived differences between the home and country of destination cultures, and (iii) low 'geographic' distance, namely the relative ease of supplying the country concerned.

Larger, more ambitious organisations will be able to identify overseas market opportunities through a more systematic process. First, countries can be segmented according to what Hollensen (2004) describes as their 'general' and 'specific' characteristics. The first set of criteria will include the geographic location, language, political factors, demographic trends, economic development, industrial and retail structure, degree of technological advancement, social organisation, religious customs, and standards of education and literacy. Their specific characteristics will include cultural peculiarities and behaviour that drive consumer behaviour, lifestyle and consumption habits, personality traits, and general attitudes, tastes and predispositions. From such criteria an overall profile can be developed for the country or countries under consideration and their relative attractiveness defined. It goes without saying that for such a process to be effective, it will need to be conducted from a fully informed standpoint.

Another form of screening addresses the political risk of entering a particular country. The Business Environment Risk Index (BERI) developed by Frederich Haner of the University of Delaware in 1972 conducts periodic assessments of countries on various political, economic and financial factors. These include political stability, economic growth, currency convertibility, labour costs and productivity, short-term credit, long-term loans/venture capital, attitudes towards the foreign investor and profits, risk of nationalisation, inflation, balance of payments, enforceability of contracts, bureaucratic procedures and delays, quality of communications, local management and partners, and professional services and contractors. Each of these has a weighting, and scoring is on a 1–4 scale, with a maximum overall score of 100. This process will give a clear indication of the relative appeal of different countries, but a more in-depth analysis will be needed before an entry decision can be taken with confidence.

Hollensen proposes a broader approach, which will also take into account the firm's particular competences as well as its existing presence in various countries. He advocates a market attractiveness/competitive strength matrix. Criteria determining market or country attractiveness are market size, market growth, customer buying power, market seasons and fluctuations, average industry margin, competitive conditions (concentration, intensity, entry barriers, etc.), market prohibitive conditions (tariff/non-tariff barriers, import restrictions, etc.), infrastructure, economic and political stability and 'psychic' distance. A view of competitive strength will be developed via market share, marketing ability and capacity (i.e. country-specific know-how), the products' 'fit' to the market demands, price, contribution margin, image, technology position, product quality, market support, quality of distributors and service, and access to distribution channels. Both sets of criteria can be scored, and the resultant coordinates plotted on a two-dimensional matrix. This will then allow the firm to identify the clusters or sets of countries in which to invest to grow, those in which to have a more selective strategy, and those where the best option may be to harvest, exit or licence-out.

While there are several means of conducting desk research on potential markets, therefore, the key consideration is the need for factually correct information to underpin it. Some of it may be obtainable from published sources, but the company is unlikely to have the resource or the ability to provide it themselves. Consequently the services of knowledgeable consultants with in-depth market knowledge will prove invaluable, even indispensable. So too will the next stage of the exercise – conducting market research. This is detailed at length in Chapter 6, but the principle remains the same: selecting the appropriate methodology to identify the company offerings' appeal and likely demand among potential customers. Again, the sophisticated process this implies can only be conducted by experts with substantial local knowledge.

4.4   Market entry options

Having identified the country or countries offering best potential, the company has to decide on how it will develop a marketplace presence. This is the most critical phase, as it amounts in effect to the launch of a new product line. Here local knowledge is indispensable and a consultant can provide this. This in essence will require a cost/benefit analysis determined by the level of commitment and investment the company is intending to make, the level of marketplace control to which it aspires, and the level of risk it is prepared to take. As in many business contexts, the greater the investment, the greater the control, and the higher the risk, the higher the potential reward (*see* Figure 4.1).

The safest approach is indirect export, whereby the company sells to a third party export merchant based in the same country. This trading company (sometimes known as a confirming house) will then deliver the goods to the overseas customer and obtain payment. While such an arrangement allows the company quick and secure payment, and will free them from the risk of servicing politically volatile markets, and while it spares them the cost of setting up an export organisation, it has many downsides. First, the company has no control over the ultimate destination of its products and has no say over how they are sold and promoted in the marketplace. It has no contact with the customer and is entirely dependent on the exporting company. The latter is only likely to be interested in products with a ready demand, and may negotiate a low price in return for the volume it is ordering. This may well bring the additional risk of re-import into the domestic market at prices below the established market norm.

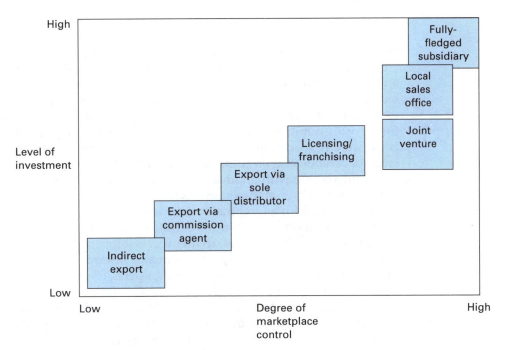

Figure 4.1 Correlation between investment and control

At the next level, the company may opt for traditional, direct export to a third party located in the country. In broad terms, this may be to a sole distributor with the capability to serve the level of market demand, or it may be on an 'open market' basis, whereby a commission agent solicits orders for direct delivery to sundry third parties who pay the exporting company direct. Of the two approaches, the sole distributor has several advantages: they are the direct link between end customers and the exporter, they control selling prices, they carry stock to ensure continuous replenishment, they are familiar with customs, banking and clearance procedures, and they will input to the local marketing programme. But title to the goods is passed to the distributor once payment has been made, pricing will need to be such that the distributor can supply the local market at an acceptable margin, the distributor's marketing and promotional skills may be limited, and the company's fortunes are dependent on the distributor's strength and competence in the marketplace.

It will be necessary to ensure adequate share of the distributor's mind, as they will carry other lines from other companies, all of whom are eager to ensure that the distributor is performing well on their behalf. Conversely, a commission agent carries little financial risk, does not hold stock, and being dependent on a percentage of the orders secured will be motivated to seek orders in large volume from reliable customers – but this carries a further risk of market saturation not necessarily related to demand, and makes forecasting particularly difficult. In both cases, though, the company will have to set up an export department, have the ability to ship its goods and process the necessary paperwork, enter into legal agreements, ensure it receives payment and undertake market visits, all of which carry further cost.

A third mode of entry is via licensing or franchising. Rather than export finished products, the licensor grants the right for a determined period of time to an overseas company to use its manufacturing process, trademark, patents and other proprietary know-how in return for an agreed royalty based on sales. It may also make additional profit through exporting particular raw materials and components. The licensor will need to undertake quality control assessments, and will have the right to receive full sales data in order to calculate their royalty entitlement. A clear understanding has to be reached over responsibility for the local marketing campaign, and the licensor will have to accept that in return for licensing out its brand it will lose marketplace control. Further, if the licensee is particularly successful, the licensor will need to appreciate that the benefit in terms of revenue and profit has accrued to the licensee rather than themselves.

A joint venture with another party may provide a further means of establishing a local presence at a reduced level of investment. In essence, the exporting company joins with a local trader or investor to establish a joint company where both share ownership and control. It will permit quick access to the market, share the investment risk, share research and development costs, possibly enjoy fiscal benefits from governments eager to encourage inward investment, and potentially have access to free circulation of goods within the economic bloc or customs union to which the country belongs.

Such a move may be necessary for economic or political reasons, the overseas company may lack the financial or managerial resources to 'go it alone', or it may be the only way to enter a country whose government prohibits direct import of finished goods. Further, a skilled local partner may prove invaluable through its knowledge and connections in negotiating the labyrinth of bureaucracy in a new and challenging market. Yet the venture has to be a meeting of minds rather than a marriage of convenience. The partners will need to adapt to and respect each other's culture. There may be disagreements over strategy, marketing or investment policy. The host country government may stipulate a majority local (possibly even government) shareholding. Further, a global organisation will be unable to impose its corporate marketing or manufacturing strategy on a reluctant partner. Identification and selection of the right partner will require particular skill and clear agreement on the details of the future *modus operandi* and indeed *modus vivendi*.

Finally, the company may decide to invest directly in establishing a wholly-owned subsidiary in the country. This may vary from a local or regional sales office supervising sales through distributors and coordinating the local marketing programmes to a fully-fledged manufacturing, selling, distributing and marketing organisation. There may be local country government incentives to take such a step, so as to provide job opportunities, or it may simply be a calculated risk by the company which considers the benefits of closeness to the market, customers, banks, government agencies and suppliers to outweigh the scale of its investment. There should be savings in the cost of freight and the cost of manufacture, and the ability to customise products to local market needs will be facilitated. Once established, the local subsidiary (sometimes known as a branch company) may also identify potential local acquisition opportunities to strengthen their leverage with the distribution chain. Locally recruited staff may prove to be of a higher calibre than those working for a distributor, since the kudos of being employed by a multinational company may prove a powerful incentive. Nonetheless, there are potential drawbacks, namely the risk of devalued currency, foreign exchange shortages, restrictions on profit remittance, protective local laws, and political-social upheaval, deteriorating markets, nationalisation or expropriation. Further, in order to entice expatriate management to what might be considered a hardship appointment, the company may need to offer a high salary, more luxurious accommodation standards, regular home visits, and a finite period of appointment with a guarantee of re-entry to the home country. This level of investment decision is clearly one that will not be taken lightly, as the ability to reduce or close down the operation if circumstances so require may prove especially costly.

4.5   Export management issues

The export manager with responsibility for a country or series of countries will need to have a wide awareness and good knowledge, though not necessarily expertise, of a plethora of subjects specific to the daily reality of exporting. Exotic new terms such as drawback, incoterms, demurrage, groupage, letters of hypothecation, general average and del credere risk will enter the exporter's lexicon. The ability to contend with these, in addition to skills in negotiation, distributor motivation, marketing planning and sales forecasting will be crucial to a successful performance. It is not the intention in this section to give a comprehensive exposition of all aspects of export practice so much as to highlight the more important areas and to indicate how consultants can help.

The exporter needs to decide on what basis a price quotation will be given to the importer. First, there is the price itself, that upon which the exporting company will realise its profit. Will it be based on the published wholesale price in the home country, will it be expressed in a standard export price list, will it relate to an increase (or not) over the price previously used, will it be established from an in-market price to the customer worked backwards down the price structure, will it have to take account of price controls in the overseas country, or will it be negotiated or offered as a tender bid? Having determined this price, it will be necessary to agree what element of freight, insurance, duty or other factors to include in the quotation. In the majority of cases, price will be quoted as either FOB (Free On Board), i.e. once loaded on to the carrying vessel, C&F (Cost and Freight) or CIF (Cost, Insurance and Freight) at a named port of destination, or in order to prevent loading of the C&F price, FOB plus Freight to a named port of destination. Alternatively, the importer may prefer an ex-works price (i.e. at the factory gates), or delivery franco domicile, i.e. to their warehouse inclusive of duty, clearance charges and onward transportation. Each has its particular merits, and it is very much a matter for both parties to agree upon. Consultants can provide valuable assistance – for example in identifying the most competitive insurance and freight rates.

The means whereby the exporting company will be paid have an obvious importance. Though desirable, cash in advance or cash with order are somewhat unlikely in view of the credit implications for the importer. Some companies with an established system of trading may have an open account arrangement, but it is generally the case that each order will have to be paid via an individual transaction. One that affords greatest protection to the exporting company is the Confirmed and Irrevocable Letter of Credit. In essence, this is a pledge via the importer's correspondent bank to pay the exporter at the time of shipment provided all the terms of the order have been complied with, and the correct documentation is provided. This may not be especially attractive to either party, as the process is complex and the scope for errors to be made is considerable. Moreover, for the importer it implies parting with their funds before taking possession of the goods.

An alternative method involves use of a Bill of Exchange. Under this circumstance, the exporter draws a bill on the importing customer which may be payable upon presentation (D/P), or against acceptance (D/A) with a stated term of credit. In order to take possession of the goods, the importer will have to accept and honour the Bill of Exchange, thus guaranteeing payment to the exporter. While this is more straightforward, it may not always be acceptable to certain countries wishing to regulate the flow of remittances abroad. Most commercial banks will provide guidance on method of payment issues, but a consultant may also have specialist knowledge.

Another area where expertise will be needed concerns shipping – identifying the most appropriate carrier, deciding the preferred routing, negotiating the particular freight rates, booking the order for shipment, assembling the necessary paperwork, and appreciating the particular issues of hazardous or inflammable goods, those requiring special stowage etc.

In this particular area, a shipping and forwarding agent can be of considerable assistance, especially to a small or medium enterprise or those new to exporting. Such agents are experts in their field, and will have an up-to-date and thorough knowledge of transport methods and the relevant carriage rates. They will be aware of port conditions and specific customs requirements, and they may be able to consolidate small shipments from different exporting companies into a single 'groupage' consignment, thereby enjoying more favourable freight rates (Walker, 1970).

Additionally, the exporter should have a good awareness of aspects of mercantile law. This will include the law of contract, laws governing agency, the sale of goods, negotiable instruments, marine insurance and the carriage of goods by land, sea and air. Access to expert legal knowledge will, however, be indispensable in cases of dispute. Further, the importing country may have additional laws of their own regarding the legal status of agents, the payment of commission, corporate liability, trademark protection, trade with countries with whom they disagree politically and other commercial practices.

Products may need to be modified or given special packaging not for any particular consumer benefit but rather due to specific local laws or by virtue of the rigours of the physical distribution process. Consider the food industry: innocuous products such as prepared mustard bound for Sweden have in the past needed to have the tartrazine colouring agent removed. The same country had more stringent rules on the level of permitted impurities in peanut butter than did the UK.

Consumer products intended for sale in Israel quite understandably require labelling in Hebrew. Foodstuffs destined for the same country need a kosher certificate, which might require the visit of a rabbi to the manufacturing plant. Labelling laws, expiry dates, distributors' addresses, safety warnings etc. all need to be accommodated. Clear honey shipped at times of severe cold can set, and soft drinks stored in containers at high temperatures on vessels plying the Arab Gulf can boil and flocculate. Cereals may be prone to infestation from weevils and therefore require additional protection. All of these are the facts of life of exporting, and all will add cost and complexity to the manufacturing operation. Yet again, without specialist knowledge of such requirements, the exporter will be at a considerable risk.

Pharmaceutical products attract further regulatory issues. Most countries will require registration even though the item in question is freely on sale in its country of origin. A certified Free Sale Certificate may be sufficient, but it may be necessary also to provide raw material specifications, the method of manufacture, the product ingredients and a certified statement of the consumer price in the country of origin. The documentation will need to be processed, and it may take two years or more before approval is given. Access to informed regulatory affairs knowledge will be crucial.

4.6   Culture

One of the biggest issues facing a consultant with a multinational assignment is the different cultures involved. Good consultants recognise these early on in the consulting process and ensure they adapt their way of working without compromising the project. Cultural differences may be national cultural differences in a largely homogeneous society, or there may be important subcultures – such as Latinos in the USA, Turkish immigrants in Germany, or the differing ethnic communities in South Africa. These differences will manifest themselves both in consumer and business behaviour. Managers and consultants should develop a keen awareness of these cultural differences, and respect them, for they will be the rules by which they will need to play if they intend to compete successfully.

One example of cultural diversity is the strong influence of Islam on daily life in the Arab world, the emphasis on observing prayer times, modesty of dress, and the avoidance of alcohol and pigmeat. A Westerner who is not a Muslim will still need to observe the Ramadan fast if he is in an Arab country at the time. But he will also enjoy a greater degree of hospitality and personal attention than may be the norm in his home country. In Chinese culture, 5,000 years of Confucianism, which seeks harmony and equilibrium, place great importance on connections (*guanxi*), interpersonal relationships (*renqing*), courteous and refined behaviour (*keqi*) and the need to preserve face (*mianxi*). In Latin societies, attitudes to time (the *hora latina*) are often more casual than in 'low context' cultures such as Germany or Switzerland. Haggling and bargaining are part of the way of life in Turkey, India and the Middle East. German companies are especially formal in conduct, and colleagues within the same organisation are likely to be known by their titles and surnames: people may spend ten years working together without knowing one another's first name. Israelis pride themselves on straight, blunt talking almost to the point of rudeness, and expect the same in return: they will have little patience with subtlety and understatement. In Holland and Scandinavia, the concept of companionship is more greatly refined than in the UK or USA: the Dutch concept of *gezellig* implies sharing one's personal feelings in a very personal way while being together in a small group (Arnould, Price & Zinkhan, 2004). National spirit is implied in untranslatable words such as *sisu* (Finland), *hwyl* (Wales), or *lagom* (Sweden). Finally, there is the facilitating role of *bakhsheesh* in Turkey and the Levant, *dash* in West Africa, or *coffee money* in Malaysia and Singapore: what Western attitudes might consider to be bribery.

Much has been written on the determinants, characteristics and elements of culture. In 1983 Geert Hofstede identified four dimensions determining national culture, adding a fifth in a further piece of research with Bond in 1988 (in Hollensen, 2004). The five elements are power distance – the degree of inequality between people in physical and educational terms; uncertainty avoidance – the degree to which people prefer formal rules and fixed patterns of life; individualism – the degree to which people in a country learn to act as individuals rather than members of groups; masculinity – the degree to which 'masculine' values such as achievement, performance, competition and success outweigh 'feminine' values such as quality of life, warmth of relationships, care and concern, and the environment; and time perspective – whether the tendency is for pragmatic long-term thinking as opposed to a conventional, short-term time horizon. Hampden-Turner and Trompenaars' 1994 model identifies eight 'value dilemmas' driving national cultural features (in Morden, 2007). These are (at either end of the spectrum) strict adherence to rules as opposed to flexibility and exceptions; analysis of concepts or events versus their integration into wholes (deconstructionism and constructionism); communal as opposed to individual focus; internal focus on the society in contrast to an external orientation of people to their environment; the perspective of time as a linear rather than a cyclical concept; status based on age, education, class or race as opposed to status on the basis of achievement or merit; emphasis on hierarchy versus equality within the community; and affective, expressive and emotional behaviour rather than neutral, subdued and controlled emotion.

Finally, and of particular value to the international manager, Mead (1990, in Brassington and Pettitt, 2006) groups eight behavioural factors influencing business conduct. These are: time – attitudes to punctuality, the sanctity of deadlines, discussion time and acquaintance time; business cards – when to offer them, whether to have them translated, who gives first, and how much attention to give them when received; gifts – whether they should be given, their size and value, and whether they should be opened in front of the donor; dress – dress codes and levels of formality; entertainment – the type and formality of social occasions, table manners and etiquette, cuisine, cultural and religious taboos, and venues (e.g. restaurant or private house); space – the meaning of office size and location, and the selection, quality and arrangement of furniture; body language – greeting conventions, facial and hand gestures, physical proximity, touching and posture; and material possessions – whether or not it is polite to comment on them or admire them. Managers intending to spend time in different business cultures would do well to seek expert advice on such issues.

4.7   International marketing

For many large companies, such as Unilever, international marketing is firmly established and the consultant needs to understand the key processes that are operated. It could be argued that the ideal prospect for a company intending to market its brands internationally would be that it will be able to sell the same product as in the home market, without any form of adaptation, using the same brand name, the same graphic design, and the same advertising message – although the more enlightened company may concede that it will be necessary to communicate in a language the consumer will understand! In a celebrated article in the *Harvard Business Review* in 1983, Theodore Levitt challenged the accepted marketing wisdom of providing products and marketing programmes specific to particular consumer requirements when he wrote, 'The world is becoming a common marketplace in which people – no matter where they live – desire the same products and lifestyles. Global companies must forget the idiosyncratic differences between countries and cultures and instead concentrate on satisfying universal drives.' He foresaw a convergence of lifestyles and a homogeneous, American-influenced global market. Joseph Quinlan, a senior economist at Dean, Witter Reynolds called the emerging consumers in this new world the 'global MTV generation' who 'prefer Coke to tea, Nikes to sandals, and Chicken McNuggets to rice, credit cards to cash' (Kotler, 2000).

In today's de-massified, individualistic global marketplace, such views now seem simplistic, even flawed. No company sets out deliberately to make life difficult for themselves, but they would ignore at their peril real differences and factors that militate against total standardisation. First, consumer habits and spending power do vary: for example, less affluent consumers in the developing world may seek shampoo in sachets rather than more expensive larger sizes, hand-held items such as cups or razors may need to be made smaller for Japanese hands, ketchup may need to be spicier in a country such as Mexico, taste in confectionery will vary considerably between the USA, France and the UK, and a powdered chocolate drink to which boiling water is added in the UK may need to be re-positioned quite differently in France where ownership of kettles is lower and the product is a milk-based breakfast drink for children. It will therefore be imperative to research consumer attitudes both to avoid expensive blunders and to identify genuine differences in habit.

Brand names may also prove a challenge. Just as English-speakers may snigger at brands such as Bum snack foods (Spain), Sor-Bits chewing gum (Denmark), Aseol toilet cleaner (Spain), Plopsies chocolate cereals (France), Pschitt carbonated drinks (France) or Kuk & Fuk pasta (Slovakia), so seemingly innocuous brands such as the Vauxhall Nova ('won't go' in Spanish), Mist (dung in German), Zip, Nike and Aero (all of which have obscene meanings in Arabic) and the direct Spanish translation of Airwick's Magic Mushroom (Seta Mágica) will cause amusement, even offence in some countries. Again, careful research or simply reference to a linguist with a good knowledge of colloquialisms and slang will help to prevent embarrassment.

Similar considerations apply to the advertising and promotional message. Clever, subtle tag lines in one language or culture may not transfer to another. A rational scientific approach may be preferred in one society, a humorous one in another. There may be laws forbidding the use of white-coated laboratory 'experts' promoting a personal care product, children may not be used in advertising in some countries, beer may be advertised but may not be shown actually being drunk in some parts of the world, superlative statements may be disallowed, comparative advertising may be illegal, nudity may be appropriate to one culture but gratuitously offensive to another, and in some Islamic countries it is forbidden to feature women in advertising. The company therefore faces a dilemma: on the one hand it will not wish to produce an advertisement so bland that it lacks any cut-through, yet on the other it will need to avoid wasting money unnecessarily on too many different creative executions for the same brand. To quote Kotler (2000) on Levitt, therefore 'so perhaps Levitt's globalization dictum should be re-phrased. Global marketing, yes. Global standardization, not necessarily.'

Keegan (1995) has identified five possible strategies that may be appropriate for products and promotion in overseas markets, as shown in Figure 4.2.

A feature of today's world is the spectre of consumer retaliation against global brands and their owners if they believe they are acting unethically. This was most apparent in the Seattle riots in 1999, when symbols of globalisation were attacked. A further example was the action by French sheep farmer José Bové who in 1999 dismantled his local branch of McDonald's in protest against a US hike in the tariff on Roquefort cheese. Similarly, 'anti-brand' websites have been spawned against brands/companies accused of unethical practices such as animal testing, animal

	Do Not Change Product	Adapt Product	Develop New Product
Do Not Change Promotion	Straight Extension	Product Adaptation	Product Invention
Adapt Promotion	Communication Adaptation	Dual Adaptation	Product Invention

Figure 4.2 Keegan's five international product and promotion strategies

Source: Kotler, Philip; Keller, Kevin Lane, *Marketing Management: Analysis, Planning, Implementation and Control*, 12th Edition, © 2006, p. 680. Reprinted by permission of Pearson Education, Inc., Upper Saddle River, NJ.

cruelty, use of child labour, heavy-handed 'brainwashing' marketing campaigns, damage to the environment, paying low prices to farmers and growers in the developing world, or association with dictatorial political regimes. In her seminal polemic *No Logo* (2000), Naomi Klein castigates many well-known brands and companies for what she considers inappropriate global marketing behaviour.

Similarly, in the conclusion to his searing indictment of the American fast food industry *Fast Food Nation* (2001) Eric Schlosser writes, 'Future historians, I hope, will consider the American fast food industry a relic of the twentieth century – a set of attitudes, systems and beliefs that emerged from post-war southern California, that embodied its limitless faith in technology, that quickly spread across the globe, flourished briefly, and then receded, once its true costs became clear and its thinking became obsolete.' He goes on to say, 'This new century may bring an impatience with conformity, a refusal to be kept in the dark, less greed, more compassion, less speed, more common sense, a sense of humour about brand essences and loyalties, a view of food as more than just fuel.' In other words, the global marketing company should remember to respect basic human values and not to ride roughshod over ethical concerns in its pursuit of profit. Companies should be prepared to be challenged on this issue by the consultant.

4.8   Global marketing planning process

For successful international marketing, planning processes are important and should be understood by the consultant. A company whose business success depends on the ability to coordinate and manage its key product categories across a number of regions faces a considerable challenge in the strategic planning process. Yet it need not be overwhelmed by it if the process is clear and logical, roles and responsibilities are understood, there is constructive iteration between the centre and the operating units, and 'sign-off' authority is clearly demarcated. Let us consider the situation of a global organisation whose brands are in No. 1 or No. 2 position in most of its key categories. They will be at differing stages of the life cycle, be contending with different competitors and will not carry the same product range in each country. Some may seek growth through a market penetration strategy, others may call for a product development strategy.

The task of those responsible will be to allocate global resources in order to deliver the best result. In addition to the global product categories there may well be strong pockets of business in non-global categories in particular countries. This may be due to past entrepreneurialism or acquisition. The appropriate growth and investment support for these businesses will need to be integrated with the global categories (*see* Figure 4.3).

An effective process should start with the corporate HQ defining the overall growth and profit objectives for the business that will satisfy the investor and analyst community. Thereafter, they should review and challenge interim proposals, and they will set the final targets and budgets. The executive directors should normally include global directors responsible for operations (sales) and marketing. The global operations director should be able to propose to his various regional directors the initial targets necessary to deliver the overall objectives. He will review their proposals, decide on prioritisation between regions and major countries, arbitrate and

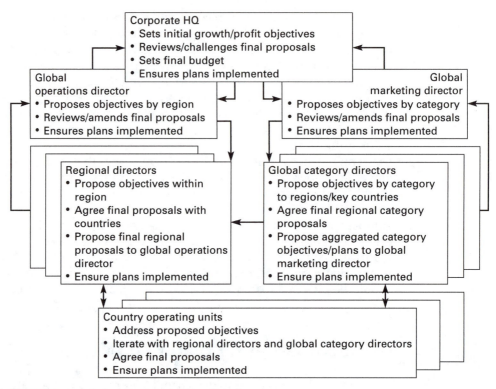

Figure 4.3 A global marketing planning 'loop'

resolve issues of conflict, and ensure the delivery of the targets, including making necessary changes to the investment plans in order to achieve the profit commitment. His marketing counterpart, responsible for global categories, will need to outline the broad category growth and profit targets, review and challenge his global category directors' proposals, prioritise between categories, validate the quality of the proposed marketing programme, and closely monitor its implementation.

Global category directors responsible for specific categories will respond to the global marketing director's initial growth targets, and will discuss individual category growth and investment plans with the various regional directors. They will establish outline category priorities in the larger countries, coordinate new product launch programmes, develop global advertising campaigns, and ensure a healthy programme of research and development activity. Thereafter they will monitor progress in their respective categories, identify such 'course correction' measures as may be necessary to deliver the target, and support and encourage regional and country implementation of the marketing mix.

The regional director should prioritise his target across the various countries reporting to him, assign an overall strategic role to each country, ensure there are appropriate plans to deliver the necessary results from the important non-global category businesses, monitor and deliver implementation of the plans, and address and resolve operational, fixed cost and other organisational issues. But only the operating units in the respective countries and regions will deliver the results needed. Corporate HQ, executive directors, regional and category directors do not sell anything to anyone. It is therefore vital that the countries are able to respond purposefully to the broad targets that cascade down to them from corporate HQ. It is equally vital that their responses are given a fair hearing, and that they can in due course agree local sales targets, investment needs and marketing programmes which will enable them to deliver a satisfactory result. This may take more than one iteration, but it is a critical phase. Once these plans have been finalised and are owned by the operating units, the latter will need to apply themselves to the specific tasks required to implement the local sales and marketing programme. In addition, they will be able to identify new opportunities and to develop contingency plans.

For such a process to run smoothly, it is imperative that the approach should not change from year to year, that each participant recognises and values the others' roles, that discussions are open and honest, and that there is a strict timetable for completion. An important role that can be played by a consultant is to act as a challenging partner, questioning constructively the various assumptions behind the sundry growth plans and investment needs.

4.9   Managing the client/consultant relationship

As this chapter has illustrated, there is no shortage of subjects in the international business world that need to be known and understood by the effective consultant. Clients will need help and advice on a number of topics. Whether it is understanding if general average can be declared over a jettisoned cargo or whether the act will in fact be construed as barratry, whether it is to appreciate that a two-litre bottle will not fit easily inside the average Spanish refrigerator, whether it is to realise that the English advertising slogan will have an unfortunate *double entendre* in another language, whether it is to learn the ways of conducting business with an Indian counterpart, whether it is to be taught the key principles of key account management in the USA, or whether it is the need for a second pair of eyes to assess the intended business plan, there are very many opportunities for consultant advice.

The challenge, though, must be whether the consultant will add value. If they are no more than discussion facilitators, or if they merely provide the information and opinions the company could have found out for themselves had they taken the trouble to ask (and indeed believe) their own staff, the investment will have been costly and unnecessary. What is sought from the consultant is genuine expertise, particular subject knowledge, the application of best practice and rigorous, high standards. In short, the provision of superior knowledge and skill not generally available within the company.

To succeed, the relationship must be professional, based on mutual respect. The consultant is neither a hired hand nor a white knight coming to an ailing company's rescue. A company capable of utilising this expertise has appointed them because of their perceived ability. But the personal chemistry must be good. An arrogant, overbearing and inflexible consultant will not endear themselves to the company with whom they are working. Nor will one who trades on their international reputation and assigns inexperienced staff to the project. Nor will one who sets out to make themselves indispensable to the company and who draws out the time and scope of the project, still less will one who feels it appropriate to involve themselves in the internal politics of the organisation. For they will only be as good as the way in which they deliver the brief they have been given. Consultants play a pivotal role in guiding and assisting companies in aspects of their international operation, but in the final event it is the job of the company to ensure that they derive the maximum value from their investment.

Team discussion points	1 What value can the right consultant deliver to an international firm that the company's own management could not provide for themselves?
	2 What do you think would be additional challenges in managing a multinational team for a consulting project?

Summary of key ideas

- The role of the consultant in helping firms with their international strategies can be a major area of work; however, this brings with it additional complexities.
- Operating internationally has great appeal, but implies considerable additional complexity and risk for the company.
- The company needs to be fully informed in order to take overseas investment decisions with confidence.
- Specialist agencies and consultants play a key role in providing information and expertise.
- A company operating internationally needs to understand and to defer to the differing cultures in the countries where it is present, and should behave as a responsible global citizen.
- Clear rules and defined responsibilities are vital for an efficient performance.

Key reading

Hollensen, S. (2004) *Global Marketing: A Decision Oriented Approach.* Harlow, Essex: FT Prentice Hall.

Noonan, C. (1999) *The CIM Handbook of Export Marketing.* London: Butterworth Heinemann.

Further reading

Albaum, G., Duerr, E. and Strandskov, J. (2004) *International Marketing and Export Management.* Harlow, Essex: Financial Times Prentice Hall.

Arnould, E., Price L. and Zinkhan G.M. (2004) *Consumers.* New York: McGraw-Hill.

Bradley, F. (2002) *International Marketing Strategy.* Harlow, Essex: Pearson Education.

Branch, A.E. (2006) *Export Practice and Management.* London: Thomson Learning.

Brassington, F. and Pettitt, S. (2006) *Principles of Marketing.* Harlow, Essex: Prentice Hall.

Johanson, J. and Vahlne, J.E. (1977) 'The internationalization process of the firm: a model of knowledge development and increasing foreign market commitment', *Journal of International Business Studies,* 8 (1), 23–32.

Katrak, H. (1971) *International Trade and the Balance of Payments.* London: Fontana.

Keegan, W.J. (1995) *Multinational Marketing Management,* 5th edn. Upper Saddle River, NJ: Prentice Hall, pp. 378–81.

Klein, N. (2000) *No Logo.* London: Flamingo.

Kotler, P. (2000) *Marketing Management.* Harlow, Essex: Prentice Hall.

Levitt, T. (1983) 'The globalization of markets', *Harvard Business Review*, May–June, 92–102.

Morden, A. (2007) *Principles of Strategic Management.* London: Ashgate Publishing.

Schlosser, E. (2001) *Fast Food Nation.* London: Penguin Books.

Sherlock, J. (2006) 'Be prepared – it's a jungle out there', *Exporting World*, Sept/Oct, pp. 30–31.

Usunier, J-C. and Lee, J. (2005) *Marketing Across Cultures.* Harlow, Essex: Financial Times Prentice Hall.

Walker, A. (1970) *Export Practice and Documentation.* London: Butterworth Heinemann.

Case exercise

Bill Chieftain

The *Bill Chieftain* brand of clothing originated in the 1960s and was best known for its buttoned-down, narrow collared shirt that was beloved of the 'Mods'. Throughout the 70s and 80s, it became part of the 'uniform' of the skinheads and other groups of young men seeking to define their identity. By the 1990s, however, the company that made them in Ireland was suffering, like many of its competitors, from cheap, foreign competition and was struggling to survive. A white knight arrived in 1995 in the shape of 2B venture capitalists who saw an opportunity to make the *Bill Chieftain* brand popular once more, and they bought the company. 2B employed a dynamic new management team who brought with them extensive experience of the fashion industry.

In the following five years, sales and profits rose fivefold as the brand was extended into menswear, womenswear, shoes and other accessories. This was on the back of a successful campaign that highlighted the heritage of the brand. Practically all the sales came from the UK as the management team concentrated on developing the brand there. There always had been a small amount of sales abroad, particularly to Germany and the US, through small specialist retailers, catering to young men who followed the 'skinhead' fashions.

In 2000, 2B were reviewing their investments and asked the management team to put together a three-year plan. In order to continue with their investment in the company, 2B required that sales and profits be doubled to £200 million and £40 million respectively. The management team's response was to expand internationally, building on the business that they already had in their two main export markets of Germany and the US. Their reasoning was that these were two of the biggest markets in the world and they would only need to get a 1 per cent market share in both countries to achieve their targets. They also felt that they did not need to change their strategy that was to exploit the 'Britishness' of the brand and in particular to use the advertising that highlighted *Bill Chieftain*'s appeal among young men of a certain type. They argued that as it had worked so well in the UK, it was bound to work elsewhere.

2B are not entirely convinced by the management team's arguments and decide to employ some external consultants to look at the strategy and advise whether 2B should continue their investment or sell up now.

Q1 You are the consultant employed by 2B. What information would you ask the management team to consider to evaluate their international marketing strategy?

Q2 The management team are advocating setting up sales offices in these two countries. What other alternatives should they look at and why?

Q3 The majority of their production is moving to the Far East, principally China for the clothes and Vietnam for the leather goods: what impact do you think this may have on their strategy?

Robinson Mason case study: Part 1

This case study is split into four sections, one in each part. It is designed to complement the short case exercises at the end of each chapter, by providing the student an exercise in which to use all the information and skills contained in this part and subsequently throughout the book. It also reflects a large complex organisation that is a regular user of consultancy and therefore balances the smaller firms portrayed in the case exercises.

In the early 1990s Robinson Mason was a long-established UK multinational with a stable of very well-known consumer brands, enjoying a presence in much of Western Europe. This ranged from fully-fledged manufacturing, marketing and distribution operations in some countries to local sales offices in others. Considerable autonomy was granted to the country general managers, who were able to operate freely within their own fiefdoms and, provided that the financial targets were met, the European regional director did not tend to impose his will on the day-to-day activity or marketing priorities. Europe accounted for more than a third of the Robinson Mason corporate total global business. Consequently attainment of its aggregate sales and profit targets was crucial.

Manufacturing took place at a number of sites. As a result, the same basic consumer offering could be produced in differing formulae and packaging in as many as three different countries, and contract packed in others. Factories competed with each other to obtain supply business within the group, and where there was spare capacity they would also seek trade own-label contracts.

Marketing was not coordinated between countries. There was no formal commonality of positioning, pricing or consumer proposition, and it could quite often be the case that a new product was launched as and when the local country decided, in pack designs, pack sizes and labels that differed in each country. Generally, the individual countries would also develop their own advertising. The degree of freedom they were allowed was seen by many of the company's young marketers as the reason why they preferred Robinson Mason to some of its more hierarchical and dictatorial competitors. Some discussion of marketing activity did take place, however, at the country general managers' bi-monthly meetings. These occasions were more for information sharing than decision-making, and as much as anything were most memorable for the quality of restaurant meals enjoyed in the evenings.

By the mid 1990s, the company's performance was beginning to stall.

■ The UK suffered a disastrous trading result due to management failings, a rash of poorly executed new product launches, neglect of the core brands, and a breakdown in planning and supply performance.

■ France, the star of the group with many highly talented and innovative marketers, had a wide range of brands requiring support, and was also moving into further new categories that it had identified as growth opportunities.

■ Spain had a good track record, built upon seven strong brands, and had recently acquired a large local brand in a further new category.

- Germany, Switzerland and Austria had hitherto been sub-critical mass, but a recent acquisition of a German-based business had strongly increased their local presence.

- Holland had a tradition of reluctance to expand, and half its business was in a category peculiar to the country.

- Italy was run as a sales office, although it too had increased its market presence thanks to the further acquisition of local brands and businesses specific to Italy.

- Belgium, Ireland, Greece, Portugal and Denmark all had a relatively wide range of products, none of which they manufactured themselves, but which provided them with some degree of strength in the marketplace.

- The rest of Scandinavia, the Mediterranean islands, Israel and the Middle East were supplied through distributors as export territories managed by the UK.

- Eastern Europe was entrusted to a commission agent in Vienna, and there was no presence in Turkey.

The company's more focused multinational and local competitors took advantage of its inefficient way of operating and started to make serious inroads into its market shares. Its customers also began to demand improved terms as the company had chosen to cut back on brand support in order to meet its profit commitments against the background of stagnating, even declining revenue.

Eventually, the regional director called 150 of his European staff to a two-day meeting at Heathrow, to share the bleak picture with them. 'Business as usual won't do,' he asserted. He then went on to say that he would be rationalising the number of manufacturing operations, placing them under the authority of a European supply director rather than the local general manager. Privately, though, he reassured the larger countries' somewhat aggrieved general managers (many of whom were long-standing friends) that of course there would still be a manufacturing presence in their particular country.

Marketing was also to be coordinated more effectively, via the creation of 'category teams' made up of middle-ranking marketing and R&D representatives from the businesses involved, reporting informally to the category team leader, who would normally be a country general manager who had been asked to take on this additional role. Their function was collaborative and cooperative, taken forward through occasional meetings in various parts of Europe and by interim correspondence. They could not commit to any decisions without the approval of their local marketing director, who was still in charge of the deployment of budgets, the prioritisation of local country marketing activity and local advertising campaigns.

The mid 1990s was also bringing other challenges in the business environment, seen by some as opportunities and others as threats. With the collapse of communism, the economies of Eastern Europe were becoming accessible. The Single European Act made easier the movement of goods across frontiers. The impending introduction of the euro would make pricing more transparent. Customers were expanding across frontiers and seeking the most favourable supply terms. Satellite television raised the prospect of advertising across national boundaries, and the rapid development of technology posed further issues. The future was another country, and business as usual certainly wouldn't do!

Discussion questions

1 Need Robinson Mason European businesses have found themselves in the unenviable predicament that now confronted them? What might have been done to prevent such a situation from occurring?

2 Critically appraise the management style applied in the Robinson Mason European business.

3 What are the consultancy challenges and issues offered by Robinson Mason Europe? Write an outline brief that can be used to solicit proposals from interested consultants.

PART TWO

Project evaluation and analysis

CHAPTER 5

Defining the destination, developing a strategy and understanding change

The learning outcomes from this chapter are to:

■ recognise the *rational*, *cognitive* and *political* dimensions of a business problem;

■ understand how a problem may be *defined* to make it amenable to resolution;

■ understand the distinction between the aim, objectives and outcomes of the consulting project;

■ be able to define an effective aim, objectives and outcomes for the project;

■ be able to articulate the aim, objectives and outcomes in a convincing and influential way;

■ develop a project charter;

■ use the principles from the Six Sigma DMAIC process;

■ understand the levels of client–consultant interaction depending on the type of consulting project undertaken;

■ recognise the drivers of organisational change.

5.1 Identification of opportunities and issues with the client organisation

Evaluating the problem

Consultants are usually called in to the client business in order to address some 'problem' the business has, or at least that its managers perceive to have. The problem will be defined as something that stops the business reaching the potential that it feels it should have. The word 'problem' has a negative connotation. To a consultant and the client business, a problem may actually be *positive*. A problem might well be an opportunity the business could potentially exploit as much as an issue that restricts the business. Problems do not present themselves. The firm's managers identify them. Managers interpret problems and decide to address them.

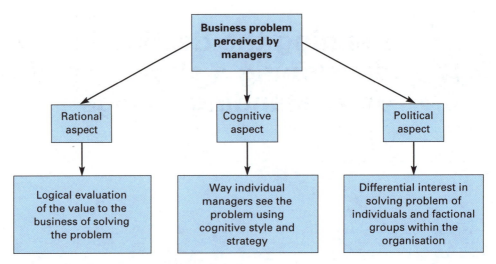

Figure 5.1 The facets of a business problem

A problem has three facets that determine the way in which it will be understood and acted upon by managers (*see* Figure 5.1). We may label these the *rational*, the *cognitive* and the *political*.

The *rational* facet refers to the way in which the problem is seen in a logical manner. It reflects a formal or semi-formal evaluation of the way in which resolution of the problem might affect the business. It will be based on a dispassionate consideration of the economic 'value' or cost of the problem and the business's capability to deal with it or, if it is an opportunity, to exploit it. The *cognitive* facet refers to the way in which individual managers see a problem. It reflects the way in which the problem is processed by a manager's mental faculties. Cognitive style and strategy determine the way in which managers see the world, process information about it and deal with challenges. The manager's cognitive style and strategy will influence the way in which the problem appears in the manager's mental landscape and determine the priority the manager will give it.

Ultimately, the problems that a firm faces must be dealt with by the business as a whole. The *political* facet reflects the way in which a problem is received and processed by the individuals who make up the organisation. Not all managers have the same objectives. Different individuals and groups have different interests. A particular problem will affect different managers in different ways, and some more than others. Some issues may be problems for some managers and opportunities for others. These differences will affect the way in which the managers work together as a team to address the problem. Ultimately, if the organisation's politics become pernicious, managers may actually work against each other.

The astute consultant recognises each of these facets. The rational is important because it determines the value the consultant can create by resolving the problem. The cognitive is relevant because it affects the way in which the consultant communicates with the client and can positively influence him or her. The political is significant because the success or otherwise of a project will depend on getting the whole organisation to see the benefits of a particular course of action and to unite behind it. Four dimensions of a problem will be relevant to its definition (*see*

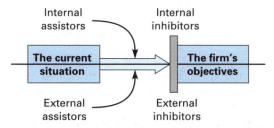

Figure 5.2 Framework for analysing business problems

Figure 5.2). These are the *current situation* of the business, the *goals* of the business (that is, the state it aspires to achieve), the *assistors* (things which help the business achieve its goals) and the *inhibitors* (those things which limit the firm and stop it achieving its goals). Assistors and inhibitors may be internal to the firm (that is, under the direct control of the firm's managers) or external to it (that is, *not* directly under the control of the firm's managers). Some important assistors and inhibitors are listed in Table 5.1.

The challenge for the consultant is to define the business problem in the following terms.

How can assistors be used and developed to achieve the set objectives?

The key issues are how the business can capitalise on internal assistors and how the firm's managers can take advantage of external assistors. It is important to ask whether the problem can be defined to enable managers to take control of external assistors and bring them in: turning external assistors into internal ones. An example is taking control of customer demand through an effective marketing campaign. Here the external assistor of customer goodwill is converted into an internal assistor of marketing capability.

Table 5.1 Assistors and inhibitors

	Internal	**External**
Assistors	Cost advantages (scale/experience)	Relationships with customers
	Unique resources	Investor's goodwill
	Innovative products	Location in business network
	Knowledge of products	Expanding market potential
	Knowledge of markets	High profit margins
	Business location (especially for distributors)	
Inhibitors	Lack of management experience	Limited market potential (market decline)
	Lack of capital	Competitor activity
	Lack of knowledge about products	Changes in customer interest (particularly for fashion-sensitive products)
	Limited knowledge about the environment	High entry costs

How can inhibitors be overcome or avoided so that the business can move forward?

Inhibitors limit the business. An internal inhibitor is the responsibility of the firm's managers. It is they who must take the initiative and address the problem. The priority given to this will depend on the business's plans and the significance of the inhibitor. An external inhibitor is a given. It is outside the control of the firm's managers. The firm must develop strategies that take account of the external inhibitors in the environment and avoid their impact. For example, a lack of knowledge must be addressed through organisational learning. Sectors in which competitors (especially stronger competitors) are active should be given lower priority than those in which absence of competitors creates an opportunity. A problem is best defined in relation to these four facets. They can be used to guide investigation of the problem and to specify the information that is required in order to define it. This framework works well as the basis of a brainstorming session. This is best undertaken with members of the consulting team and with key information providers from the client business.

Reinterpreting problems as opportunities

Problems, by their very nature, are negative. They demand to be solved, but they do not inspire. Opportunities, however, are positive. They call to be exploited. Problems, especially when their resolution is difficult, tend to be divisive. Managers may work at devising solutions. However, energy will also be diverted into avoiding recrimination. After all, a problem is 'internal' to the business. Someone, somewhere must have caused it. A problem is someone's *fault*. Rather than solve the problem, a manager may think it a better strategy to ensure that someone else gets the blame for it. This is a self-defence mechanism. Problems get caught up in the internal politics of the organisation and can exacerbate them. An opportunity, however, is external to the firm. It comes from 'outside'. It is there to be exploited. It is not anyone's fault. Managers will resist identification of problems. They will minimise them or even deny their existence. Yet they will queue up to take credit for identifying an opportunity. Managers can rally round and work together to take advantage of an opportunity. In general, people are constrained to deal with problems; they are motivated to capitalise on opportunities. For these reasons it is better, whenever possible, to talk about taking advantage of opportunities rather than addressing problems.

In many respects problems and opportunities are the two sides of one coin. It depends on whether one looks towards what has been achieved from the perspective of what might have been achieved or from the starting point. Translating one to the other is often a matter of rhetorical approach. The old adage of the half-filled glass applies: is it half-full or half-empty? For example, a new product launch has not gone as well as expected. This is a problem: the return on the investment is not as good as expected. However, it represents an opportunity to understand customer demand better and come up with an improved product. A competitor moves into a market. This is a problem – it will increase competition – but it confirms that the sector is an attractive one for the player who can get it right.

A word of caution here: although it is better, for the reasons given, to talk about opportunities rather than problems, it is important to be realistic. Too much emphasis on the positives can make someone seem glib and unable to come to terms with the real world. People may begin to doubt the decision-making ability of the person. If the person cannot see the problem, how can his or her decisions address it? If the person does not allow himself or herself to talk about problems, this limits the call to action he or she can make to others. Further, individuals who tend to see problems rather than opportunities (and this is to some extent a part of the cognitive perspective discussed above) may feel that those who emphasise the positive are ignoring their concerns.

Turning problems into opportunities – negatives into positives – should not be a mantra; it should be a tool used as part of an overall communication strategy. It should not be used to deny problems but to put them into context. Revealing the opportunity makes the problem seem tractable and tackling it even enjoyable. It also takes the sting out of responsibility (real or imagined) for the problem in the first place.

5.2   Problem analysis, specification and quantification

The consultant is presented with a 'problem' by member(s) of the client organisation. Before he or she can start to solve this problem, they need to analyse it and discover whether the client has correctly identified the problem and its 'root cause'. Ideally this should be done before any formal proposal is given to the client.

Stage 1: Brainstorm the causes

Using members of the consulting team and, if possible, clients as well, you need to explore some of the causes of the problem. You need to clearly state the chosen problem and follow the rules of *brainstorming* (*see* Section 9.7) to answer the question. For example, the question could be: *Why is the response to my questionnaire too low*? See Table 5.2 for some responses to the question.

Table 5.2 Possible causes of a poor response rate

Not going to a named person
Survey is too long
The language used is too complicated
The incentives are not large enough
It is not clear on how the interviewee should respond
The person to whom the completed questionnaire should be sent is not obvious
It has not been sent to enough people
The mailing list details are out of date
The information requested is confidential or too personal
The target is too busy
The respondent is suspicious of the survey's motives
Our organisation has failed to process the completed questionnaire

Stage 2: Group the causes into major categories

This is often a helpful way to sort a lot of ideas that have come from the brainstorming session. Kerri Simon (www.isixsigma.com/library/content/t000827.asp, consulted 20 March 2007) describes two sets of categories for service and manufacturing which may prove a useful guide (*see* Table 5.3).

Table 5.3 Suggested categories for service and manufacturing

Service industries *(The 4 Ps)*	Manufacturing industries *(The 6 Ms)*
■ Policies	■ Machines
■ Procedures	■ Methods
■ People	■ Materials
■ Plant/Technology	■ Measurements
	■ Mother nature (environment)
	■ Manpower (people)

Source: The Cause and Effect Diagram (aka Fishbone), by Kerri Simon. Copyright © 2000–2007 iSixSigma LLC – all rights reserved. Reproduced with permission.

So, using our example from above, we could group our responses in the way described in Table 5.4.

Table 5.4 Major causes of poor response

Not getting to the right person	Not going to a named person It has not been sent to enough people The mailing list details are out of date
Target not completing the survey	Survey is too long The language used is too complicated The incentives are not large enough The information requested is confidential or too personal The target is too busy The respondent is suspicious of the survey's motives
Survey completed but not processed	It is not clear on how the interviewee should respond The person to whom the completed questionnaire should be sent is not obvious Our organisation has failed to process the completed questionnaire

Stage 3: Construct a 'cause and effect' diagram

This useful tool (often called a 'fishbone diagram') was developed by Kaoru Ishikawa, a Japanese management guru who was particularly concerned with the achievement of total quality within the workplace. For this and other problem-solving techniques, you should refer to Ishikawa's book *What is Total Quality Control? The Japanese Way*.

Here it provides a picture of the problem ('effect') and the likely causes. By using this, you can challenge further the groupings and identify the *major* causes. The minor causes should be ones that are easily resolved or do not have a significant impact on the problem. Figure 5.3 takes our example and uses the cause and effect tool.

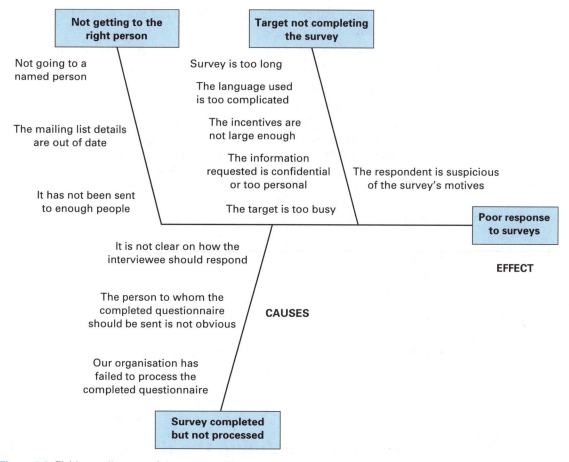

Figure 5.3 Fishbone diagram of the causes of low response to surveys

Stage 4: Getting to the root cause of the major problems

Having established the major causes of the problem, it is important to determine the *root* causes. The '5 Whys' tool is useful here to challenge thinking and undercover the true root of the problem. It keeps asking 'why' until a meaningful answer to the root cause is uncovered. Sometimes it takes less than 5 whys and sometimes more to reach an answer. An example of this process follows, based on the analysis of an unsuccessful sales call.

Problem statement: The last sales call was not successful.

1 *Why?* Because the customer did not buy.

2 *Why did the customer not buy?* Because the product did not seem right for her.

3 *Why was the product not right for her?* Because it did not address any needs she had.

4 *Why did the product not address any needs she had?* Because it was too complex for her business.

5 *Why did you not know this before the call?* Because I did not know about the business she was running.

6 *Why did you not know about the business she was running?* Because no research had been done in advance.

The solution to this problem is clear!

In our example, if we decide that the mailing list being out of date is a major cause of the problem, we can explore the root cause of this (Table 5.5). In this example, it is the last answer that gives us something to work on as including an update of the mailing list *is* within our control and therefore can be fixed. In comparison, if we had stopped at answer 4, we would be trying to change the budget we were given, which is harder or impossible to achieve.

Table 5.5 Root cause of why the mailing list is out of date

1 **Why** is the mailing list out of date?
  - Because we haven't updated it
2 **Why** did you not update it?
  - Because we cannot afford it
3 **Why** can you not afford it?
  - Because we did not put it in our budget for the year
4 **Why** did you not put it in your budget for the year?
  - Because we had no room in the budget we were given
5 **Why** did you have no room in the budget you were given?
  - Because we thought it was not necessary

5.3 Objective setting: defining the desired end-state

Aims, objectives, outcomes and actions

When we engage in conscious action we do so with a view of what the future will be like. We anticipate future conditions when we make a decision and act on it. For example, an investor is not just interested in the current profitability of a company. He or she is also interested in what the company's profitability in the *future* will be. Managers do not simply accept what the future conditions might be like. They try to control them. Good managers actively *shape* the future. Managers operate with a conscious picture of the state they wish to create: where they want their organisation to be, what they want the organisation to do, what they want it to be like. This desire colours management language. Managers talk in explicit terms about what they and their organisations wish to achieve. They use a variety of words to describe these ambitions. They will talk, for example, about their *goals*, *aims*, *objectives*, *missions* and *outcomes*.

Sometimes these words are taken to be synonymous with each other. At other times, users imply subtle distinctions between them. It is useful for the consultant to recognise differences in meaning between such terms. This aids thinking about the rationale for the consulting project and makes communication more efficient and likely to have an impact. Appropriate and well-defined aims, objectives and outcomes are the cornerstone of effective project management. They are worth investing in. They provide the solid platform on which a successful project can be built. The consultant develops aims, objectives and outcomes in the preliminary analysis phase of the consulting project. They are communicated to the client through the proposal. They function to keep the project on track and help the consulting team maintain focus during the process of delivery. They can then be used to assess what the project has actually achieved at delivery. The following discussion highlights the differences between aims, objectives and outcomes and how that difference might be used to aid the consultant in analysis and communication with the client at the different stages of the project.

Aims

The aim of the project is its *overall goal*. It is the *broad* scope of what that project aspires to achieve. An aim is the starting point of a project. It is first articulated as a desire: a sense that things might be different and better. Most businesses share a set of common desires, for example to grow, to be more profitable, to be more secure, to compete more effectively and so on. It is from these general desires that the aim of a consulting project can be distilled. In defining an aim, a consultant is refining the desires of the firm's managers. The way in which this will be done will depend on a number of factors. Some of those the consultant needs to take into account include the following.

The extent to which managers have already articulated their desires for the business

Some managers have a clear view of what they want to achieve. Others only harbour a vague sense of the direction they want to take their business. The consultant may obtain a well-specified project. Often, though, the consultant must help the client comprehend and articulate what he or she wants to achieve on behalf of the firm. This does not mean that the consultant imposes an aim and objectives on the client. Rather the consultant must *facilitate* the client's articulation of what he or she wishes to do.

The level of detail in that articulation

As a business moves forward to pursue its aims, it changes. It modifies its internal processes. It must adjust the structures that give the business its form. It develops its relationships with external stakeholders. Sometimes managers have thought these things through in detail. At other times they will have given them little thought. Consideration must be given to the *detailed* implications of pursuing and achieving particular goals for the firm as a whole. If managers have not done this, the consultant must encourage them to do so and support them to appreciate these changes.

How appropriate the aims are for the business

Not all aims are appropriate for a business. A detailed consideration of what will happen if the business actually achieves the aims that managers are specifying may indicate that the outcomes might not help, and could even damage, the business. The outcomes may, for example, move the business into an area where competitive pressures are unsustainable. They may expose the business to too high a level of risk. In short, they may reduce rather than increase its ability to reward its stakeholders. In this case, the consultant is obliged to inform the client that, in his or her opinion, the aim is not appropriate for the business. This will usually result in a reconsideration of the aims.

The extent to which aims are realistic, given the firm and its situation

Even if the aims are *appropriate* for the business, consideration must be given to how *realistic* they are. Can the business *really* deliver them? Two factors are important to this consideration. First: can the aims realistically be achieved given the situation in the market in which the firm operates? Aims must reflect the reality of the demand of the firm's customers. It is pointless having an aim of achieving sales of £10 million with a product whose total market is worth only £5 million. Second: are the aims reasonable, given the resources the firm has available to pursue them? It is not usually realistic for a small firm to aspire to market leadership using just its own cash flow. It might do so if sufficient new investment capital can be found. If this is the course decided upon, acquiring this additional capital will need to be incorporated in the project.

The way in which the desires are particular to the firm and are distinguished from the general desires all firms have

All firms have ambitions of some sort. 'Generic aims' include a desire to grow, to increase profits, to make cash flow more stable and so on. These are common to most, if not all, businesses. The consultant must be careful to distinguish between those aims the firm will share with all other firms in its sector and those that can properly be said to be exclusive to the business. The distinction is important because businesses pursuing shared aims tend to meet in head-to-head competition. Aims that are exclusive may be a way of differentiating the firm and so reducing competitive pressures.

The scope of the consulting project relative to the business as a whole

Some aims are general. They relate to what the business as a whole wishes to achieve. Other aims may be more localised. They will relate to a limited part of the firm only. There are three dimensions along which aims usually become specific to a part of the business. If the firm is large enough, they may relate to one particular part of the business or business unit within the firm as a whole. In addition, they may refer to the development of a particular product range out of the firm's entire product scope. Finally, they may refer to a particular functional activity within the firm, such as marketing, production or human resource management. These three dimensions are illustrated in Figure 5.4.

A project should be summarised by a *single* aim, not a list. The important thing is that the aim summarises the project in a succinct way so that all involved can recognise it. It might even be thought of as the *mission* for the project. It is not necessary that the aim quantifies the project or gives away all the details. That is the job of objectives and outcomes, discussed below.

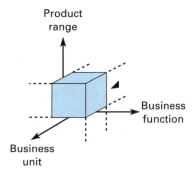

Figure 5.4 The scope of a consulting project

The best way to start the aim is with a phrase like:

It is the aim of this project to . . .

or:

This project aims to . . .

For example:

This consulting project aims to give New Firm Ltd an analysis of its main competitors to aid decision-making about competitive positioning.

Or:

It is the aim of this consulting project to develop a promotional plan for the effective launch of the Ideal product range.

Mission

In many ways, a business may be thought of as a permanent and ongoing project. Certainly, an entrepreneur will see the development of his or her venture as a project of great importance. In the case of the whole business as a project the overall aim of the business may be defined in terms of the business's *mission*. A mission is the reason for the firm's existence. It is a statement of *what* it will achieve and *how*. A mission can include a statement of what the firm offers, to whom it is offering it, the source of its advantages in the marketplace, its aspirations and the ethical values it will uphold. (*See* Wickham (1997) for a review of business missions.) If a business has a stated mission it is a good idea to test the aims of a particular consulting project against it. They should resonate. The consulting project should help the firm achieve its mission. If it is recognised that it does, it can be a positive selling point for the project.

Objectives

An aim is a *broad* statement. It is a *wish*. Objectives provide the details of how this wish will be made into reality. A single aim may be split into a number of objectives. These may be listed. A good way to start the objective list is with the phrase:

The objectives of the consulting project are to . . .

The specific objectives may be put into a bullet-point list after this statement. A number of tests should be applied to an objective list to ensure that the objectives provide the basis for a good project. Good objectives must meet the following criteria.

Consistency

Consistency is the first and most fundamental test. Are the objectives consistent with the agreed aim? Will they deliver it? If not, they must be revised.

Definition

An objective must be well defined: it should not be ambiguous. A great number of problems can arise if the consultant and the client (or different members of the consulting team) read objectives in different ways. Avoid words that mean different things to different people. For example, the word 'profitability' often appears in objectives. Improving it would certainly seem to be a good thing to do. Yet what does the word refer to? Is it profit margin? Or return on capital employed? Or cash flow? The simple rule is: if in doubt – spell it out!

Desirability

The test of desirability relates to the point about the appropriateness of aims discussed above. Will achieving the objectives actually be good for the firm? If the aim is appropriate and the objectives are consistent, then logically they should also be desirable. This allows a double-check that what the consultant is doing for the firm is worthwhile.

Feasibility

Feasibility asks whether the objectives are likely to be achieved given the environmental conditions the firm faces. For example, can sales be achieved given the size of markets, product advantages and competitive pressures? Always ask challenging questions. For example, if the business is to grow, can margins be sustained given the strengths of suppliers and buyers? Can new business be delivered in the face of competitor responses?

Achievability

If an objective is feasible, it can be achieved in *principle*. For an objective to be achievable in *practice*, the firm must dedicate resources to pursuing it. Does the firm have the necessary resources? If it has, is this project the best available use for them? Account must be taken of productive resources and people as well as money. If the firm does not have the resources to hand, can it obtain them? Is obtaining these additional resources part of the consulting project or is it a separate project? Care needs to be taken to clarify and agree whether the project is just about identifying and recommending a direction for the business or actually implementing the project and taking the business there.

Quantified

Ideally, objectives should be quantified. To 'grow the business' does not mean very much. To 'grow the business by 20 per cent' does. Whenever possible, objectives should be quantified by numbers. It is not just *what* will be achieved, but *when* it will be achieved and, critically, *what it will be worth when it is*. Not all objectives can easily be quantified. Objectives such as 'to make our human resource management more effective' or 'to make employees' working time happier' do not offer easy numerical targets. Some would argue that they can, ultimately, be quantified. A starting point might be the actual costs of the human resource management function and staff turnover. Others may argue for the inherently qualitative nature of such objectives. Quantitative information may be difficult (that is, expensive) to obtain. In any case, they may argue, forcing artificial numerical targets on such objectives robs them of their essence.

If objectives are left unquantified it is particularly important that the client's expectations are carefully managed and not allowed to become unrealistic. Some understanding of what these objectives mean for the firm must be found. It is important that what the project can achieve is communicated in an unambiguous way.

Signposted

An objective is *signposted* if it will be clear when it has been achieved. As the word implies, a signpost indicates that the project is going, or has gone, in the right direction. Signposts take a number of forms. They may be a physical output (a report presented, for example) or may be indicated by a numerical measure (say, an increase in sales). Occasionally they may be revealed through qualitative information, for example a survey of employee satisfaction. Quantified objectives have inherent signposts. Qualitative objectives need signposts to be assigned to them. Good signposts are definite, are easily recognised and are agreed by all who have an interest in the consulting project. Do not assume that signposts are recognised and accepted by all involved. If in doubt, highlight the signpost and make sure it is agreed to. Clearly, aims and objectives are involved in describing the same thing: the direction the business wishes to move in. They say this in different ways, though. In a 1977 article, James Brian Quinn makes a powerful case as to why broad goals and specific objectives should be separately articulated. Three reasons are important.

First, goals can be used to give a sense of direction without over-centralising decision-making. Individuals contributing to the project can set their own objectives or sub-objectives and check them against the goal rather than have them set by the project leadership. For example, a goal might be set to generate sales from a new product. If so, decisions must be made about what the product will be like, its features, its price and so on. But the goal does not set these as specified objectives. The managers launching the product are free to use their experiences and local knowledge to set these themselves. An aim offers direction without dictating individual contribution. Second, goals, being broad and unquantified, do not allow conflict over detail. It is details people often object to. For example, an objective to increase sales by 15 per cent might easily start an argument. Should it be 10 per cent or 20 per cent? Such a debate obscures the fact that there is unanimity on the central point: that growth is wanted. Recognising this as a general aim is a starting point for agreement on the detail.

Third, goals define broad 'spaces' for achievement whereas objectives are narrow. Objectives are rigid, especially when they have agreed signposts attached to them. The point about objectives is that they be strived for. An objective is of little use if it can be changed easily. However, there are circumstances in which it might be legitimate to change objectives. The client may alter the requirements of the project. There may be a change in the resources available for the project. New information may become available which indicates a change in direction is judicious. Situations in which objectives might be changed are discussed later in this chapter. In such cases the best move is to go back to the original aim and use it to devise new objectives in light of the new situation. This is much easier, and prone to less disagreement than starting from scratch and establishing entirely new objectives in the absence of an overall goal.

Actions

Good objectives inspire managers to follow them through. They are a *call to action*. Actions are what managers actually do in order to achieve objectives. A collection of coordinated actions is a *plan*. It is implementing a plan of actions that actually consumes resources. Plans organise actions in two dimensions. The first is linearly, as a *sequence in time*. Actions follow one another. Some actions can be undertaken only after others have been completed. Actions must be properly sequenced. The stages of the consulting project reviewed in Chapter 2 are an example. The second dimension is *coordination*, the ordering of actions between individuals. The advantage of team working is that it allows individuals to distinguish and differentiate the contribution they make. If the value this potentially offers is to be realised then individual contributions must be properly integrated. Planning will be dealt with in more detail in Chapter 11.

Outcomes

Outcomes are what will be *made possible* if the objectives are achieved. Outcomes are the difference that is made by achieving the objectives. An outcome is something that takes the business along the road to achieving its organisational mission. It is the outcomes of a project that really sell it to the client. The outcomes define the value of the project to the client. A good way to start an outcome statement is:

> *As a result of this project the business will be able to . . .*

Defining outcomes gives the consultant a chance to check the value of what is being offered to the client. Three important aspects to question are as follows.

Are outcomes consistent with aims?

Are the outcomes of the project in line with the aims agreed for the project? Is the outcome the fulfilment of an aim? Will the outcomes take the business along the road that it wants to go? Critically, will the outcomes help the business deliver its mission?

Are outcomes attractive?

Will the client business and the decision-making unit involved in bringing in the consultant recognise the outcomes as ones which are right for the business and which they desire to see happen? Don't forget, managers are not always rational. They don't always do what the consultant might see as being in the best interests of the firm. Consultants drive change and change is usually political. Different managers see the benefits of change in different ways. If there is an issue, question how different individuals and groups might see the project outcomes. One approach is to consider the different types of client involved in the project (*see* Section 1.5).

Will the client recognise the value created by the consultant?

If managers find the outcomes attractive, do they recognise the contribution the consultant is making to their delivery? Do they feel that they can achieve them unaided? If not, why not? The process consulting mode (*see* Section 1.6) can be particularly prone to leaving managers feeling that the consultant has not made a contribution, especially when process consulting is at its most effective!

Understanding your own objectives

People work together because this allows greater value to be created. In working together, they agree to the aims and objectives of a project. However, individuals will have their own personal objectives that are distinct from those of others involved in the project. Managers pursue their own interests as well as the interests of the organisations they work for and with. The consulting project is no different. The consultant will have objectives that are distinct from those of the client. This does not detract from the potential for working together. Far from it. It is the fact that the client and consultant have distinct objectives that allows them to work together and create value for each other.

Gaining a valuable managerial experience

A consulting project is an opportunity to engage in a high-profile, senior-level managerial experience. If it is to be a valuable part of an overall management education, it needs to be an experience of a particular sort. It should involve contact with senior managers. It should demand that a strategic perspective be taken. It should require that initiative and innovation be brought to bear. Formal managerial skills should be used and developed. If any of these things are missing, the value of the consulting experience will be reduced. Ensuring that the project will have these elements should be an objective for any student undertaking a consulting project.

Practising particular skills

The consulting project provides an opportunity to apply in a real business situation the ideas and skills developed throughout a formal business education. It calls in equal measure on all of the skill areas that mark the effective manager: *analysis skills*, which enable opportunities to be spotted; *project management skills*, which can be used to exploit those opportunities; and the *relationship-building skills*, which enable the value of those opportunities to be communicated and used to motivate others. The consulting project is a chance to see that these skills are of value and to refine their use. It is a proper personal objective that the project be pursued in such a way that these skills are called on in a meaningful and balanced way.

Gaining evidence of achievement

The consulting experience also provides an opportunity to demonstrate managerial ability. The skills used in consulting are transferable to a variety of managerial roles. Successfully completed, the consulting project is something that can be used to enhance the curriculum vitae when applying for positions in the future. It is something that can be related at interviews. It is a very reasonable objective to view the consulting exercise as a way of gaining real and visible evidence of managerial competence. How this can be done is discussed fully in Chapter 13.

Understanding the client's objectives

Clearly, the main objective of the client is to develop the business in a particular direction. However, this is not the client's only objective. They may also have a number of subsidiary objectives that will colour the way he or she approaches the project. Whereas the formal objectives of the project will be explicit, discussed and documented, the client's subsidiary objectives will usually be implicit. It is worthwhile to develop an understanding of them. Recognising the client's subsidiary objectives gives the consultant an insight into how a good working relationship can be developed. Some important subsidiary objectives for the client might be as follows.

An opportunity to develop general understanding

Consultants are experts. Experts have interesting things to say. The manager may regard working with consultants as an opportunity to explore and develop his or her understanding of management in general and the specific management tasks he or she faces. This general understanding will develop in areas that go well beyond the bounds of the particular project.

An opportunity to explore the business in general terms

Managers must be close to their businesses. Their success depends on an intimate knowledge of and sensitivity to the details of the business they are managing and the specific features of the sector in which it is operating. However, by being so close the manager may not find it easy to stand back and view the business as a whole. It is, as the saying goes, easy to lose sight of the wood for the trees. Working with a consultant is an opportunity to redress this situation.

An opportunity to talk about the business

Managers are usually proud of the businesses they work for. An entrepreneur will be very pleased with what he or she has achieved. The interest the consultant shows is flattering. The consulting project gives the manager a chance to talk about the business in which he or she is involved. This is something most will relish. It is something the consultant can use. Asking the manager to talk about the business will be the first step in building a positive relationship and engendering rapport. It will give the manager the confidence to be open and provide the consultant with the information needed to do the project well. As will be discussed in Section 7.6, rapport can be built and openness encouraged through an effective questioning technique.

Reconciling your own objectives with those of the client

In a good consulting exercise, the client and the consulting group work together as part of a team. This does not mean that the client and consultant share every objective, however. As discussed above, the client and consultant bring along their own, distinct objectives to the project. Usually these will be compatible: the client and the consultant team can agree on a set of coordinated actions and common outcomes which will deliver the objectives desired by both parties. Occasionally, however, there will be a misalignment and the consultant and client must negotiate the objectives of the project so that they are reconciled. This process is illustrated in Figure 5.5.

Misalignments occur for a number of reasons. Some of the most common are as follows.

The client expects too much of the consulting team

The client may harbour unrealistic expectations about what the consulting team can achieve. The kind of problem that is highlighted may be of a highly technical nature. The project may require specific industry knowledge to be applied. Often, the client will expect the consulting team to build relationships with outside agencies (particularly customers and investors) in a way that the team simply does not have the experience or time to manage properly. Projects which demand that the consulting team go out and act as a sales force selling products to customers (rather than just develop and advise on a marketing or selling strategy) are examples of this kind of demand.

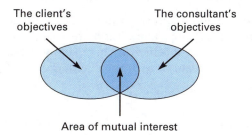

Figure 5.5 Negotiating objectives

The client expects too much of the project

The outcomes expected may be unrealistic given the resources the client is willing to put into the project. Unfortunately, whereas most managers recognise their own resource limitations, some think that consultants either have access to an unlimited supply or are superhumanly efficient with those they have! Typical here are market research projects. The client may be quite clear about the market information wanted but may not recognise the cost involved in gaining that information. It is not unknown for a market research company to be approached and, after its quotation has been found to be too expensive, for a consulting team to be offered the same project without resources made available. The cost of promotional campaigns may also be underestimated.

The project does not have sufficient scope

It is easy for the client manager to look upon the consulting team as an additional, low-cost resource rather than as partners in the development of the business. It is tempting for client managers to hand over jobs that are important, but of low level. Such jobs may involve repetitive tasks. They will not demand that interpretive skills be brought to bear on information obtained. They will not challenge at a sufficiently intellectual level. Such jobs are of such limited scope that they do not demand the full range of skills and insights that would be expected of a consulting challenge. Such jobs should really be undertaken by the business itself. An example would be a project that involves simply creating a list of potential customers rather than developing an understanding of a new customer segment.

The client is not willing to define specific outcomes

Not everybody works to objectives. Some managers simply don't bother. Others make a policy of not setting them. They prefer to deal with things on a contingency basis as they arise. They may present this as 'flexibility'. Problems will arise if the client resists setting objectives for the project. Without clear objectives, the consulting team has no idea of what to aim for. Expectations cannot be managed properly. It will be tempting for the client to simply see the consultant team as an extra resource, to be called upon to do jobs that should be done by the business itself. If objectives are not set, the quality of the consulting exercise as a learning experience must be in doubt. With a little thought, it is quite easy to deal with these situations. Some useful rules of thumb are as follows.

Agree on aims before discussing objectives

As noted above, aims, because they are broad in scope, tend to be less contentious than detailed objectives. It is better to agree on the overall aim of the project before moving on to specifics. If there is any debate about objectives, either within the consulting team or with the client, then the agreed aim can be used as a reference point.

Break down projects into sub-projects

If the client is too ambitious about the project, or expects too much from it, then expectations must be managed. Don't reject the idea for the project out of hand.

Rather, get the manager to explore the project he or she is proposing. Break the project down into relevant sub-projects. It may be that one of these will present a more realistic project.

Get the client to prioritise outcomes

Having broken the project down, assign objectives to each sub-project. Get the client to prioritise. If they must choose, which is most important to them? The argument to use is that it will be better for a realistic project to be done well rather than risk disappointment at the outcomes of one that is too ambitious.

Use the proposal

The proposal documents the project's aims, objectives and outcomes (*see* Section 3.7). If these are written and communicated, the client must recognise them. The aims and objectives of the project must reflect the interests of the manager. However, it is the consultancy team that will actually articulate and document them. This is an advantage, which might be used positively. In the preliminary discussions with the manager it is likely that a lot of ideas will come out. In distilling these into the proposal, the consultant has an opportunity to emphasise and prioritise. Avoid the temptation to impose ideas on the client though. The latitude available here should not be used simply as an opportunity for the team to present the project they believe to be appropriate. The best projects are those to which the client has a genuine commitment.

Understand the client's desired outcomes

Ultimately, it is the project's *outcomes* – the things that the business will be able to do as a result of the project – that are important. This is the difference that the project will make to the business. It is these that the client ultimately 'buys'. Emphasise the importance of this. Understand what it is that the client wants the business to do. Once this understanding is in place the project can be designed to achieve the outcomes. If the client has unrealistic ambitions, break the outcomes down and get the client to prioritise. Again, a good small project is better than a large mediocre one.

Focus on win–win outcomes

Ultimately, the client and consulting team must work together. The manager will be getting insights of value to his or her business. The consulting team will be gaining a valuable learning experience. There is mutual benefit, not conflict. The consulting team should not hesitate to explain that they are seeking a project that will add to their experience in a meaningful way. The team should make it plain that the manager's knowledge and experience will be an important part of this. Most managers will be flattered that their insights are valuable in this way. It will certainly encourage them to shape the project so that it will provide a good learning experience. A general point: focusing on win–win scenarios like this is the essence of good negotiating practice. Negotiating objectives is about aligning the project so that the outcomes desired by the client and those desired by the consulting team are achieved.

5.4   Developing a strategy for the destination

As discussed in earlier, clarifying the causes of the problem is vital. This is also true for the end-point or destination. You need to understand what you are trying to improve or change and when you have achieved your aim.

A good way to start is to develop a 'project charter'. An example is given in Table 5.6.

Project information

This provides a quick summary such as the name of the leader, in case someone needs to contact them, the timing of the product and a brief description.

Team members

As well as a team leader, it is often useful to have a sponsor for the project. This person usually is someone senior within the organisation who can help if there are issues in delivering the project and who can ultimately influence upwards to gain implementation. Team size should be as restricted as possible (no more than six) but it may be necessary to involve others on an ad hoc basis, particularly if expert guidance is required.

Scope of the project

Sometimes an issue may be part of a larger problem within the organisation. For example, poor sales may be down to ineffective sales technique (which a project could address) but it may also be due to the wrong type of salespeople being recruited, which may be beyond the control of the team. It is therefore important that it is clearly stated what is part of the project and what is not. However, at the end recommendations could be made if such wider issues were highlighted.

Table 5.6 Example of a project charter

Project information	**Case for project**
Leader:	*(Why are we doing this?)*
Project start:	
Project end:	
Brief description:	
Team members	**Problem to be solved**
Sponsor:	*(What will be the benefit to us?)*
Leader:	
Core team:	
Ad hoc members:	
Scope of the project	**Project goals**
(What should and should not be included)	*(What are your objectives?)*
Project time frame	**Project measurements**
(Key milestones and dates)	*(What tools will you use to know whether you are successful?)*

Project time frame

This should detail the date of the final delivery of the project outputs together with key events along the way. Pay attention to events that will entail a lot of involvement with the client managers so that they can timetable this into their schedules. Also detail any points at which the client managers will be expected to make expenditure so that they can manage their budgets. Finally, consider any events, such as interim reports and presentations, which will reassure the client managers that the project is on track.

Case for project

It is rare that a consulting project is done for its own sake as it usually has wider implications. For example, a project to improve the effectiveness of your advertising will have the ultimate aim of increasing your sales and profits.

Problem to be solved

This is a detailed description of the problem and its root causes that are to be investigated. By solving this problem, it will bring benefits to the organisation that should be articulated.

Project goals

This is a clear statement of what you are trying to achieve that is measurable.

Project measurements

In general all objectives should be measurable but it is sometimes difficult to put hard numbers on everything or the cost of doing so may be prohibitive. In these circumstances, you look for tools that will give you some indication of whether you are successful or not. This also links back to the case for the project.

5.5   Developing the strategy for the journey

No two consulting projects are alike but there are some common processes which consultants can adopt to form the basis of a framework. One that is popular at the time of writing is the 'Six Sigma' methodology.

Six Sigma

This was originated by Bill Smith at Motorola who developed a means of increasing profitability by reducing defects in manufacturing and services. He said that there should not be more than 3.4 million defects per million opportunities to achieve 'Six Sigma', with defects being defined as anything outside customer specifications. In order to achieve this, the Six Sigma methodology is a measurement-based strategy that looks at process improvement through defined projects. Bill

Smith's ideas were first adopted by Allied Signal (now Honeywell) and General Electric. The latter has estimated benefits of $10 billion in the first five years of operation (*source*: www.isixsigma.com/sixsigma/six_sigma.asp (consulted 20 March 2007). For more information, please refer to *Six Sigma Way* by Peter S. Panda (2000) and *The New Six Sigma* by Matt Barney and Tom McCarty (2003). At the heart of these are two methodologies: the DMAIC (define, measure, analyse, improve and control) process and the DMADV (define, measure, analyse, design and verify) process. The first is for existing processes and is the most widely used. We will concentrate on this one. The latter is for new processes or products.

DMAIC process

Figure 5.6 shows the outline process.

Define

The requirements for this phase include understanding the real problem and its causes and the objectives of the consulting exercise. These have been described above. Also, any current processes may be mapped out to get a common view of the 'way things are done now'. Consultants often refer to this as the 'as is' processes. The project charter outlined in Section 5.4 is the document issued after the 'define' phase has been completed.

Measure

Having defined in your project charter what measurements you are going to use, you need to start collecting some historical data to use as a benchmark. When doing this, you need to challenge whether the data:

- continues to be key to the project;
- is reliable and not liable to interpretation;
- is cost effective to collect;
- is able to be collected in the future.

Is the measure sensitive enough to answer whether you are making proper progress? Ask how the measure will change if the project goes off schedule. Will it change a lot or only a little for minor delays, moderate delays or major delays?

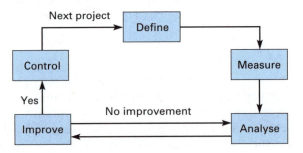

Figure 5.6 The Six Sigma DMAIC process

Analyse

This is the critical phase as you assess what is wrong with the current process and what you need to do in order to improve things. Consultants often call the resulting improved process the 'to be' process. Key questions that you need to ask are:

- Who do we need to involve to make the changes happen?
- What other resources do we need?
- What are the potential pitfalls we may face?
- What are the downsides if we fail to implement?
- What are the risks to the other parts of the business in implementation?

Improve

Here you draw up an implementation plan of how you will introduce the improved processes. This plan would include the breakdown of work required by sub-project if necessary. The implementation plan would then be carried out and the results of the improved process monitored using the measurement tools described in the 'measure' phase. If the initial results were not as expected, it may be necessary to go back to the 'analyse' phase to ensure that the correct problems with the current process and solutions have been identified.

Control

This is the final phase where the consultant will usually hand control back to the process owner within the client company. In order for this to be done, the consultant (and his or her team) needs to ensure that the changes in the process are well embedded in the client organisation and all relevant personnel are trained in the new process. Any auditing of the process will now be the responsibility of the client process owner and this is critical to ensure that the improvements are maintained.

It is often at this stage that the next project is defined which relates to further improvements in this process or related processes. In this case a lot of the learning in the original project should be used, so as not to reinvent the wheel.

5.6 The need for change in the client organisation

Organisations undergo continual change. For most of the time this change is incremental. It takes place in a gradual way with small steps. Managers may not recognise change is taking place unless they specifically reflect upon it. At intervals, though, the change is more radical and is manifest as a specific management project. Given that change is often difficult, both in terms of the best direction for change and the implementation of that change, consultants are often called in to support the project. John P. Kotter, in his book *Leading Change* (1996), has a useful discussion as to why organisations need to change and how to be successful at it.

Change is often forced upon an organisation by factors such as:

- being loss-making, or facing other financial difficulties;
- large new competitors successfully entering the marketplace;
- new regulations or other restrictions on trade;
- changes in purchasing habits by major customers;
- new technology that changes the way the business operates;
- growth driven through delivering new products or serving new markets;
- new managerial approaches (often associated with political manoeuvring).

When an organisation is in such a crisis the first stage of change is usually a turn-around effort that aims primarily to stabilise the organisation. The objectives and the projects involved are very clear. Although this phase often involves recrimination – individuals look for someone to blame for the crisis – eventually all involved are motivated to meet this challenge.

This may be followed by an attempt to implement a radically new strategic approach that aims to put the organisation back on a growth track. This is usually harder to implement, as it demands major structural or cultural change. Here there are multiple objectives and projects, resulting in a complex and dynamic situation that is more difficult for participants to follow. In this case, Kotter emphasises the importance of leadership, as opposed to management of change. Leadership establishes direction, aligns people, motivates and inspires to create change. Management in a period of change is about planning, organising and problem solving to produce some degree of order and coherence during the change episode.

Team discussion points	Discuss the following statements. Argue as to whether they might be true or not:

Discuss the following statements. Argue as to whether they might be true or not:

- Only an outsider can really see the problems an organisation faces.
- Change is always good for an organisation.
- A consultant and client's objectives can always be reconciled.
- Always turning problems into opportunities can sometimes be seen as unrealistically optimistic or naive.

 ## Summary of key ideas

- The problem a consultant has been called in to address has three facets:
  - the rational: the value the resolution of the problem will create for the business;
  - the cognitive: the way the problem is perceived by individual managers;
  - the political: the way the organisation as a whole reacts to the problem and the impact it (and its resolution) will have on different individuals.
- The consultant must be aware of each of these facets.
- When defining the problem it is useful to consider four dimensions:
  - the *current state* of the business;
  - the *desired goals* of the business;

- *assistors*: those things which will help the business achieve its goals;
- *inhibitors*: those things which will restrict the business and stop it achieving its goals.

■ Assistors and inhibitors may both be further divided into internal and external dimensions. Those that are *internal* are part of the firm and are under the control of managers. Those that are *external* are given by the environment and must be accepted by managers.

■ On being presented with the 'problem' by the client, it is important to go through a process to get to the root causes.

■ Getting to the root causes involves challenging the reasons why there is a problem, uncovering the *major* causes and then asking 'why' until the answer is able to be 'solved' by the consulting team.

■ A consulting project is defined in terms of its *aim*, *objectives* and *outcomes*.

■ The aim of the project is a single statement of the project's broad goal, what it aims to achieve. The aim need not be quantified or have a lot of detail. It is important that all involved in the project recognise the aim and agree to it.

■ A statement of an aim might start: *'It is the aim of this project to . . .'*

■ The objectives of the project are a detailed list of the things the project aims to achieve.

■ Good objectives are:
- consistent: they will lead to the aim being fulfilled;
- well defined: they are unambiguous; they can be read only one way;
- desirable: they will lead to outcomes wanted by all involved;
- feasible: they are realistic, given the firm's environment;
- achievable: they can be delivered, given the firm's resources;
- quantified: it is agreed when they will be delivered and what it will be worth when they are delivered;
- signposted: it will be recognised when the objective has been achieved.

■ The list of objectives can be started with the statement: *'The objectives of this project are to . . .'*

■ Objectives are a call to action and to initiate a plan.

■ The outcomes of a project are what the business will be able to do if the objectives are delivered. Outcomes are the *difference* the project will make to the client business.

■ The statement of outcomes can be started with the phrase: *'As a result of this project the business will be able to . . .'*

■ A consulting project has both a destination and a journey.

■ The destination can be defined through the use of a project charter.

■ The project charter includes information on the team members, project goals and scope, the problem the project sets out to resolve, and how outcomes will be measured.

■ The project journey can be defined using the Six Sigma DMAIC process.

■ Change is important for organisations if they are to maintain their competitive position in a dynamic marketplace.

■ External forces and internal crises often force change upon organisations.

Key reading

Kluckler, J. and Armbruster, T. (2003) 'Bridging uncertainty in management consulting: The mechanisms of trust and networked reputation', *Organization Studies*, 24 (2), 787–94.

Quinn, J.B. (1977) 'Strategic goals: Process and politics', *Sloan Management Review*, Fall, 21–37.

Further reading

Andreas, S. and Andreas, C. (1987) *Change Your Mind – And Keep the Change*. Moad, UT: Real People Press.

Barney, M. and McCarty, T. (2003) *The New Six Sigma*. Harlow, Essex: Prentice Hall.

Drennan, D. (1992) *Transforming Company Culture*. Maidenhead, Berkshire: McGraw-Hill Education Europe.

French, W.L. and Bell, C.H. Jr (1990) *Organization Development*. Upper Saddle River, NJ: Prentice-Hall.

Hayes, J. (2002) *The Theory and Practice of Change Management*. Basingstoke, Hampshire: Palgrave.

Ishikawa, K. (1988) *What is Total Quality Control? The Japanese Way*. Harlow, Essex: Prentice Hall.

Kotter, J.P. (1996) *Leading Change*. Boston, MA: Harvard Business School Press.

Moss Kanter, R. (1988) *Changemasters*. Chichester, West Sussex: Jossey Bass Wiley.

Panda, P.S. (2000) *Six Sigma Way*. Maidenhead, Berkshire: McGraw-Hill Education Europe.

Pyzdek, T. (2003) *The Six Sigma Project Handbook*. New York: McGraw-Hill Education.

Silberman, M. (ed.) (2000) *Consultant's Tool Kit: 50 High-impact Questionnaires, Activities and How-to Guides for Diagnosing and Solving Client Problems*. New York: McGraw-Hill Education.

Silberman, M. (ed.) (2002) *Consultant's Big Book of Organizational Development Tools*. New York: McGraw-Hill Education.

Werr, A., Stjernberg, T. and Docherty, P. (1997) 'The functions of methods of change in management consulting', *Journal of Organizational Change Management*, 10 (4), 288–307.

Wickham, P.A. (1997) 'Developing a mission for an entrepreneurial venture', *Management Decision*, 35 (5), 373–81.

Exconom

Exconom is a company specialising in cable and small-bore pipe-laying technology. The company started life as a technical division of a major utility. It gained its independence as the result of a venture capital backed management buyout (MBO) three years ago. The company now has 21 employees and a turnover of just over £4 million. The company's competitive edge comes from its technological capabilities with 'mole' excavating tools. This is equipment that can lay cables and pipes underground without the need to dig a trench first. This reduces cost and disruption. Exconom contracts its services to companies which need to lay cables. Electrical and gas utilities provide the core of business. This business is largely based on historical relationships with these customers developed prior to the MBO. Marketing activities are limited. An as yet small but high-growth sector which is expected to be important in the future is cable television, though the company has not won any contracts here yet.

Alan, the business development manager, explains that the business is sound and has a lot of potential. However, the rest of the management team are limited in their ambitions. While they talk about the business moving into new areas, in practice they resist practical moves. They prefer to stick to the business applications they know and understand. The attitude tends to be one of not taking unnecessary risks while the company is under the 'control' of venture capitalists. In fact, Alan explains, although the venture capitalists will see a reasonable return on their investment (they have a five-year exit plan),

they are a little disappointed that the company has not grown as much as initially suggested by the original business plan.

So far, Alan has argued for diversification of the customer base on an ad hoc basis in meetings. This has not really worked. Now he wants to put forward a proposal in the form of a cohesive plan. He wants the team to undertake the research necessary to develop this plan. His brief includes the comment that the management team tend to focus on details. They will make a move only if all implications have been considered. If he is to get his plan implemented he will need a lot of reliable information which makes the opportunities clear and unambiguous. Also, the emphasis should be on why the company's technology will work in the new application and will be attractive to customers.

Alan also mentions in passing the fact that he has heard of a couple of new companies in the sector using the same technology as Exconom. He would be interested in anything the team can pick up on these competitors.

Q1 Analyse the problem presented by the client. Can Alan's problem(s) be re-presented as opportunities?

Q2 Formalise four objectives for the project.

Q3 Consider what problems might emerge in reconciling the client's objectives with your own as a consulting team.

CHAPTER 6

Evaluating client capabilities and business opportunities

Margaret Dewhurst and Tony Kellett

Learning outcomes

The learning outcomes from this chapter are to:

- introduce a range of analysis techniques to review the business and its environment;
- understand what is meant by and what is the basis for building a business's success (competitive advantage);
- illustrate how to use a range of techniques in order to identify strategic options for the business;
- identify the qualitative and quantitative market research techniques that can aid decision-making.

6.1 Preliminary analysis techniques

We need to start by asking why the business organisation or system exists. What is its mission or purpose and what are its objectives? We also need to establish how this business system fits externally – not just in comparison with competitors but in the 'bigger picture'. Two useful techniques to help set the scene are SWOT and STEEPLE.

SWOT and STEEPLE

The *SWOT analysis* is a good, basic technique for getting the analysis started. SWOT is an acronym standing for 'strengths, weaknesses, opportunities and threats'. The SWOT analysis provides the consultant with a concise and comprehensive summary of a business. It offers an immediate and accessible insight into the capabilities of the business and ways in which it might use them. Normally presented as a four-box matrix, typically, a SWOT analysis will identify a broad-based group of strengths and weaknesses coupled with a number of opportunities and threats (Figure 6.1). The SWOT analysis can be generated through a brainstorming session. It can also be used to keep a summary of features identified by other

Strengths Things under the control of managers which will help the business achieve its goals.	**Weaknesses** Things outside the control of managers which will hinder the business and prevent it from achieving its goals.
Opportunities Things under the control of managers which will offer the business a means of achieving its goals.	**Threats** Things outside the control of managers which will hinder the business and prevent it achieving its goals.

Figure 6.1 SWOT analysis

analysis techniques. However, it should be recognised that the opportunities and threats side of the SWOT analysis is a 'wish list'. This side of the equation should be kept realistic.

In order to take a closer look at the business system and 'bigger picture' factors in which the business operates, it is useful to use a technique like the *STEEPLE analysis*. STEEPLE, like SWOT, is an acronym. It stands for 'social (demographic), technological, economic, environmental (natural), political, legal and ethical' factors. The analysis is sometimes referred to as the *PLEEST analysis* (in which the same terms are used, but in a different order. It is also known as the PEST or STEP analysis, where the factors have been grouped). Essentially, *sociological factors* are those that relate to the societal development of buying groups. Look for changes in social trends and attitudes that will affect consumption.

Technological factors are those that relate to the knowledge used in the design, production and delivery of outputs. Technology is changing continually. New products are constantly being developed and existing ones are redesigned. There are broad technological trends, which will have an impact on every business in some way or other. Each industry and sector has its own 'proprietary' technological base where the effects of technological developments are localised.

Economic factors are those that relate to the overall economy. Look for growth in economic wealth (GDP) and its distribution in relation to customer groups. Consider the effects of economic booms and recessions. Other important factors include the impact of interest rates (which make borrowing more expensive) and exchange rates. A strengthening of a currency makes imports cheaper and exports more expensive. Exporters are hit when a currency strengthens; importers benefit. A weakening of the currency has the reverse effect.

Environmental factors refer to what are nowadays dubbed 'green' issues. These tend to have more importance in some industry sectors than others, like chemicals or packaging, but are always worth considering. A good example is the disposal of toxic waste. *Political and legal* factors are those that relate to governance and the attitudes of government agencies. Look for political favour and disfavour, influence with government, lobbying and potential new laws that may give or take away legislative monopolies or change the conditions under which trading will take place. *Ethical* factors, like environmental, play more of a part in medical and food related businesses, for example, but again should be considered as a matter of course even when their influence is not believed to be strong. An example is the use of human genome data.

6.2 Strategic capabilities of businesses

There are a number of ways in which business strategy can be defined. At one level, a strategy is simply the consistency of the actions the business takes, the fact that it sells a particular range of products to a definite customer group. In this respect all businesses have a strategy of sorts. At another level, a strategy is the way in which the business will compete and beat its competitors. It is the way in which it develops an edge in the marketplace. Ultimately a strategy must dictate the way the business behaves, it must become a plan – a 'recipe for action' to succeed in the marketplace. A firm's competitive advantage is the basis on which the performance of the business is built. A competitive advantage is something that:

- the firm *possesses*;
- creates *value* for its customers;
- in a way is *unique*; and
- competitors find it difficult *to imitate*.

A firm can be said to have competitive advantage when it is *able to sustain profits that exceed the average for the industry*. A good place to start the process of identifying the source of competitive advantage (if any) is by asking a few key questions about the reason for the business's existence or the *business idea*. It is valuable to distil the responses to these questions to a key sentence or maximum two for each question:

- What is the need or behaviour in the market that the type of product or service the firm is providing satisfies?
- What is the basic (existing) offer out there in the marketplace that satisfies this need?
- How does the firm's offering differ or how is it special in a way that the customer values?

Analysing the answers to these questions should provide a clear insight into what the source of competitive advantage is or might be: remember, it must meet the criteria listed above.

Porter's five forces

Michael Porter originally identified three basic types of competitive advantage, namely *cost* (lower cost advantage), *differentiation* (delivery of benefits that exceed those of competing products) and *focus* (focusing on a particular buying group, segment or product line – servicing a market particularly well). These are known as *positional advantages*. There is also a *resource-based view* that emphasises that a firm utilises its resources and capabilities to create advantage that results in superior *value chain* creation (see later). This view suggests that a firm must have resources and capabilities that are collectively superior to those of its competitors. Examples of the source of such resource-based advantage include: patents and trademarks, proprietary know-how, installed customer base, reputation of the firm and brand equity. Together these resources and capabilities form the firm's *core competencies*.

The model for industry analysis – *Porter's five forces* – still offers a useful means for understanding the industry context in which a company operates and may help suggest how to develop an edge over rivals (*see* Figure 6.2).

What this model offers is an insight into the drivers of competition:

■ *Intensity of rivalry among players*: influenced by the number of firms, their market share and cost bases, switching costs (when a customer can freely move from one product to another), levels of product differentiation and exit barriers (the cost of abandoning a product).

■ *Threat of substitutes*: price changes in products in other industries affecting the industry under scrutiny, substitution of one product by another in a different industry (one example is the advent of personal digital assistants supplanting diaries and calculators).

■ *Buyer power*: the impact customers have on an industry. Where there is one buyer and many suppliers, the buyer has the real power, for example.

■ *Supplier power*: the impact suppliers have on an industry. Where a supplier holds a company to ransom over a critical resource, the supplier exerts real control.

■ *Barriers to entry*: the possibility that new firms may enter the industry also affects competition. There may be high barriers to entry if there are considerable costs associated with entering a market or where the prices are too low to attract new entrants (a deterrent) or where there are patents in place. The government can create such barriers through regulation too.

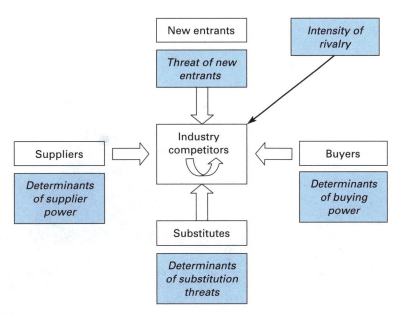

Figure 6.2 Five forces

Source: Adapted with the permission of The Free Press, a Division of Simon & Schuster Adult Publishing Group, from *Competitive Strategy: Techniques for Analyzing Industries and Competitors* by Michael E. Porter. Copyright © 1980, 1998 by The Free Press. All rights reserved.

The Delta model (and sixth force)

Hax and Wilde in *The Delta Project* argue that their model provides a means of unifying the Porter framework ('five forces', as above, and value chain – see later) with the resource-based view to developing strategy (*see* Figure 6.3). They identify three distinctive strategic positions offering very different approaches to achieve 'customer bonding'. These go beyond the 'best product' (i.e. low cost/differentiated option, mentioned earlier) and further develop the 'focus' option to give 'total customer solutions' and 'system lock-in'. The Delta model also offers a 'sixth force' to add to Porter's five forces, namely, *complementors*. A complementor is a firm engaged in the delivery of products and services that enhance the firm's product and service portfolio. These are typically, though not necessarily, external and are easily overlooked. A classic example of this is the Microsoft Windows operating system and software companies. To get the best coverage and market penetration, a software company needs to be compatible with Windows.

Market segmentation

Market segmentation is the process of dividing a market into distinct subsets (segments) that behave in the same way or have similar needs. Because each segment is fairly homogeneous in their needs and attitudes, they are likely to respond similarly to a given *marketing mix* (also known as *the 4 Ps*): **p**roduct or service, **p**lace – including demographics as well as geography, **p**romotion, and **p**rice). Broadly, markets can be divided according to a number of general criteria, such as by industry, geography or profession. Small segments are often termed niche markets or speciality markets. However, all segments fall into either consumer or

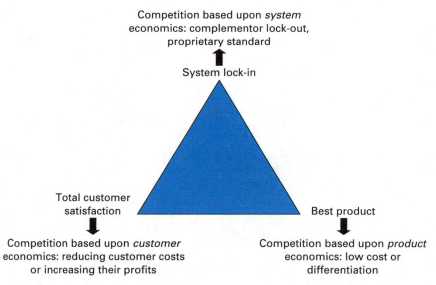

Figure 6.3 Delta model

Source: Hax, A.C. and Wilde, D.L., *The Delta Project: Discovering New Sources of Profitability in a Networked Economy*, 2001, Palgrave Macmillan. Figure 1.1, page 10. Republished with permission of Palgrave Macmillan.

industrial markets. Although it has similar objectives and it overlaps with consumer markets in many ways, the process of industrial markets is quite different. The overall intent is to identify groups of similar customers and potential customers; to prioritise the groups to address; to understand their behaviour; and to respond with appropriate marketing strategies that satisfy the different preferences of each chosen segment.

Successful segmentation requires that segments be:

- Substantial – large and profitable enough.
- Accessible – can be reached efficiently.
- Different – will respond to a different marketing mix.
- Actionable – the firm must have a product for this segment.
- Measureable – the size and purchasing power of the segment can be measured.

There is another way of looking at segmentation – called defining by *centre points*. This technique looks at segments in a different way, taking an ideal customer as the centre of the hypothesised segment and envisaging segments like a swarm of bees or school of fish with an identifiable centre. The market strategy is then focused on that centre with communications and a range of products/services dedicated to addressing that ideal customer's needs and wants, what is known as the *whole product*.

6.3 Financial and business performance

The financial situation of a firm is fundamental. The health of a firm's finances is not just an indication of how successful it has been in the past, it is also an indication of the resources it has available to reward its stakeholders and to invest in new projects. In making an evaluation of a business, its performance and its potential for the future the consultant must be cognisant of its financial situation. Finance and accounting are disciplines in their own right. All that is necessary here is to outline the principles of financial analysis and give a flavour of the approach to analysis that is important to the consultant. Businesses are required by law to keep accurate records of their income and expenditure and to produce accounts. The complexity of the accounts will depend on the business and its legal status. They are quite straightforward for a small sole trader; they are extensive and complex for a publicly quoted multinational.

Whilst accounting practices vary between countries, the principles behind all company accounts are the same. There are three fundamental financial documents: the *balance sheet*, the *profit and loss account* and the *cash flow statement*.

The balance sheet

The balance sheet is a statement of what the firm owns (its *assets*) and what it owes (its *liabilities*). The balance sheet represents a snapshot in time. It is a statement of what is owned and owed at the time the balance sheet is produced. Accounts usually have two balance sheets (or the balance sheet quotes two columns of figures), an *opening set* and a *closing set*. The closing set is for the date of the balance sheet, the opening set for an earlier point in time (usually one year before). Comparison between the two gives an indication of the changes in the firm's assets and liabilities over the period. There are various sorts of assets. They are usually classified in terms of *liquidity*: that is, how easy it is to convert them to cash should the need arise. *Tangible assets* are things that have a physical form, such as buildings and machinery. These are normally considered to be less liquid than any *stock* stored by the business. Stock is those things that the firm normally exists to trade in, or materials that can be converted into stock. The most liquid assets are cash and investments held by the business, as well as any debts owed to the business. (Care needs to be taken in respect of 'bad debt' that cannot be called in.) Assets that could, in principle, be turned into cash within one year are called *current assets*. Current assets are normally taken to be cash, liquidisable investments, stock and outstanding debts owed to the company.

Intangible assets are things which do not have a physical form but which may, potentially, be sold. Important examples are brand names, copyrights and patents. *Liabilities* are things to which the firm has access but which (technically at least) it owes to outside parties. Liabilities are of two sorts. *Short-term liabilities* are due for settlement within the normal accounting period, usually one year. *Long-term liabilities* are due for settlement after that. The key liabilities are *debts* owed to creditors (suppliers, including employees), *interest* owed to those who have lent to the company, outstanding *tax* owed to the government and *dividends* due to shareholders. As it is the shareholders who actually own a company, they own the difference between its assets and its liabilities. This difference is included in the balance sheet as *shareholders' funds*. It is included as a liability so that the two halves of the balance sheet are equal – so that they actually balance.

The profit and loss account

The *profit and loss account* is a statement of the trading activity of the business over a period, again usually one year. It relates to the balance between the income and outgoings of the business. *Income* is the revenue gained from normal trading activity, that is, sales. Exceptional income from sources that do not represent normal trading activity (for example, investments) will also be included but will be indicated separately in the accounts. *Outgoings* are the expenditures on those things that are needed to keep the business running. Immediate costs are for raw materials, productive equipment and services and salaries of production staff. Together these immediate costs are known as the *cost of sales*. Costs for administration and central staff are known as *overheads*. Other expenditure is on paying the *interest* on loans, *tax* to governments and *dividends* to shareholders. The difference between income and expenditure is the *profit* generated by the business. Different types of profit are quoted after the deduction of different types of outgoings. These are described in Table 6.1.

The different levels of expenditure included in the profit and loss account give an indication of the *cost structure* of the business. It is common, especially in the US, to refer to earnings rather than profit. A common version of earnings used for comparing different types of business is earnings before interest, tax, depreciation and amortisation (abbreviated to EBITDA).

Table 6.1 Outgoings and profit

Total income minus	Equals
Cost of sales (raw materials + production salaries + production services + depreciation)	Gross margin
Distribution costs (distribution materials + distribution salaries + depreciation on distribution equipment)	Operating profit
Administrative costs (overheads + all other costs not disclosed elsewhere)	Profit before interest and tax (PBIT)
Interest on loans	Profit before tax (PBT)
Tax to government (national and local)	Profit after tax (PAT)
Dividends to shareholders	Retained profits

Cash flow statement

Many profitable businesses fail because they do not manage their cash resources properly, hence the dictum 'cash is king'. This is particularly important for businesses in early stage or high growth phases. The cash flow statement is normally used as an internal forecasting tool. The forecast takes into account not only the elements of income, outgoings and assets that appear in the profit and loss statement but also their timing. A sale is typically registered on the profit and loss account when the invoice is issued but it will be some time before payment is received. This interval is known as *days receivable*. The gap between being invoiced by a supplier and the firm paying the invoice is called *days payable*. Salaries and other administrative costs are scheduled and predictable in cash flow terms. Long-term projects have complex cash flows that can be input to the forecast. Purchasing major capital items also has a significant impact on the cash flow. These factors are used to develop a model of when cash flows into and out of the business and hence determine the ongoing cash position of the firm. This in turn determines what payment terms are acceptable to the firm and what additional finance it may need to maintain adequate liquidity.

Financial ratios

The figures in the balance sheet and profit and loss account do not, in themselves, offer a full picture of the firm in relation to its competitors and its sector. What is important is how they relate to each other. The figures are related to each other through *financial ratios*. Financial ratios fall into three types. *Performance* (or *operating*) *ratios* measure how well the firm is using the resources it has to hand. *Financial status ratios* measure the stability of the business and indicate how well it could weather a financial storm affecting income or expenditure. The third type is used by investors to get an external view of the firm for comparative purposes. They give an indication of its performance as an investment vehicle. The key performance ratios are those that relate to profitability. This may be measured in two ways. The first is the profit margin, the ratio between profit and total sales, also called *return on sales* (ROS).

Profit margin = Profit/Sales

Different profit margins use different profit lines (such as operating, PBT, PAT, as outlined in Table 6.1).

The most fundamental measure of performance is *return on capital*. *Return on capital employed* (ROCE) gives an indication to managers of the profits they are generating for the money they are using. It is defined as:

ROCE = Operating profit/Capital employed

where capital employed is usually defined as total assets minus short-term liabilities.

Return on equity (ROE) is of interest to investors. It indicates the way in which an investment in the firm is generating a yield. It is defined as:

ROE = PAT/Shareholder funds

Two financial stability ratios are particularly important. The *debt ratio* measures the balance between equity capital provided by investors and loan capital provided by lenders. This is defined as:

Debt ratio = (Long-term debt + Short-term debt)/Capital employed

This ratio is important because interest on debt must be paid, whatever the business's performance. If the company has a high debt ratio, it may face cash flow problems and pressure from its debt providers if profits are squeezed.

Interest cover is a measure of how much 'room' the profits give to pay off interest on loans. It is defined as:

Interest cover = Operating profit/Interest owed

Two ratios are used to measure the *liquidity* of the firm. Liquidity is the ability of the firm to pay off its debts at short notice. The *current ratio* measures the extent to which short-term or current assets can be used to pay off short-term liabilities. It is defined as:

Current ratio = Current assets/Current liabilities

The *quick ratio* is a much tougher test. It is a measure of a company's ability to pay off its liabilities *immediately*. The *liquid assets* are cash, liquidisable investments and debt owed to the company (after allowing for bad debts). It is defined as:

Quick ratio = Liquid assets/Current liabilities

The third type of ratios give an indication of how well a firm's stock (its shares) is performing as an investment opportunity. If a firm is publicly quoted then its shares will be traded in a market which gives them a price. The price of shares for private companies is set by closed transactions.

Shareholders are rewarded in two ways. The first is by means of *capital growth*, the increase in the underlying value of the company's share, which enables a profit to be made when the shares are sold. The second is through *income*. This is the flow of *dividends* paid out of company profits. Each share entitles its owner to a particular cash dividend. One form of reward can be played off against the other. If the firm's managers hold back profits (so do not pay dividends), they can use the money to invest in the firm's growth (so increasing share capital value).

The main metrics for investors are:

Earnings per share (EPS) = PAT/Number of shares issued

Price/earnings ratio (P/E) = Market price of share/EPS

Market capitalisation = Market value of shares × Number of shares

Dividend cover = EPS/Dividend per share

Dividend yield = Dividend per share/Market price per share

A P/E ratio is a kind of market rating. A high P/E ratio suggests that the market places a high value on a firm even though its current earnings are relatively low. First, the firm may have quite low risks. Second, the market may expect the firm's earnings to grow in the future.

Care should be taken when using ratios. They give absolute indications of a business's performance. They can be revealing. Yet they provide a full picture only when they are compared with other ratios. This comparison may be *historical*, as a trend in the ratios of a particular firm over time, or *cross-sectional*, as a comparison at a particular time of the ratios of a number of firms in the same or related sectors.

The Balanced Scorecard

Traditionally, approaches to performance measurement have relied heavily on financial accounting measures. Motivated by the belief that this approach was obsolete, a study sponsored in the early 1990s by the Nolan Norton Institute (part of KPMG) revealed that reliance on summary financial measures was hindering organisations' ability to create future economic value. The outcome of this and subsequent work is captured in the *Balanced Scorecard* (*see* Figure 6.4). The Balanced Scorecard is a balanced set of measures and a management system that emphasises that financial and non-financial measures must be part of the information system for employees at all levels in the organisation. Front-line employees must understand the financial consequences of their actions, for example, it argues. The scorecard is designed to translate a company or business unit's mission into tangible objectives and measures. The 'balance' is between outcome or lagging measures (financial) and the drive for future performance or leading measures (driven by the internal activities that give rise to the financial results). Most scorecards have four 'perspectives' with typical generic measures like:

- *Financial*: return on investment and economic value-added.
- *Customer*: satisfaction, retention, market and account share.
- *Internal*: quality, response time, cost of new product introductions.
- *Learning and growth*: employee satisfaction and information system availability.

The 'trick' with the scorecard is to find and use the most appropriate measures for a firm or organisation for its specific objectives and with its mission in mind. When looking at a firm, it is worth considering what metrics are used and why,

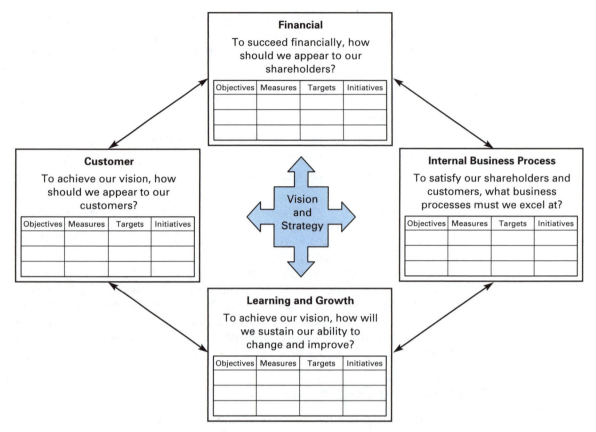

Figure 6.4 Balanced Scorecard

Source: Reprinted by permission of *Harvard Business Review*. Adapted from Figure 1.1: Translating Vision and Strategy –
Four Perspectives from 'Using the balanced scorecard as a strategic management system' by Kaplan, R.S. and Norton, D.P.
(Jan–Feb 1996). Copyright © 1996 by the Harvard Business School Publishing Corporation; all rights reserved.

bearing in mind the old adage 'you get what you measure'. So ask: are the factors
that are being measured the right ones for the organisation and are they right
at this time?

Pareto analysis

Every business is different. However, the contribution to sales (or profits) of different lines in a multi-product firm follows quite a consistent pattern: a (relatively)
small number of leading lines will make a large contribution while a (relatively)
large number of low-volume lines will make a small contribution. This is called
the Pareto rule. It is sometimes called the '80–20' rule because often the top 20 per
cent of lines make a contribution of 80 per cent to sales and profits. A Pareto
curve can be drawn by listing the product lines in order of sales (or profits), with
those that make the highest contribution being first. A graph can then be drawn
with the cumulative contribution on the vertical axis and the percentage of total
product lines on the horizontal axis. The curve will look something like that
in Figure 6.5. A Pareto analysis is useful if a firm is considering rationalisation.
Whereas different product lines make different levels of contribution, each line

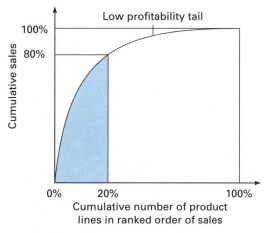

Figure 6.5 Pareto analysis

accounts for a fairly similar level of costs, particularly fixed costs. In general, profitability will be increased by divesting of product lines in the 'tail' of the curve. As with any general recommendation, though, this should be judged in light of the business, its situation and the product concerned.

S-curve analysis

Most living creatures exhibit a characteristic growth curve with an early stage with increasing growth, a middle stage with high growth and a final stage where growth drops to zero. This pattern is depicted in graphical form and appears as an S-curve. The life of most products takes a similar form and is depicted as a graph of total sales against time. The early stage has high risk. The middle stage consumes a lot of resources to expand production and the sales platform. Mature products are usually the profitable 'cash cows' but with a finite life. A balanced product portfolio should contain a range of products at different stages in their life cycle. S-curve analysis reviews the sales profile of each product to identify their stage in the life cycle. This allows the product portfolio to be adjusted to achieve a balance between risk, resource requirements and profits that is consistent with the firm's strategic objectives.

6.4   Identification and evaluation of strategic options

A number of techniques are available that are designed to help with the identification and evaluation of options for development.

The Ansoff matrix

One of the best known frameworks for deciding upon strategies for growth is the Ansoff matrix (see Figure 6.6). This offers strategic choices for achieving the company's objectives. There are four main categories for selection:

Product / Market	Present	New
Present	Market penetration	Product development
New	Market development	Diversification

Figure 6.6 Ansoff matrix

Source: Reprinted by permission of *Harvard Business Review*. Exhibit 1: The Ansoff Matrix from 'Strategies of diversification' by Ansoff, H.I. Issue No. 25(5), Sept/Oct 1957. Copyright © 1957 by the Harvard Business School Publishing Corporation; all rights reserved.

- *Market penetration*: Here the firm markets its existing products to its existing customers. This means increasing revenue by, for example, promoting the product, repositioning the brand, and so on. However, the product is not altered and no new customers are sought.
- *Market development*: Here the firm markets its existing product range in a new market. This means that the product remains the same, but it is marketed to a new audience. Exporting the product, or marketing it in a new region, are examples of market development.
- *Product development*: This is a new product to be marketed to existing customers. Here the firm develops and innovates new product offerings to replace existing ones. Such products are then marketed to existing customers.
- *Diversification*: This is where the firm markets completely new products to new customers. There are two types of diversification, namely related and unrelated diversification. Related diversification means that the firm remains in a market or industry with which it is familiar. Unrelated diversification is where the firm has neither previous industry nor market experience.

The Boston Consulting Group (BCG) matrix

This matrix aims to give an indication of cash flow stability in a firm by illustrating how cash-generating and cash-absorbing parts of the product portfolio are in balance (*see* Figure 6.7). The key dimensions of the matrix are the growth rate of the sector in which the product range lies (plotted vertically) and the competitive index – the ratio between the market share of the range in its sector divided by that of the most important competitor (plotted horizontally). The BCG matrix assumes that market share relates to profitability, an assumption that has validity but must be challenged for specific businesses.

The four quadrants are given evocative labels and the BCG makes recommendations about the product range based on its position in the matrix. Products in the low-growth, high-competitive index quadrant are called *cash cows*. These can generate – be milked for – cash. Above these, in the quadrant for high-growth, high-competitive index products, are the *stars* – the company's success stories. Stars

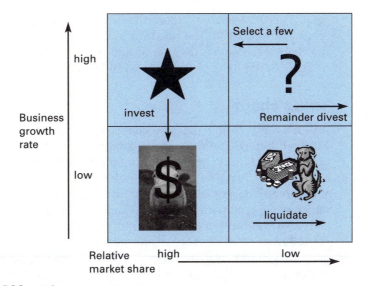

Figure 6.7 BCG matrix

Source: Boston Consulting Group. Adapted from *The Product Portfolio* (1970). The Star, the Dog, the Cow and the Question Mark – The Growth Share Matrix.

may generate some cash but they are equally likely to need investment in order to protect them from competitive attack. In the high-growth, low-competitive index quadrant are the *question marks* (sometimes called *problem children*). These are products about which a decision must be made – to invest in improving the competitive position (to make them stars) or to divest (to drop the product). The final quadrant contains the low-growth, low-competitive index products. The products here – called *dogs* – are said to be cash sinks. They take up more cash than they generate and have poor prospects. The recommendation is to divest these.

The dividing lines between the quadrants are to some extent dependent on industry conditions. Often a 10 per cent growth rate is used to separate high from low growth. A competitive index of one (i.e. a market share equal to competitors) is used to separate a good from a bad competitive position. More information can be obtained by means of the BCG matrix if circles of different sizes, reflecting the sales or profit contribution that they make, represent products. The BCG matrix offers broad recommendations. However, like any analytical method, its recommendations should not be followed blindly but interpreted in light of the particular features of the company's situation.

The directional policy matrix

The directional policy matrix (DPM) is similar to the BCG matrix, but it uses more general factors to determine market attractiveness (plotted vertically) and competitive position (plotted horizontally). Important factors in determining market attractiveness are market growth rate, profitability, stability of profits, customer strengths and environmental conditions (defined by means of the STEEPLE analysis – *see earlier*). Important factors in determining competitive position are market share, production and technical expertise and relationships with distributors and buyers. Different factors can be weighted if they differ in significance. Each axis is divided into three levels – labelled high, medium and low – giving nine sectors in total. The DPM enables recommendations to be made on investment and divestment on the basis of the position of the product in the matrix. As with the BCG matrix, the recommendations should not be followed blindly but used to provide insights in the light of the context of the business.

Value chain

Another very useful concept is that of the *value chain* (a term coined originally by Michael Porter). The value chain analysis describes the activities the organisation performs and links them to the organisation's competitive position. Value chain analysis describes the activities within and around an organisation and relates them to an analysis of the competitive strength of the organisation. It evaluates which value each particular activity adds to the organisation's products or services. This idea was built upon the insight that an organisation is more than a random compilation of machinery, equipment, people and money. Only if these things are arranged into systems will it become possible to produce something for which customers are willing to pay a price. Porter argues that the ability to perform particular activities and to manage the linkages between these activities is a source of competitive advantage.

Porter distinguishes between primary activities and support activities. Primary activities are directly concerned with the creation or delivery of a product or service. They can be grouped into five main areas: inbound logistics, operations, outbound logistics, marketing and sales, and service. Each of these primary activities is linked to support activities that help to improve their effectiveness or efficiency. There are four main areas of support activities: procurement, technology development (including R&D), human resource management, and infrastructure (systems for planning, finance, quality, information management etc.). In most industries, it is rather unusual that a single company performs all activities from product design, production of components and final assembly to delivery to the final user by itself. Most often, organisations are elements of a value system or supply chain. Hence, value chain analysis should cover the whole value system in which the organisation operates.

A typical value chain analysis can be performed in the following steps:

- Analysis of own value chain – which costs are related to every single activity?
- Analysis of customers' value chains – how does our product fit into their value chain?
- Identification of potential cost advantages in comparison with competitors.
- Identification of potential value added for the customer – how can a product add value to the customer's value chain (e.g. lower costs or higher performance)? Where does the customer see such potential?

6.5 Planning for the future

Rapid change, new technology and increased competition are some of the factors making for unprecedented uncertainty in today's markets. Planning for the future has never been so difficult. One well-documented and well-established approach to planning for the future is that of *scenario planning*. A scenario is a story. It is a tool for ordering perceptions about alternative future environments in which today's decisions may play out, described as 'an outline of future development which shows the operation of causes' by the *Chambers English Dictionary*. Scenario planning is an 'outside-in' approach to strategic management. A scenario describes a possible future business environment but is not a prediction. It explores the extremes that challenge the existing business model.

Creating a scenario

A scenario should be engaging, interesting, challenging and credible, as well as logically consistent with the known facts. It is useful to create a set of scenarios describing a range of possible futures that are ideally mutually exclusive and collectively exhaustive – no more than four scenarios is the norm. Scenarios can be presented in many different forms, such as in a script or a timeline, or within a discussion. The descriptive scenarios need to be supported by some numerical analysis, which should test the credibility of each scenario, explore the magnitude of changes in the environment and evaluate the impact of those changes.

Using scenarios for business planning

The scenarios are then used to challenge existing business models and stimulate new ideas. They form the basis of a strategic debate that is radically different to the traditional business planning cycle. Scenario planning creates a flexible plan for the business that is composed of a variety of options. The business moves forward by shifting its weight between these options. This enables the business to adapt its plans to the evolving environment.

Evaluating future plans

The evaluation of future investments, for example new product developments or capital investments, requires financial analysis to review the expected risk and returns. The core issue is how to compare a real cash outlay today with a potential return in the future. The common method for addressing this problem is to apply a discount rate to the future returns using a discounted cash flow (DCF) model. For example, it is proposed that a £100 investment today will produce a return of £150 in the future. A discount factor of 20 per cent per annum is used. If the £150 is returned in one year, the DCF is £150 × 80% = £120 and a gain of £20 is predicted. If the £150 is returned in two years, the DCF is £150 × 80% × 80% = £96 and a loss of £4 is made.

DCF models are summarised in one of two forms. Net present value (NPV) uses an agreed discount rate. It gives the total of the discounted cash values throughout the life of the investment, as per the gain and loss example given above. The discount rate is chosen to reflect the level of risk in the project. A low rate would be appropriate for buying equipment to build a standard product but a high rate would be appropriate for developing a product using new technology. NPV gives an absolute indication of the potential return on an investment. Internal rate of return (IRR) works in a slightly different way. The discount rate is varied to achieve an NPV of zero. The rate that achieves this is the IRR. If a bank account had the IRR as its interest rate then it would be able to generate the same cash flow as the project. IRR is a relative indication of the potential return. It can be compared with the perceived level of risk in the investment to decide whether the investment is justified. All DCF models carry a high level of risk and their results should be interpreted with caution.

<table>
<tr><td>**6.6**</td><td># Opportunity, innovation and information</td></tr>
</table>

As mentioned in Chapter 2, marketing research is the process through which managers discover the nature of the competitive environment in which they are operating. Managers make decisions about the direction in which their organisations are to move. Those decisions relate to the selection of strategic options, the implementation of plans and the allocation of resources. If those decisions are to be the right ones they must be informed. If the decisions are to be good ones, managers need information. Market research is a discipline that has developed a number of very powerful techniques for evaluating the market context of a business. This gives managers clear insights into the dynamics of the markets in which they operate and the behaviour of the customers they serve. These insights underpin effective decision-making.

Market research falls into two types. *Qualitative research* aims to answer questions about individual attitudes and orientations. It answers the 'who?' 'why?' and 'what?' questions. *Quantitative research* aims to answer questions about collections of individuals. It answers the 'how much?' and 'how many?' questions. The two forms of research work together. In combination they can provide a picture of the market in which the firm operates and flesh out the details of a market opportunity. Qualitative methods define the nature of the opportunity. Quantitative methods give an indication of its worth. Market research calls on a variety of sophisticated techniques. It is a specialist area, of which few managers have the relevant knowledge. Supporting managers in developing an insight into market opportunities is something which consultants are often called on to do.

Market research can be expensive. It is an investment in the business. Like any investment it should be undertaken only if the returns are appropriate. Managers must consider the nature of the decisions they are facing, the value of the resources involved and the risks to which they will be exposed and then decide what it will be worth to invest in information that will improve those decisions. A sales representative visiting a prospective customer may dedicate an hour or so researching the company by reading the annual report and a few newspaper articles. A business making a major launch of a new consumer brand may spend millions in analysing market potential, customer buying behaviour and perhaps advertising effectiveness. A firm aiming to buy another will undertake an extensive programme of evaluation – called *due diligence* – involving commercial, finance and legal specialists in order to be sure of the other company's fitness and potential.

When the level of expenditure available for market research has been decided, it is important that that investment is used wisely. The objectives of the research must be clear. The questions it aims to answer must be made explicit, the right techniques for answering those questions must be selected, and the appropriate groups of customers must be selected for investigation. Consultants may or may not themselves be conversant with the details of various market research techniques, though it is certainly useful for them to be able to undertake some of the more straightforward methods. What they must be able to do, however, is recognise how market research can illuminate a management issue and be used to support better decision-making. They must be able to help managers formulate their problems so that a cost-effective, informative marketing research exercise can be devised. The following is intended merely as an overview of market research techniques: an indication of the approaches available. It is recommended that should students be called upon to implement an extensive market research programme, they consult a specialist market research text.

Secondary research

Secondary research uses already published information (as opposed to *primary research* which is original material gathered directly for the task in hand). The amount of information in the world relevant to business is vast and it is growing. Already published information, because it has not been undertaken specifically for the purpose, varies enormously in its relevance. But it is of low cost and it can be very informative. It should always be the first source consulted by the researcher. Some of the most valuable sources are as follows.

The Internet

The first port of call is the Internet. In addition to individual company websites and sectoral reports, there are a number of good sources of business information that are either free or available by subscription. Examples include:

ft.com – general business information;

hoovers.com – worldwide company information, concentrating on larger organisations;

reuters.com – the well-known news service;

dnb.com – information on every registered company worldwide;

hemscott.net – information on UK publicly quoted companies.

Market sector reports

A number of companies routinely publish reports on market sectors. Mintel and Keynote in the UK cover important areas of consumer spending. Euromonitor and Datamonitor look at developments in European and worldwide markets. In addition there are a number of *ad hoc* reports on specific sectors. Many of these are held by the British Library and can be accessed through listings in a good business library.

Company annual reports and websites

Company annual reports and reviews serve a specific and legally defined function, primarily for publicly quoted companies. They must inform investors of the financial state of the business through the balance sheet and profit and loss account. However, most annual reports go beyond just fulfilling this basic function.

They are exercises in public relations, promoting the company as a whole to all its stakeholders. The chairman's statement gives an indication of the prospects for the sector. In these company documents and especially on the website there may be information on political, technological and social developments in the business's spheres of operation. They may also provide an insight into those areas where the business is investing in the future. Much information relevant to a small business client will be gleaned through a detailed and insightful reading of the information sources of some of the large players in its sector.

Newspaper articles

Quality newspapers regularly feature articles that are of relevance to a consulting project. The *Financial Times* not only covers ongoing events in the world of business, but it also includes regular surveys dedicated to specific business areas, topical issues and geographic regions. *The Economist* (a weekly newspaper with a magazine format) provides a good, succinct and accessible guide to what is going on in the world of international politics, finance and business. This also has regular business and geographical surveys. Profiles of publicly traded companies can be found in the *Investors Chronicle* along with commentary on general developments in the world's stock markets. Most consultants read these publications regularly. Many keep a cuttings file on topics of interest. Business libraries keep back copies and have key word indexes.

6.7 Qualitative methods for evaluating opportunities

Markets are made up of individual decision-makers. The dynamics of a market must be understood in terms of both the influences on individual decision-making and the way individuals aggregate to generate overall demand. A number of techniques are available to explore the nature of individual needs, buying and product selection.

Depth interviews

Depth interviews are one-to-one interviews in which the investigator gets the potential customer to explain how he or she makes buying decisions. The interview may be partially structured but the investigator will keep open the option of exploring interesting avenues as they are revealed. Examples of products and other stimulus materials might be used to encourage the discussion. This is usually done face to face but occasionally is conducted by telephone, although the latter method is limiting in terms of the time and the type of questions that can be asked.

Focus group discussions

Focus group discussions involve a small group of potential customers (usually about four to seven people) who are invited to explore their views on a product category. The session will usually last between two and three hours. A facilitator who will be responsible for interpreting the findings afterwards leads the discussion. Again, product examples and stimulus materials may be used.

Product placements

With product placement the customer is exposed to the product in a normal usage situation before being questioned via one of the above techniques. This technique can give an insightful picture of the customer's reaction to the product on which to base further development and promotion. It does, however, demand that a product, or a prototype, be available. This can prove to be expensive and may present security issues if the product is in a development stage. Each of these techniques has its strengths and weaknesses. They may be used in combination to give a full picture of the buying behaviour of potential customers. Often a small number of flexible but relatively expensive techniques (e.g. depth interviews, focus groups) will be used to establish broad issues which can then be explored in more depth using quantitative methods as described below.

6.8   Quantitative methods for evaluating opportunities

Once the character of the individual buying process has been established, the researcher must move on and establish how buyers as a group present an opportunity to a particular business. This calls for quantitative techniques: the most important are as follows.

Postal or email surveys

A representative sample of customers is mailed or emailed a questionnaire. This will include questions relating to what products they buy, from what suppliers, how often they buy, how much they use and how frequently they use them. This is often the cheapest cost in total, but as response rates are often low, it might not be the most cost effective in the long run.

Omnibus surveys

In omnibus surveys, a representative sample is asked similar questions to those used in the postal survey. As speed is of the essence, the telephone is the usual means of communication, although increasingly electronic means are used if appropriate to the target audience. There may be more potential to open up new lines of enquiry here than in the postal survey. However, consumers may not have time to reflect on their consumption (as they will have with a postal survey) and a follow-up call may be needed.

In-hall or on-street testing

This is a familiar method, whereby respondents are recruited on the street and interviewed directly or are asked to attend a short session in a local building. Despite costing more than postal or telephone surveys, you do have the advantage of being able to ask different questions as respondents can see the new product or other stimulus material. This technique is used for consumer products in particular.

Distributor or retail audits

Distributor or retail audits are a particularly important source of information on markets, their structure, size and growth. The technique used requires a representative sample of distributors (who may be wholesalers or retailers) to keep a record of their purchases and sales. This information, which can nowadays be kept electronically, can be supplemented by direct outlet audits. A distributor audit allows a market to be broken down in a number of ways. The overall market can be represented as the product of *rate of sale* (the number of units a typical distributor sells) and *distribution* (the proportion of distributors selling the stock). Other information includes *stock holding* (the amount of a product a typical distributor holds) and *forward stocking* (the amount on display to the buyer). Information of this type allows the business to make subtle decisions about its distribution strategy and how to manage its relationship with distributors. A meaningful distributor audit is likely to be time consuming and expensive. A number of companies offer store audits on a commercial basis, the leading two being A.C. Nielsen and Information Resources.

Team discussion points

1 Read the following short case study.

Halifax Foods is an upper-medium-sized supplier of own-label canned goods to major supermarkets. It has ten key product categories. The firm is concerned about its costs and a consulting team has been called in to help the company develop a rationalisation plan. The team has held a brainstorming session with key players in the firm. Using the factors discussed above, the team has established the ratings (out of ten) shown in Table 6.2 for market attractiveness and competitive position for each product category. These are listed with the sales for each category.

Table 6.2 Market attractiveness and competitive position

Category	Annual sales (£m)	Market attractiveness	Competitive position
Fruit	11	5	4
Baked beans	2	4	2
Traditional soups	39	7	8
Ethnic soups	1	10	2
Mixed vegetables	24	3	7
Carrots	7	2	4
Peas	6	1	3
Stir-fry vegetables	1	8	1
Broad beans	2	6	4
Flavoured beans	1	8	2
Total sales	94		

Construct a Pareto analysis and a DPM matrix for the firm. What strategic recommendations would these analysis methods suggest?

2 Consider the decision you made to undertake your course in management consulting. What market research methods would you adopt to evaluate the interests of your colleagues in such a course within your institution? How would you measure the overall demand for such a course? How would you investigate ways in which the course might be modified to make it more attractive in the future?

Discuss your ideas in a group.

 ## Summary of key ideas

A number of techniques are available to the consultant to aid analysis of a business and its environment. An evaluation might include the following:

- A simple summary of the business's capabilities and the environment in which it operates.
- A review of the business's source of competitive advantage and the environment in which it operates.
- An evaluation of the firm's performance and product performance.
- Identification and evaluation of strategic options.
- Planning for the future.
- An assessment of markets and their segmentation.
- The use of market research techniques both qualitative and quantitative.

Key reading

Coyle, G. (2004) *Practical Strategy: Structured Tools and Techniques*. Harlow, Essex: FT Prentice Hall.

Housden, M. (2006) *Marketing Research and Information (CIM Coursebook 06/07)*. Oxford: Butterworth-Heineman.

Further reading

Ansoff, I.H. (1957) 'Strategies of diversification', *Harvard Business Review*, September–October, 25 (5).

Bryman, A. and Bell, E. (2003) *Business Research Methods*. Oxford: Oxford University Press.

Hax, A.C. and Wilde, D.L. (2001) *The Delta Project: Discovering New Sources of Profitability in a Networked Economy*. Basingstoke, Hampshire: Palgrave Macmillan.

Heijden, K. van der (2004) *Scenarios: The Art of Strategic Conversation*. Chichester, West Sussex: John Wiley & Sons.

Kaplan, R.S. and Norton, D.P. (1996) *The Balanced Scorecard: Translating Strategy into Action*. Boston, MA: Harvard Business School Press.

Kaplan, R.S. and Norton, D.P. (1996) 'Using the balanced scorecard as a strategic management system', *Harvard Business Review*, January–February, 75–85.

Porter, M.E. (2004) *Competitive Strategy – Techniques for Analyzing Industries and Competitors*. New York: Free Press.

Porter, M.E. (2004) *Competitive Advantage – Creating and Sustaining Superior Performance.* New York: Free Press.

Wilson, A. (2006) *Marketing Research: An Integrated Approach.* Harlow, Essex: FT Prentice Hall.

Case exercise

DQS

DQS is a large Asian display manufacturer that has a strong position in the declining market for cathode ray tubes (CRT) for televisions. It has developed a good position in supplying LCD panels, up to 21 inch diagonal, for use in laptop computers and computer monitors. The majority of their sales are to European Original Equipment Manufacturers (OEM) for building into complete products. A small proportion of output is sold as finished products using the company's own brand names.

The company's CEO, John Shih, sees the future for the company's television business as being in large flat-panel products of at least 40 inch diagonal. He has a dilemma because the established technology in the large flat TV sector is plasma display panels although LCD TVs are starting to make inroads. The investment in building a new production line for large panels of any type is several billion pounds. He can only afford one and the choice has to be right.

John has worked in the US and has used consultants before. He calls you and asks you to look at the following questions:

- What is the consumer perspective on the two alternative technical solutions?

- What is the market size and expected growth?
- What are the market drivers?
- What sizes of TV should DQS build?
- What performance is required?
- What is a reasonable target market share and how does this split between own-brand and OEM?
- What price does DQS need to sell at to establish a sustainable competitive position?
- Can DQS achieve a return on investment that is acceptable to its board and investors?

Q1 What analysis techniques would you use and why?

Q2 What would a SWOT analysis covering DQS's entry into the large flat panel television market tell John?

Q3 What market research material would be required to support the choice of technology and define the product specification?

CHAPTER 7

Contracting, influence and team leadership

Kevin Parker

Learning outcomes

The key learning outcomes of this chapter are to understand:

- how the consultant contracts with the client to ensure success of the project;
- how the consultant can influence the client to ensure a win–win outcome;
- team dynamics and what is successful for team leadership, particularly in a consulting environment.

7.1 Contracting

Often the hardest part of being a consultant is learning to effectively use the 'soft' skills of contracting, influence and team leadership. Establishing and maintaining a good relationship with the client is the goal of an effective contract; in order to understand why, here are a couple of scenarios.

- The first scenario is that the consultant has been asked to help manage a task force charged with designing some new procedures as part of some organisational change. The organisation has never had a task force, but the consultant has been told that their role is simply to 'sit in from time to time and make comments' as needed. The consultant does not think that provides enough support to ensure success in this important aspect of the change process.

- The second scenario is that the consultant has been asked to provide some 'skills training' to a work group with a history of conflict and dissension. The consultant suspects that training at this point may not be well received by the group and that the causes of the problem are deeper than skill deficits.

Both these situations illustrate a dilemma. In both, the consultant's initial view of the relationship and the intervention that will be required differs from what the client thinks is needed or wanted. Such situations are likely to end with disappointing results. Consultants – internal and external – often talk about getting 'burned'. Usually it happens when the way the consultants' role has been structured leads to no-win situations. Much advice is available to new and practising consultants on how to be effective practitioners, but not much of it focused on the special problem of contracting with the client on the best role to adopt. Champion, Kiel and McLendon (1990), in an article called 'Choosing a consulting role', provide clear guidance for the consultant and client as to whether the role being played is the right one.

In order to do this kind of practical assessment and to facilitate collaborative agreements between clients and consultants, three things are needed:

- A clear understanding of the purposes of a consulting relationship.
- A language for talking about consulting roles.
- The criteria for determining which roles are appropriate in a given situation.

In any consultation, the clients will have two types of need:

- The need for results refers to concrete outcomes associated with a project. These might include changes in the bottom line, organisational structure, information transmitted, skills learned or behaviour and attitudes.
- The need for growth means increased capacity to perform new functions or behaviours on a continuing basis. In other words, if a high level of growth is achieved in the consultation, then the client will be able to do the job the next time with less or no outside help.

The need for results and the need for growth will vary depending on the nature of the consulting project. For example, in performing a one-time service with which the client is unfamiliar, the consultant's major focus is likely to be 'getting the job done' for the client. However, in helping the client perform an important and recurring – but new – task, the appropriate emphasis is on helping the client to learn how to perform that task over the long haul, instead of merely producing an immediate result. When project outcomes are specified in that way, it is easier to determine what services are needed from the consultant and what contributions are needed from the client system to bring about the desired changes. Champion *et al.* proposed that by constructing a grid model of consulting, using as the two axes, consultant responsibility for growth and consultant responsibility for results, one could specify the consulting roles appropriate for the mix of services that the consultant is expected to provide. Champion *et al.* developed a nine-box grid, but for simplicity a four-box grid is used here (*see* Figure 7.1).

- **The partner role** implies high responsibility for results and growth. It assumes that both the client and the consultant have the capacity to successfully perform aspects of the task and that both will share the responsibility for the results. It also assumes that a big jump in the client's capacity to do the task is an important goal. The partner role means that the client is ready to learn in a hands-on way and that the consultant can teach effectively in this mode, as well as guide the task to successful completion.
- **In the coach role**, the consultant's concern is almost entirely for the capacity of the client to perform the task. The coach tries constantly to help the client clarify and set goals, maintain positive motivation and develop and implement effective plans. The coach often is removed from the performance of the situation. He or she may have to rely on the client's data about what is happening in the project. Hence much of the counsellor's skill is in helping the client to gather, analyse and develop conclusions from his or her own experience.

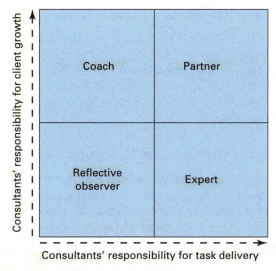

Figure 7.1 Consultants' responsibility for growth and results model

Source: After Champion, D.P., Kiel D.H. and McLendon, J.A. (1990) 'Choosing a consulting role', *Training and Development Journal*, 1 February.

■ With **the reflective observer role** the client is most responsible for results and capacity building; the consultant is least responsible. The consultant's task is limited to feeding back observations and impressions. In spite of the low activity level of the consultant, this role can have a dynamic effect on a client system that is skilled in using such assistance. The reflective observer can help clients monitor themselves on such ambiguous but crucial indicators as trust, team-work and openness.

■ The consultant who takes on **the hands-on expert role** actually undertakes the task on behalf of the client. In this role the consultant has most, if not all, of the responsibility for producing good results. The client is not expected to grow in capacity very much. He or she will need the consultant again next time in order to perform the task equally well.

A consultant may play multiple roles simultaneously within a client system, but with different clients. He or she might be a coach to one manager, a reflective observer for the team the manager leads and a partner for a task force of other managers. In this framework, the consulting role is always defined situationally with a specific client or client group. Ideally, roles should be defined and clearly understood by both the client and consultant. Many errors arise from the consultant's attempt to play more than one role simultaneously with the same client without clear agreement to do so.

Choosing the right role for the right situation is obviously a key skill. Four key areas can be identified, building on Robert Tannenbaum and Warren Schmidt's classic formulation of criteria in determining behavioural choice for leadership roles. The areas to consider are as follows.

The organisational situation

The roles of partner and hands-on expert are likely to be appropriate in cases where there is immediate need for results. If client capacity is low, then roles of coach and reflective observer may make more sense.

Characteristics of the client

In determining an acceptable role relationship, the client ought to ask the following questions: Will the proposed consulting relationship be likely to achieve the results that the organisation needs? Will I be helped to grow in the process, in a direction that is in my long-term interests? Will the skills that I already possess be used to their fullest extent? Are the skills that the consultant possesses being used in the best way?

Characteristics of the consultant

The capacity of the consultant is the most obvious limiting factor in determining a consultant role. Consultants cannot take on the more results or growth-oriented roles if they lack the experience, knowledge and confidence to do so. But if the consultant is competent to take on various roles, how should he or she choose among them? Willingness, interest and time are factors. The consultant needs to ask themselves not only 'Can I do this?' but also 'Do I want to serve in this role?' A role that is unwanted will probably not be well performed.

The client–consultant relationship

A relationship of trust and openness permits collaborative determination of the appropriate client–consultant role. Too often, the client's unwillingness to ask for help leads to an insufficient consulting role, or the consultant's need for business results leads to an unhealthy dependency. But most relationships don't begin with the necessary trust to permit open discussion and negotiation or roles. The grid model, by providing a common language for clients and consultants, may help overcome some initial barriers. Here are five steps for agreeing the most effective roles for the consultant and the client.

1 Clarify the organisation's need for results and capacity for each client or client group.
2 Discuss the current capacities of the clients and consultants.
3 Identify a match between client needs and consultant capacities relative to the various tasks and client groups, using the consulting role grid.
4 Check that all parties have the support they need in the situation to deliver on their responsibilities for results and growth.
5 Commit jointly to your respective role responsibilities in the consultation.

Consultants and clients can do a better job of negotiating roles, and increase their chances for successful project outcomes. But that can only happen if both parties are clear about the outcomes the organisation needs and the capacities they both have. The consulting role grid can help match needed outcomes with appropriate levels of consultant involvement. The five-step model above can help ensure that the agreements reached can be successfully carried out. By using this simple framework, consultants and clients may be able to avoid some of the game playing and misperceptions that can handicap consulting relationships from the early stages. The result is openness about what is needed and about how the client and consultant can meet those needs. That openness can set the stage for a collaborative relationship for the duration of the project.

7.2   Influencing

As in any aspect of business, effectively influencing others makes the task easier: this is particularly true for consulting projects. There is no right way, nor is there only one way to influence others. Everything, but everything, is a factor when influencing people. People, places, events and situations at all times influence everyone. Sometimes people are affected more or less by these things, but they are continually being influenced by what happens around them. So what about the specifics in the workplace? A job requires people to influence others just about all of the time. It may take the form of gaining support, inspiring others, persuading other people to become their champions, engaging someone's imagination, creating relationships. Whatever form it takes, being an excellent influencer makes a job easier.

An interesting point about people who use their influencing skills well is that others like being around them. There's a kind of exciting buzz, or sense that things happen when they're about. It's because they don't sit around wishing things were different while moaning there's nothing they can do about it. They don't sit around blaming others or complaining about what needs fixing that will make things better. They see what needs doing and set about getting it done. Truly excellent influencing skills require a healthy combination of interpersonal, communication, presentation and assertiveness techniques. It's about adapting and modifying one's personal style after becoming aware of the effect it is having on others, while still being true to themselves. Behaviour and attitude change are what's important, not changing who the person is or how they feel and think.

People may try to exert your influence through coercion and manipulation and they might even succeed in getting things done; but that isn't really influencing. That's forcing others to do what they want, often against the former's will. They won't have succeeded in winning support. Pushing, bullying, bludgeoning or haranguing DO NOT WORK! Like elephants, people will remember the experience. Indeed, if someone forces another to do something the former wants, without taking the latter's point of view into consideration, then the impression that they is left with is how they will see the former forever. They are stuck with it, unless they deliberately change what they do in order to be seen differently. People are far more willing to come halfway (or more) if they feel acknowledged, understood and appreciated. They may even end up doing or agreeing to something they wouldn't previously have done because they feel good about making the choice. Influencing is about understanding oneself and the effect or impact one has on others. Though it can, on occasion, be one way, the primary relationship is two way, and it is about changing how others perceive them. In other words, the cliché, perception is reality, makes perfect sense in the context of influencing. It doesn't matter what's going on internally for someone – if it is not perceived by the other person, then it doesn't exist, other than in the former's mind.

A consultant could be doing the most brilliant presentation they have ever created, but if they have not brought their 'audience' with them, the brilliance is wasted. And that's about being able to see what's going on for the audience, which will be different, however much they may have in common. Influencing can sometimes be looked at as the ability to 'finesse', almost sleight of hand. The other person is not prodded into seeing their view of the world, but is persuaded, often unconsciously, into understanding it. Sometimes people can get so used to their own personal style, or way of being or pattern of communicating, that do not think of how it is being received, and do not think of behaving in any other way. Influencing is about being able to move things forward, without pushing, forcing or telling others what to do. One of the most powerful forces that affect people's behaviour is the avoidance of humiliation. No one wants to embarrass themselves if they can help it. So changing their own behaviour entails a certain risk. But if that behaviour change is deliberate, and they have made an effort to see the world from the other person's point of view, then humiliation can be avoided on both sides. Whatever the arena a consultant works in, influencing others is about having the confidence and willingness to use themselves to make things happen.

7.3 Fundamentals of rapport and key skills

Communicating effectively is the main skill the consultant needs to get by in the world. The words actually spoken really count for very little in terms of the total message. For example, voice tone and body language account for far more. What everyone needs to do is get their message across quickly and effectively and in a way that the other person relates to and wants to act on positively.

Rapport is the skill of building cooperative relationships. Rapport skills enable the consultant to quickly put others at ease and create trust. Mastering the skill of building physical rapport requires being able to sense what is going on quickly and accurately, and behavioural flexibility on their part. These are the only two limits to the consultant's ability to produce results in this area: the degree to which they can perceive other people's postures, gestures and speech patterns; and the elegance with which they can match them in the dance of rapport. Physical matching is only one aspect of rapport. Being aware of a person's inner reality is another. Establishing rapport creates an environment of trust, confidence and participation. Remember, *'if you ain't got rapport, you ain't got nothing . . .'*

Mastery of rapport skills:

- allows the consultant to get on with anyone anywhere;
- greatly increases the consultant's confidence and effectiveness;
- makes it easier for others to communicate with the consultant.

Matching

The building blocks of matching are:

Body language

Posture	Orientation
Weight distribution	Gestures – arms and hands
Legs and feet	Facial expression
Eye contact	Breathing rate

Voice quality

Tone	Volume
Tempo	Pitch
Sounds	

Leading

Changes the other person's behaviour by getting them to follow a lead (e.g. leading them from slumping into a more upright posture, or leading them from speaking quietly to speaking more loudly). This is one way to test that they do indeed have rapport. Having rapport, and hence being able to lead others, makes it easier to achieve mutually desired outcomes (e.g. reaching agreement!). It also allows them to take responsibility for the outcome of all their interactions. It is, however, a *choice*. There may be some people with whom they would choose not to be in rapport. In which case you have the choice of mismatching.

Mismatching

Allows a person to break rapport, to interrupt or to avoid communicating. To mismatch, someone needs to alter their body and/or voice to make them different from the other person's. This will subtly and unconsciously interrupt the flow of communication, giving them the opportunity to redirect the interaction. (NB. If rapport is well established, they may find that the other person follows their behaviour as the former mismatches, i.e. they are effectively leading them; they will then have to keep changing their behaviour until they cease to follow the former and they achieve a conclusive mismatch.) Warning! Mismatching can seriously damage relationships – only use when direct requests fail!

General points about rapport skills

1   The dance of rapport is what people do naturally.

2   Rapport needs flexibility of thought and behaviour.

3   Notice what happens when people get on well. They tend to match.

4   Notice the opposite: when people are in disagreement, they mismatch.

5   Notice when someone is not getting on well with someone else and try matching.

6   Make it *easy* for others to communicate with you by practising rapport.

7   Notice how you feel when you are matching different people.

8   Ask yourself, 'How will I know when it is time to get in rapport?'

9   Experience the world as others do. Rapport makes them and their experiences/difficulties/joys much more understandable. All sorts of information is gained from body and voice that is not there in the words.

10   Notice when you are uncomfortable matching – use that as an opportunity to stretch yourself, choose that as homework/practice, seek out people who behave in that way to develop your own flexibility.

11   Liking the other person is not necessary for rapport. Both having confidence in competence for the task in hand is. If credibility for the task in hand cannot be established, consider changing the task or person.

7.4   Change-limiting assumptions

Unresolved conflict between individuals or groups in an organisation can block the fresh thinking that leads to innovation and learning. This conflict tends to rise from unexpressed underlying assumptions and beliefs. All human actions are based on assumptions – some are positive and true, some are negative and untrue. Positive ones do not need to be removed. Blocking assumptions should be identified and removed to free up thinking for individuals, groups and whole organisations.

Any one of these three types of limiting assumption may occur:

A fact:	something that is true.
A possible fact:	something that could be true, or true in specific circumstances – a bedrock assumption.
A bedrock assumption:	something to do with the nature of things rather than circumstances, how the world works or a chosen truth for an individual in their life.

When the possible-fact assumption is removed and changed, new ideas emerge. But the endurance of those ideas and the courage to act on them are limited because you know that there is still a chance the assumption is fact. The something that makes a possible-fact stop someone is another, more subjective assumption or belief – the bedrock assumption. The bedrock assumption is a limiting subjective perception, usually of the self but sometimes of how life works. For example:

Subjective perception of self: I don't deserve to have work I enjoy.

Subjective perception of how life works: Work is not meant to be enjoyed.

The bedrock assumption, according to the practical and positive view of human nature and life, is of little use. When the bedrock assumption is removed, the thinker's mind is freed from limitations in many areas, not just in the specific area that is the subject of the current thinking. The bedrock level, therefore, is one of the most far-reaching levels at which to make change. When willing – and this permission is important because working at the bedrock level requires willingness to address the issues on your part – a consultant can ask the question that takes them from the possible-fact to the underlying bedrock assumption.

Ask: *'That's possible, but what are you assuming that makes that possibility stop you from doing what you want to do?'*

When the consultant has identified the bedrock assumption, they can then ask the incisive question that removes and changes the bedrock assumption. In phrasing the incisive question they have to develop a more freeing assumption. The client does not have to believe it at this stage. A good way to start is simply to take the opposite of the limiting assumption. For example, instead of 'I don't deserve to have work I enjoy' simply change it to 'I do deserve work I enjoy'. Now when you ask the incisive question, the client lets go of their previous beliefs and assume that just for the purposes of this process – wild and wacky though it may seem – they knew this more freeing assumption was true. What would be the result, and what might be happening differently?

Ask: If you knew the opposite to be true for you, what would you be doing, or what would be happening differently? For example: *'If you knew that you do deserve work that you enjoy, what job would you be proposing?'* or *'If you knew that work is something to be enjoyed, what would change for you?'*

It is at this level that people sometimes experience an explosion of creativity. Possibilities and ideas emerge that were unavailable before. Also, when groups explore the limiting bedrock assumptions that have driven them, new structures and systemic changes become possible. This new freedom that results is what we experience increasingly as the heart of innovation. Tables 7.1, 7.2 and 7.3 explore some examples to illustrate the above points.

In order to explore some of the issues raised by possible fact assumptions and limiting bedrock assumptions, Table 7.4 gives some sample incisive questions which a consultant can use to free a client's thinking.

Table 7.1 Possible fact assumptions

They might laugh	They might think I'm stupid
They will say no	They might select someone else
They will fire me	I might fail
They do not care about this as much as I do	It will be difficult
I might cry	Things will never be the same again
Nothing will change anyway	

Table 7.2 Limiting bedrock assumptions

Perception of self	Perceptions of how life works
I am stupid	It is not OK to get it wrong or not to know
I cannot handle the outcome	Change is always difficult and takes a long time
I am trapped. I have no choice. I have no power here	Men (white, able-bodied, adult, Western, university-educated, handsome, heterosexual) are smarter and more important
I am not loveable	Certainty is achievable
I cannot make everyone's life right	Because the experts haven't figured it out, I can't
I cannot make a difference	It isn't possible
I am not worthy	The way to prevent disaster is to be constantly vigilant
I do not matter here	Acknowledging one's success precipitates decline
I do not have a right to say what I think	Peace is better than honesty
I am a bother	Talking to someone about a problem means you are weak
I have to take responsibility for everyone	You can't have it both ways
I cannot lead	Competition among people leads to excellence
My feelings don't count	Ordinary people cannot affect large systems
	If it is mostly for you, you have no right to do it
	Listening puts you in the weaker position

Table 7.3 Possible fact assumptions *v* Limiting bedrock assumptions

Possible fact assumptions	Limiting bedrock assumptions
I'll be laughed at	I am not worthy. I don't deserve to be listened to
I'll break down and cry	I'll never recover
I might be wrong	I'm stupid. I can't ever get it right
I might be rejected	I cannot or will not survive
They won't agree	I have to be right
They won't hire me – I have a beard, I'm too fat, the wrong colour, not qualified enough, or lack the right experience	I am inadequate. I'm not OK. I'm not worthy
I might fail	I'm not good enough
They won't want me	I'm not loveable. I'm alone
They won't change; I can't make a difference. I'm powerless	Life's hard work. Life's always unfair

Table 7.4 Sample incisive questions

If you knew you are at least as intelligent as anyone else is, what would change for you?

If you knew you have choices you have not yet considered, what would you face that you have been denying?

If you knew you are good enough, what would you do and how would you feel?

If you knew you are worthy of the best, what would you want?

If you knew working hard is not the same as working well, how would you approach your work differently?

If you knew you are significant in the world, what would change for you?

If you thought of yourself as a leader, what would you most enjoy leading?

If you were not holding back, what would you be doing?

If you could make one change in your life, what would it be?

If you were not afraid, what would you do?

For something to be exactly right for you, what would have to change?

If you began to care more about what you think than about what other people think of you, what would you think and do?

7.5 Outcome thinking, outcome-frame thinking and improving advocacy

Many consulting projects stumble mid term due to team members (often from the client) perceiving that they have to do 'business as usual' and assume that major change is not possible. Using techniques such as outcome thinking and outcome-frame thinking can help improve the process.

Between stimulus and response, man has the freedom to choose.

Victor Frankl, from *Man's Search For Meaning*

Much of what is done in terms of human actions, the decisions made and how someone responds to challenges is based more on an automatic response to the circumstances at hand than a conscious choice. These responses are preconditioned from past experience or from our personality – but are not our only option. Victor Frankl, a Jewish psychiatrist who was imprisoned in a concentration camp during the Second World War, wrote of his discovery of what he called the 'ultimate human freedom'. One day, naked and all alone in a small room and having just been tortured, he began to realise that while his captors could control his entire environment, and could do what they wanted to his body, ultimately it was up to him to decide within himself how all of this was going to affect him. Between what happened to him, or the stimulus, and his response to it was his freedom or power to choose his outcome.

The proactive model

$$E \quad + \quad R \quad = \quad O$$
$$(\text{Events} \quad + \quad \text{Response} \quad = \quad \text{Outcome})$$

People can often feel like victims or that it is the others that are difficult. This model is deceptively simple but very powerful. Take this simple example. Imagine that you'd agreed with your partner or a friend that you were going to cook them dinner at 8 p.m. that evening. They didn't turn up till 10 p.m., with no excuse and no phone call, and the dinner was ruined. That is the event – we can't change that. What reaction could you have in this situation? You could say, 'Your dinner is in the dog' or have a row and shout at them. Now of course if you make that kind of response, what is the outcome – a miserable evening, one of those rows that goes on forever, loss of friendship etc. etc? In this situation events have been allowed to drive the outcome.

Now what if someone thought about the outcome they wanted before making the response. For example, if their outcome were still to have a pleasant evening and remain friends with that person then they would think about the right response. They can still let the other know they are unhappy but in a controlled way and perhaps ask the other to go and get the takeaway/wine! Here they are far more in control of the outcome they want. Thinking about their outcome has tailored their response to meet it. So this simple formula is very powerful. One can drive one's own brain and not let others drive it for you. Starting to think in terms of the outcome they want gives them a much better chance of achieving it. As Victor Frankl showed, a person is always in charge of their response and there are many ways to adjust it.

Outcome-frame questions

This technique is useful for getting people to reframe their problems so that they see the apparent problem in a new light. The very word 'problem' creates a sense of weight, worry and difficulty. If the consultant goes down the problem route, they therefore run the risk of increasing the size, scope and depth of the problem for the person they are trying to help.

Here are some examples of problem-frame thinking:

- Whose fault is it?
- Why haven't you done anything about it yet?
- What's stopping you doing something?
- What does having this problem say about you as a person?
- What does having this problem say about you as a professional?
- What forces outside your control are contributing to this?
- What are the negative consequences?
- What further problems is this leading to?

The general effect of questions like these is to rob them of power. It increases the chances of feeling helpless and a victim.

Outcome-frame thinking

This is very different. It empowers a person. When they ask outcome-frame questions, they can often see a visible difference in the way the other person responds – for instance, they may sit up straighter, stop frowning or look somehow lighter. Here are some examples of powerful outcome-frame questions using the same themes as the problem-frame questions above:

- What do you want?
- What else will that do for you?
- What will it look, sound and feel like when you have what you want?
- What resources outside of you do you have to get what you want?
- Who else can help you?
- What will getting what you want confirm about you as a person/professional?
- What further benefits could there be?
- What is the first step to getting what you want?

Improving advocacy

Advocacy is about getting one's view across clearly and succinctly. Below are some tips and questions to help do this more effectively.

Some preliminaries

- Who is the 'audience' for your pitch?
- What services, products, ideas do they obtain from you? How happy are they with these products?
- Are you completely clear what you want from the session? What would an ideal outcome look like, sound like, feel like? How would you know you'd got it?
- Why should it matter to the person you are trying to influence to do what you want? What will be the consequences for them if they do not?
- What would be needed to support any change you are suggesting?
- If there is some underlying problem, what have you contributed to it?

Identifying shared interests

- Putting yourself in their shoes: what could explain their present behaviour?
- What, in their minds, is standing in the way of their seeing things like you do?
- What range of interests do they represent? What other players are involved?
- What other human needs is this session going to meet – e.g. for recognition, security, affection, prestige, a sense of having control over their lives?

Being assertive

Remember that assertiveness means believing in the right to be heard as well as respecting the rights of others.

You have the right to

- Be there
- Be treated respectfully
- Ask for information
- Disagree
- Change your mind
- Be listened to
- Think before reacting
- Ask for time to consider or reconsider

Making your own thinking visible

- State your assumptions – e.g. 'here's what I think and this is how I got there.'
- Make your reasoning explicit: 'I've come to this conclusion because . . .'
- Give examples of what would happen if your proposal were implemented, for instance, 'If we were to do this, you'd see something like this . . .'
- Actively encourage others to test your hypotheses, e.g. 'How does this strike you so far?' 'What flaws suggest themselves?' 'Do you have any worries about it?'
- Ask for the other person's view.

7.6 Listening, powerful questions and push and pull of influencing

More key skills for the consultant are the art of listening and asking questions: using these with the client enables the consultant to gain a much deeper insight into the client's issues. To be listened to is a striking experience – partly because it is so rare! When one person listens to another, interested in every word, eager to empathise, the former feels known and understood. People get bigger when they know they have been listened to. They have more presence and also feel safer and more secure. Not only that, listening intently to someone else provides them with a great win–win. If someone feels they have been listened to, how do they feel about listening to understand what the other person is trying to say? Listening is a talent that is given to everyone and while some are more naturally talented than others, it is certainly a skill that can be trained and developed. Most people do not listen at a very deep level. Their day-to-day occupations and preoccupations don't require more than a minimum of listening – just as most never acquire more than the minimum level of physical fitness. Muscles are not needed because they are not world-class athletes. But masterful leadership requires masterful listening. People need to exercise and develop those listening muscles.

Attention and impact

There are two aspects of listening. One is attention or awareness. It is the receiving of information through what is heard with the ears of course, but it is also listening with all the senses and with intuition. The attention is on all the information coming in, the words, the energy, and the impressions. The second aspect is what is done with the listening. This is the impact on others. The consultant needs to be conscious not only of their listening but the impact they have when they act on their listening. To understand the process of attention and impact, imagine a crowded room and smoke is smelt – it could be a fire. Attention is drawn to the smoke. It is noticed and then a decision is made. Someone might yell fire, or mention it casually to the host, or grab a fire extinguisher. Each of these choices will have a different impact.

Level 1: Internal listening

At level 1 the attention is all internal. People listen to the words of the other but focus on what it means to them. The spotlight is on the individual: their thoughts, judgements, feelings and conclusions about themselves and others. At level 1 there is only one question: What does this mean to the listener? There are many times when this is appropriate; for example, when there is a strong desire for information when travelling. Answers, explanations, details and data are needed. The flight is late – how does this affect the person? People that are led are often at level 1. That's their job, to look at themselves. But it's definitely not the place for a coach or leader. Coaching happens at level 2.

Level 2: Focused listening

At level 2 there is a sharp focus on the other person. It can be seen in people's posture when they are listening at this level – for example, leaning towards each other. There is a great deal of attention on the other person and little on the outside world. All listening at level 2 is directed at the speaker; the listener's awareness is totally on the other person. They listen for their words, their expression, their emotion, everything they bring. At this level people are unattached to their own agenda. They are no longer trying to figure out what to say next; it will come spontaneously from the absolute curiosity about what the other person is saying. As a coach at level 2, a person listens to the speaker's words, tone, pace and emotion. Then they choose what to respond to and how to respond. Then they notice the impact of their response on the speaker. Its as though they listen twice before the speaker responds again.

Level 3: Global listening

At level 3 a person listens at 360 degrees. They listen and are aware of everything that is going on around them. If level 2 is like being 'hard wired' to the other person, level 3 is like a radio field. The radio waves are completely invisible, yet they know they are there because they can hear music coming from the radio. Level 3 is like the radio waves; they cross the antenna and become information to be used. It takes a special receiver to pick up level 3 signals, and practice to learn how to tune it properly. For many people this is a new realm of listening, but then imagine the surprise when people discovered that Marconi was right: signals travel through air on invisible waves and can be received by tuning an antenna and receiver.

Powerful questions

Questions focus another person's attention in a way that a statement or presentation would find much harder to achieve. Why? Because of the way the brain works. At the end of the day, people make decisions and take actions based on their own logical and intuitive reasoning. A presentation or statement may engage someone's thinking, but a question *always* does.

Consider this question: *What's the weather like right now?*

Even though it's a pretty routine question, your mind went straight away to consider it. So even though you knew you were unlikely to have to come up with an answer you still did this. People love answering questions. Quiz shows are some of the most popular shows on television and many of the most successful board games like Trivial Pursuit are about questions. But this is not about simple questions or ones that test general knowledge. This is about questions that challenge a person's thinking, that get them to think about something differently, that increase their self-awareness or that build their responsibility. Since being small children, everyone has been taught to pursue the right answer. At job interviews, people hope to answer the interviewers' questions correctly and at work they are constantly being asked to solve problems. It is really quite amazing how much value people place on answers, considering an answer is only as good as the question that spurred it. An answer's value comes from its ability to solve a problem. A useful answer is more likely if the problem is properly defined, and a well-defined problem is usually stated in the form of a question.

To understand the effectiveness, begin evaluating the quality of the questions asked. Successful people not only ask a lot of questions, but they also learn to ask powerful questions. What would happen then if a very incisive question were asked, one that would really make someone think about something? The most effective leaders are inevitably the ones that ask the best questions, and the way questions are asked and the type of questions will determine the response received. The way in which a question is framed sets the direction for the conversation. The intent of a powerful question is to reveal more, to learn more, to open people up to see new possibilities and new solutions; thus, powerful questions lead to greater creativity. Like many paradoxes of leadership, powerful questions gain their power from their simplicity. A powerful question is usually short and seemingly even 'dumb'. For example, 'What outcome do you want?' or 'What's the next step?' or 'What did you learn?' appear simple on the surface. But these questions cause people to become introspective and more reflective; thus, they are able to get to the heart of the matter. Notice that powerful questions are open-ended and 'what' questions. They move a conversation forward because they require reflection and more than a 'yes' or 'no' answer. Their intent is to go beyond getting information – it's to provide focus and to help gain both insight and clarity.

Many clients come to consultants because they are looking for greater fulfilment at work, and one of the first questions a consultant asks, is 'What would being fulfilled look like to you?' When the client gets to the point where they can give the consultant a fairly complete description, the latter asks, 'What do you need to do to make that happen?' And then the consultant begins creating the steps they must take. The strength of this type of inquiry comes from its ability to elicit more authentic responses and to get people to think in a way that leads them to action. Powerful questions also support collaboration because they enable everyone involved in the conversation to learn. They are great tools to use with teams in problem solving. They make people stop and think. Because they arise from true curiosity, powerful questions are non-judgemental. There is no right or wrong answer. A simple question such as 'What would that get us?' frees up people to contemplate the possibilities. If this type of inquiry were used more often in corporate settings, it would help to shift beliefs. Questions can be one of the most effective communication tools available. Strong relationships, strategic plans, award-winning collateral and meaningful exchange of ideas and information are all products of asking skilful questions. If they're not, communications could be weak or worthless, and miscommunications may be experienced more often than necessary.

Why is the ability to ask skilful questions so powerful? Questions are the means used to excavate new information, to compare someone's perspective with reality, and to learn more about what others are thinking and perceiving. When someone does not ask questions, the assumption is that everything there is to know is known about the subject or the person. Is this ever the case? Rarely.

Push and pull of influencing

There are two main sets of skills for influencing and they are classified under push and pull skills. Pull skills are essentially about trying to understand the other person's agenda through questioning and listening so that one can understand the other person's point of view and, as a result, position one's proposal to meet their needs. The other benefit of listening first to understand is that if one is listened to, one tends to feel very positive to the other person. Thus, in listening to someone first, they understand the other's point of view and have built the conditions for their proposal to be more easily accepted. Push skills involve being a better advocate of a point of view. It means being specific, stating views clearly, and being prepared to specifically request what is wanted.

As Figure 7.2 shows, there are effective and ineffective push and pull skills. Typically starting initially down the push route, when someone is not successful in persuading the other person, the tendency is to 'push' harder and as a result start moving into the ineffective area. Similarly with pull skills, the tendency can be to get so aware and understanding of the other person's point of view that people become reluctant to assert their own views. On the left-hand side of the circle are the push skills starting in the top left quadrant with the positive ones and bottom left side being the ineffective skills. Similarly the right-hand side shows the pull skills in the same way.

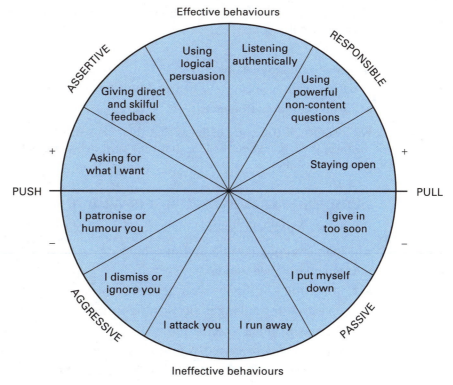

Figure 7.2 Push–Pull model

The lesson from this is if 'pushing' is not successful, then switch to 'pull' and vice versa.

7.7   Team leadership and climate

Often a consultant is called upon to lead a team and they sometimes describe a feeling of helplessness about leading effectively, as expressed below:

They [more senior managers] won't let me get on with things my way.

There's so much change and reorganisation around here, no one can settle down . . .

The good news is that research clearly demonstrates that the consultant can lead a team in a way that creates a positive climate. Furthermore, a positive climate is not just a nice-to-have. It has a direct link with performance.

What is climate?

The metaphor is interesting: people in organisations frequently describe a kind of weather system that directly affects how they behave. Real, physical climate may be changeable or steady, stormy or sunny, hot or cold; it affects people's physical comfort and may also affect feelings of well-being. The metaphorical climate of the work unit may be almost as tangible with the same powerful impact on people's day-to-day behaviour.

Climate:

- is relatively long-lasting;
- reflects what we believe to be true about the atmosphere in a work unit;
- affects the way we behave.

For instance, if someone believes that their boss will punish them if they make a mistake, the usual effect will be that they start behaving defensively and covering up their mistakes.

Symptoms that something is wrong

If there were problems with climate, some or all of the following would be seen:

- A high level of grievance and/or complaint
- Low performance standards
- Conflict and hostility between team members
- People avoiding talking to or listening to each other
- People being afraid to speak up
- Managers being perceived as unapproachable
- Lack of effective communication with other teams
- Confusion about the overall goals of the team
- Widespread confusion about individual tasks and roles
- Apathy and lack of involvement about where the team is heading
- People failing to acknowledge each other's good work
- Confusion about working procedures as a group
- Relationships with other teams being fraught with hostility and mistrust
- Poor performance compared with other teams doing similar tasks

Climate is one of the best-researched areas of organisational behaviour and one of the few where it is possible to demonstrate a direct relationship between cause and effect. Kurt Lewin was a German Jew who fled Germany in the 1930s. His own experience of Nazism led to a lifelong interest in what made people behave the way they did. How, for instance, could a whole country have submitted to a dictator like Hitler? He did some interesting experiments in the 1940s and 1950s with boys' clubs where the only variable was the way the boys were led. There were three leadership styles:

Authoritarian: A stern I-know-best style where they were told what to do and got little praise.

Laissez-faire: A pleasant leadership style but one which gives little direction.

Democratic: A style that involved the boys and took their wishes into account.

The results were startling. The *authoritarian* leader achieved early good results, but the moment the leader left the room, chaos broke out and the boys often destroyed their work. Achievements also diminished over time. The *laissez-faire* leader created a pleasant atmosphere but little was achieved in the way of output.

The *democratic* style nearly always started with a degree of apparent excitement and perhaps confusion, but always outperformed the others over time. George Litwin and Robert Stringer continued this work at Harvard. They hired groups of students who did not know the purpose of the study and who were put into three groups. They were asked to build models using Meccano. Each group had identical goals. Again, the only variable was leadership style. The names are different, but essentially the styles were variants on Lewin's work and had similar results:

The power-led group suppressed contributions from the group, and created strict rules and regulations. The results were:

- high initial productivity;
- subversive behaviour breaking out among the group with covert or overt struggles for power with the leader;
- inability to innovate or flex production;
- inability to keep costs competitive;
- lower overall productivity;
- a conservative, formal and cold climate.

The affiliative group (cf. Lewin's laissez-faire group) stressed cooperative behaviour and participative decision-making rather than product excellence or productivity. It resulted in:

- flexibility and creativity;
- workers who enjoyed the climate and felt loyalty towards the group;
- lower output;
- frustration and struggles for leadership developing inside the group; this often took attention away from production.

The achievement-led group (cf. Lewin's democratic group) stressed participative goal-setting, competitive feedback, pride and teamwork. It resulted in:

- the highest productivity and biggest profit margins;
- loyalty to the team; a feeling of satisfaction in the work;
- high-quality products;
- people reporting a much greater feeling of individual responsibility for their work;
- a high level of innovation and creativity.

The cause and effect relationship

What both these pieces of work show is that there is a direct cause and effect relationship:

LEADERSHIP
↓
CLIMATE
↓
MOTIVATION
↓
PERFORMANCE

In other words, varying the leadership style affects the climate; the climate in its turn affects motivation and motivation affects performance.

The lessons

When someone is a team leader the lessons are clear. The achievement style is the one that makes people both happy and productive. So what are the key pieces of behaviour that are needed? Further research with real companies has shown that the climate research holds true in the 'real' world. For instance, teams whose performance was rated highly on measures such as customer satisfaction and net profit also showed that they had a positive climate along the lines of Litwin and Stringer's 'achievement' focus. There is a consistent pattern around these four areas:

Clarity

- Make it clear where people fit into the organisation and the team. If there is confusion, talk it through and sort it out.
- Clarify the boundaries of people's roles. If they are unclear, make them clear.
- Set clear objectives and expectations.
- Make it crystal clear who has what authority to make decisions.

Standards

- Establish high standards through discussion.
- Communicate the high standards.
- Challenge complacency – keep on looking for increased quality and quantity.
- Involve customers in standard-setting.

Recognition

- Give people very frequent positive feedback – catch them doing something right and do it immediately.
- Balance this with negative feedback when necessary, but keep the emphasis on the positive.
- See mistakes as opportunities to learn for the whole team.

Team working

- Talk positively about the team so that people feel proud to belong to it.
- Create an atmosphere of trust by dealing with conflict openly so that there are no hidden agendas.
- Support, encourage and reward innovation.
- Devote time to team communication – looking at feelings as well as facts.

The other good news about climate is that it can be changed quickly and that change is within any leader's control.

7.8   Accelerating team performance and dealing with conflict

In a recent study carried out by the DTI (now the DBERR) on some of the UK's top-performing companies, teams were identified as the principle building blocks for business success. The idea that teams should play such an important role in moving organisations forward is based around the principle that many minds working together on a problem or opportunity are smarter than a group of individuals working on it independently. Is this, however, always true? Clearly it depends on the team in question and, more importantly, what stage of development the team is at. The key to the success of the above quoted organisations is not just that they used teams, but that they were able to form and develop high-performing teams in a relatively short period of time. By studying the common factors within high-performing teams, some of the vital ingredients necessary for improving the performance in any team can begin to be pieced together.

Compelling purpose for being

Fundamental to any group of people working together effectively is a common vision that compels each person to take action. Victor Frankl, in his account of how people survived the terror of concentration camps, asserted that people will put up with almost any 'what' or 'how' if they have a big enough 'why'. With effective teams, it is the 'why' that fuels them to overcome obstacles, and do whatever it takes to succeed. In defining the team's purpose, two basic criteria need to be met. First of all it has to be exciting enough to make people want to give of their absolute best. Second, it needs to be sufficiently clear to align people's actions towards its achievement.

How to set up a team to win

It is absolutely vital that during the setting up of a team, time is taken to ensure that it is given the best possible chance of success from day one. Besides getting commitment through a compelling purpose, the following is needed:

1 Select the right people for the right reasons. This should include a balance between technical expertise and other skills like communication, leadership and creativity. The real genius of a great team is often in the diversity of the people it brings together.

2 Explore the current situation and any circumstances associated with it; clarify the desired outcome and what it will mean to the success of the business; and, finally, examine all plausible paths between the two before coming up with a clear strategic plan.

3 Clarify what autonomy the team has to make decisions. One secret to empowering people within teams is to give them a clear boundary of responsibility over which no one else will interfere. This symbol of trust, no matter how small the boundary, is what makes people feel as if they really make a difference.

4 Wherever possible, guarantee commitment from significant people who have an indirect influence on the success of the team. One of several ways to achieve this is to set up a 'steering' team to clear the path for the actions of the main 'project' team.

5 To increase the commitment from people within the team, begin by defining what will be required from each person in terms of time and resources etc. The benefit of this is that it will counter any fears people may have of over-committing themselves.

Finally, and above all, ensure that people begin with an expectation of success, even if the 'how to' is not yet evident. It is frightening to imagine what would not have been achieved today if people only acted on what was believed possible. In reality the only way to discover what is possible is to go beyond it into the impossible. How is it possible that a talented group of managers with individual IQs well in excess of 120 have a collective IQ of 55? The key to overcoming the above paradox is to accelerate team performance by giving each member the necessary skills and encouragement to learn from experience, surface and deal with internal conflicts, play to each person's relative strengths, and utilise advanced thinking strategies for developing innovations, problem solving, scenario planning etc. The same attributes that define a successful individual (i.e. a willingness to take responsibility for the results they produce, flexibility and a thirst for constant improvement) apply to high-performing teams. The only addition is open communication, the essential glue that brings the component parts of a team together. When the intelligence of the team exceeds the intelligence of the individual members, you get extraordinary capacity for coordinated action.

When next faced with leading a team, it would be worth thinking about the following questions:

1 If you think back to your best experience as part of a team, to what extent is the current team clear on and excited by their purpose?

2 What is the potential for your team to work together better, i.e. what is the gap between current performance and potential performance?

3 How often does your team make use of external resources to facilitate creativity and challenge traditional ways of operating?

4 To what extent would increasing resources invested in developing key skills to facilitate effective teamwork provide benefits?

5 How long does it take your team to become productive on a new project?

6 What can be learnt from those times when your team is performing at its best?

Dealing with conflict

Conflict arises in teams or between individuals primarily because of lack of understanding of each other's position or unwillingness to explore the other person's point of view and search for areas of agreement. One of the best ways to deal with conflict is to impose as a facilitator a somewhat artificial structure on the dialogue between the parties at conflict. Nancy Kline, in her superb book *Time to Think*, proposes the following structure for resolving issues. First, get the parties involved to agree to the structure below (to contract with them).

1 Explain that each party will have up to three minutes to talk and explain their view. During this time the other party can only listen. They may not ask questions or show agreement or disagreement. They simply pay attention. When each party has their turn they have the space totally to themselves. They don't need to build on or pay attention to anything the other party has said.

2 After each party has had their three minutes the drill is continued until the facilitator believes that they have reached a better understanding. Do not stop the process too soon even if one party has gone silent. It is their space.

3 Usually this simple process alone is enough to resolve many issues. If, however, there is insufficient common ground, then as a facilitator allow each party to question the other party for three minutes at a time. The rule is, though, that all questions should be to check and test understanding and the facilitator will oversee this.

This process is deceitful in its simplicity, but it has enormous power.

Team discussion points

Changing assumptions/beliefs exercise

1 Either identify a specific area you want to work on or choose one from the list of: leaders, race, nuclear weapons, marriage or divorce, food, politics, religion, dentists, the medical profession, bosses, sex, education, money, exercise, unemployment, consultants, your partner, alcohol, smoking, family, work.

2 What are some of the beliefs and messages you have about the issue you've chosen?

3 What would you like to be possible for you in relation to this issue? Phrase this as an objective in about half a dozen words.

4 Which is the main belief or message that you feel stops you achieving your objective?

5 Exploring your limiting assumption in more detail:

■ How does this assumption affect your behaviour?
■ How does it serve you or help you?
■ What does it stop you from seeing or doing about yourself and others?
■ How long have you had it?
■ How strong is it?
■ What would be a freeing assumption for you?

Note your incisive question here:

If I knew that . . .

Summary of key ideas

■ Consultants need to identify which role to adopt:
  – Partner
  – Coach
  – Reflective observer
  – Hands-on expert.

■ The right role to adopt depends on the situation; you need to consider the organisational situation, characteristics of the client and consultant and the client–consultant relationship.

- Influencing is a key consulting skill as it enables things to be moved forward.
- Rapport is the skill of building cooperative relationships done through matching your behaviour with others.
- Underlying assumptions and beliefs can limit change and impact a consulting project.
- Thinking of the possible outcome before you respond to an event can help the situation.
- Outcome-frame thinking empowers you as you get a more positive response.
- Advocacy is about getting your view across clearly and succinctly.
- Listening is a powerful tool but there are different levels:
  - Internal, centred on me
  - Focused, centred on the speaker
  - Global, on everyone.
- Powerful questions can elicit information otherwise difficult to extract.
- The most effective team leadership style has been shown to be the 'democratic' one where everyone feels involved; this in turn affects the climate positively.
- In order for a team to be successful it must be right from the start.
- Dealing with conflict can be done by the use of a facilitator and time to discuss disagreements.

Key reading

Champion, D.P., Kiel D.H. and McLendon, J.A. (1990) 'Choosing a consulting role', *Training and Development Journal*, 1 February.

Tannenbaum, R. and Schmidt, W.H. (1973) 'How to choose a leadership pattern', *Harvard Business Review*, 1 May.

Further reading

Beaver, D. (1997) *Easy Being: Making Life As Simple And As Much Fun As Possible*. Cheltenham, Gloucestershire: Useful Book Company.

Bennis, W. and Townsend, R. (2005) *Reinventing Leadership*. London: HarperCollins.

Blanchard, K., Zigarmi, D. and Zigarmi, P. (2000) *Leadership and The One-Minute Manager*. London: HarperCollins Business.

Bono, E. de (2000) *Six Thinking Hats*. London: Penguin Books.

Covey, S.R. (1999) *7 Habits of Highly Effective People*. London: Simon & Schuster.

Covey, S.R. (2004) *The 8th Habit: From Effectiveness To Greatness*. London: Simon & Schuster.

Frankl, V. (1993) *Man's Search for Meaning: Introduction to Logotherapy*. Boston, MA: Beacon Press.

Gallwey, W.T. (2003) *The Inner Game of Work: Overcoming Mental Obstacles For Maximum Performance*. Mason, OH: Texere Publishing.

Goleman, D. (2005) *Emotional Intelligence: Why It Can Matter More Than IQ*. New York: Bantam Books.

Harris, T.A. (1995) *I'm OK, You're OK*. London: Arrow.

Johnson, S. (1999) *Who Moved My Cheese? An Amazing Way to Deal With Change in Your Work and in Your Life*. London: Vermilion.

Kline, N. (1998) *Time to Think: Listening to Ignite the Human Mind*. London: Cassell Illustrated.

Knight, S. (2002) *NLP at Work: The Difference that Makes a Difference in Business*. London: Nicholas Brealey.

Lewin, K. (1997) *Resolving Social Conflicts*. Washington, DC: American Psychological Association.

Litwin, G. and Stringer, R. (1969) *Motivation and Organizational Climate*. Boston, MA: Harvard University Press.

Meyers, I.B. and Myers, P.B. (1995) *Gifts Differing: Understanding Personality Type*. Mountain View, CA: Davies-Black Publishers.

Senge, P.M. (2006) *The Fifth Discipline*. London: Random House Business Books.

Whitmore, Sir J. (2002) *Coaching for Performance: Growing People, Performance and Purpose*. London: Nicholas Brealey.

Wiseman, R. (2004) *The Luck Factor: The Scientific Study of the Lucky Mind*. London: Arrow.

Case exercise

O'Reilly Design

O'Reilly Design is a company specialising in designing interiors for leisure outlets such as pubs, bars, restaurants and nightclubs. They have been particularly successful in transforming bars worldwide into 'Irish pubs' in conjunction with a leading producer of stout. The company's owner and founder, John O'Reilly, and his marketing director, Peter Doyle, have secured funding from the local development agency for a consulting project aimed at making them more innovative.

They have asked you to bid for this work and you propose a short meeting with O'Reilly and Doyle to understand their needs better. At that meeting, a few things become clear:

1 It is John O'Reilly who is the driving force of his company in terms of creative ideas but he is a shy man and reluctant to take on day-to-day management of his 100-strong team.

2 Peter Doyle is the complete opposite of his boss in terms of being extrovert and happy to tackle man-management decisions, but he has no authority to do so.

3 The company is in reality run by O'Reilly's long-term girlfriend, Sinead Kelly, who has been with the firm from the start and while an excellent administrator has an abrupt manner which has alienated her colleagues. Furthermore, her personal relationship with the 'boss' means that the other members of the firm do not trust her.

4 On further questioning, their 'problem' is not that they are short of good business ideas; in fact, they have too many, resulting in a lack of focus and follow-through.

In considering your proposal you need to reflect the above and also stay true to the spirit of the grant that is to aid innovation. So you decide that you will work in two areas: one is the *implementation* of the ideas and the other is the ongoing *management* of projects. However, you need to involve one or more members of O'Reilly Design in order to ensure the success of the project. You decide to hold a workshop for the 'senior management team' aimed at identifying new projects and the start of an implementation plan for them. The date is duly set and you arrive to find over ▶

20 people there (one in five of the workforce). John O'Reilly is reluctant to take an active part in the proceedings and Peter Doyle and Sinead Kelly vie in their respective teams to come up with the most ideas. At the end of the day, you have over 100 new ideas generated but as John only 'approves' of ten of them, many are unnecessarily discarded. You run out of time to start building implementation plans.

You are concerned that this project is seriously off track and persuade John O'Reilly to have a one-to-one meeting with you prior to a session with the other members of the senior team. In this, you hope to find a solution to the current problems.

Q1 Use the framework in Section 7.1 to identify which role to play as a consultant and say why you chose this one.

Q2 How do you propose to get this project back on track?

Q3 What would you do to improve the senior leadership team of John O'Reilly, Peter Doyle and Sinead Kelly by playing to their strengths?

Robinson Mason case study: Part 2

The magnitude of the business transformation required across Robinson Mason's European businesses soon became clear. Put simply, a dozen countries accustomed to operating on their own would now be required to become a single, unified business with a common mission, working in complete alignment. Clearly, such a radical change posed many potentially unsettling challenges to the country general managers, whose authority and status would inevitably be affected. To indicate the seriousness of his commitment and the level of his determination, the European regional director (who was also a member of the Robinson Mason board of directors) appointed a full-time director with full authority to oversee the design and implementation of the changes needed. He was allocated a substantial budget for this purpose, but the country general managers were informed that the distraction posed by this European business transformation process would not be allowed to be used as a pretext for failure to achieve their sales and profit targets. Business as usual had to continue.

While the European regional director intended to conduct a review of the various stand-alone single country off-strategy businesses, which he intended to divest in order to generate cash and which would help to offset the lamentable trading performance, the job of the European business transformation director was to embark upon a programme to align the corporation's many business processes. Everything from writing a marketing plan to responding to consumer complaints to writing copy strategy to new product development was in due course to be conducted uniformly, as too were sales and operations planning, Human Resource procedures, strategic planning, customer management and information systems. Responsibility for the design and harmonisation of these processes was entrusted to a business transformation team drawn from various parts of the global Robinson Mason corporation and seconded full-time to the European HQ in London. It was put to these often reluctant recruits that this was a career-enhancing move. They were to be supported by a number of managers from a well-known global consultancy specialising in the business transformation process. Simultaneously, to support the streamlined manufacturing operations and to facilitate standardised financial reporting, a new integrated software system was to be introduced throughout Robinson Mason's European operations, replacing the many different legacy systems in use. This task was assigned to specialist consultants from the organisation from which the system had been purchased. They were to work together with the change management consultants and the full-time RM staff as part of one unified team, Ganymede, reporting to the European business transformation director.

It was anticipated that the programme would run in three phases. First, a two-month exploratory/familiarisation stage when the Ganymede team would split into various cohorts, visit the individual countries and engage in process mapping. This was somewhat ceremonial, as its main purpose was to prove to sceptical general managers that their systems were inefficient and unaligned, and that a team was being deployed to rectify matters. Running in parallel was an initiative to identify likely savings and opportunities for revenue growth so as to establish a business case. This was conducted purely by the change management consultants, in dialogue with financial management in the various countries and at HQ. In addition, the information systems experts began their various scoping exercises.

Once the first phase was complete, some preliminary recommendations would be made, and a large number of managers from RM's European operation would then be brought to London to participate in an intensive three-day workshop run by the Ganymede team, when the broad outline of the new operating procedures would be defined. These would then be developed into a series of specific, detailed proposals over a period of six months, using the experience and energies of multi-functional teams recruited on a part-time basis (at no additional reward) from among the operating units, who would come together at regular two-day workshops in various parts of Europe. The broad areas covered were Operations and Logistics (i.e. every aspect of the supply chain from forecasting, purchasing, production planning etc. through to warehousing and delivery), Commercialisation (i.e. sales management, customer management, sales force efficiency, business strategy, innovation, marketing planning and brand management), Accounting and Finance, Human Resources Management (as there would clearly be a number of cultural challenges and organisational design issues in the new, unified business) and Information Systems (to ensure that the new integrated software supported the redesigned business processes).

Once this stage had been completed, and the Ganymede team's various recommendations had been validated and documented, it was envisaged that they would be presented to, built upon, and eventually accepted by the European regional director and his direct reports. Thereafter, the Ganymede team would plan and facilitate implementation throughout Robinson Mason Europe, the team would be disbanded and the consultants' contracts brought to a conclusion. From end to end, the entire programme was not expected to take more than 12 months.

This was the plan. The reality was different.

Discussion questions

1 Critically evaluate the outline plan, the areas of priority, and the intended modus operandi.

2 Might the intended results have been achieved in a quicker, simpler way?

3 How might the European general managers have been more effectively engaged in order to gain their support for the Ganymede project?

PART THREE

Undertaking the project

Executing a successful project

The learning outcomes from this chapter are to:

- understand the levels of client–consultant interaction depending on the type of consulting project undertaken;
- demonstrate how benchmarking can help the smooth running of a project;
- show the different roles that members of the client organisation can play;
- understand why organisations resist change;
- appreciate the types of consultant interaction that facilitate change;
- recognise the types of *problem* that might challenge the progression of the project;
- learn the most effective *response* to make in the face of such challenges.

8.1 Consultant–client engagement for project implementation

As no two consulting projects are alike, nor is the level of engagement that a consultant has with a client. Figure 8.1 looks at the spectrum of consultant–client relationships, depending on the level of intimacy the consultant has with the client. When the consultant is briefed and delivers a report at the end, the level of intimacy with the client is low. An example of this would be a market research brief. In this case the client would tell the consultant what information they required, agree the questions and the next interaction would be the findings from the research. A more traditional view of a consulting project would be where the external consultants do most of the work but they have regular contact with the client. An example of this type of project would be a commercial due diligence. This is a review of a business that is for sale and a prospective purchaser wants to ensure that they are making a good investment. The brief is clear and the view from the consultant has to be independent, but a buyer wants to be kept informed of progress in case the consultant uncovers any major issues that would prevent the sale.

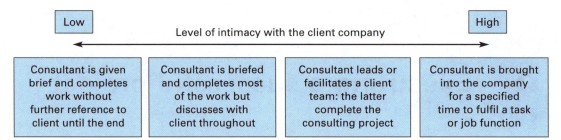

Figure 8.1 Consultant–client interaction

The bulk of the work that many professional management consultants undertake would fall into the third category where the consultant would lead or facilitate a client team. The reasons for this are:

- cost – external management consultants do not come cheap;
- a better knowledge of the issues that the client company faces;
- any solutions are likely to be better imbedded and therefore implemented;
- it is a good training for the members of the client team;
- the client has more control over the project.

The last category, where effectively the consultant becomes a full-time member of the client organisation, is often called interim management. There may be a role or specific project for a limited time that the client needs someone to fulfil but at the same time wants him or her to be part of the organisation. In cases where the client company is in dire straits, specialists called 'company doctors' are brought in to try to rescue the company.

As was discussed in Section 3.5 on the selling process, there is also the issue of whether a standardised or customised process is being offered. While standardised processes are often associated with a lower level of intimacy with the client company, as in the example above with regard to a market research project, this is not always the case. IT consultants often implement standardised computer systems in client companies where they are engaged almost as an interim manager. Having a customised process does usually mean a higher level of intimacy with the client, as the consultant needs to have a greater understanding of the client. However, there are exceptions where a customised approach is needed but little client contact is needed. This is because the client is expecting the consultant to come up with an 'answer'. The consultant in this case would probably be a leading thinker or 'guru', who would be applying their considerable skills and knowledge to provide a solution.

8.2 Benchmarking project progression

Benchmarking is a process through which specific achievements are predicted, defined and evidenced. A consulting project will have an overall set of objectives (see Section 5.4). However, these may be broken down into a series of intermediate and subsidiary objectives, based on the objectives and outcomes specified in the project charter. This is particularly useful if the project is a long or complex one.

Benchmarking involves:

1 identifying the relevant intermediate stages of the project;

2 defining specific objectives for each intermediate stage;

3 anticipating what will be appropriate evidence that each subsidiary objective has been achieved (this will be related to the means of measurement specified in the project charter);

4 delivering on the objective and producing the evidence.

What constitutes evidence will vary depending on the project and the nature of the subsidiary objective. It may be of a qualitative, numerical nature that is formally measured. It may take the form of the production of a particular document or the obtaining of a particular piece of evidence. It may be that a particular meeting has taken place, in which case notes from the meeting will constitute the evidence. The production of the evidence is a good discipline in that it substantiates progression of the project. Building on the project charter that was discussed in Section 5.4, below is an example of a benchmarking document (Table 8.1).

From Table 8.1, we can see that the large project of completing and executing a marketing plan has been split into ten subsections, each with its own goal, measurements, the date for completion and, most critically, who is ultimately responsible for delivery. The project leader, Mr Y, can ensure that the project is running smoothly by ensuring that key dates are adhered to. More critically he can ensure projects are completed in the correct order, as it would be impossible to complete a product strategy without doing an NPD review, for example. This can also flag up any potential problems to completing the whole project on time. This is discussed further in Chapter 11.

Table 8.1 Example of a benchmarking document

Project information	Team members
Leader: Mr Y (Excel Consultants)	Sponsor: Mrs G (AB Company – 'ABC')
Project start: October 2006	Leader: Mr Y
Project end: June 2007	Core team: Mr Y, Miss H and Mrs J from Excel and Mr D, Mr U and Ms X from ABC
Brief description: Marketing plan for ABC	Ad hoc members: Mrs P, Mr K and Miss L from ABC

	Project goals	Measurements	Date for completion	Responsibility
1	Market assessment	Audit data	Nov 2006	Ms X
2	Consumer assessment	Market research	Dec 2006	Mrs P
3	Product assessment	Competitive review	Nov 2006	Mr U
4	NPD review	Pipeline	Dec 2006	Mr D
5	Marketing strategy	Strategic statement	Jan 2007	Mr Y
6	Product strategy	NPD plan	Feb 2007	Mr K
7	Promotional strategy	Promotional brief	Mar 2007	Mrs J
8	Sales strategy	Sales plan	Mar 2007	Miss H
9	Pricing strategy	Pricing plan	Mar 2007	Miss L
10	Review	Sales and profits	Jun 2007	Mr Y

8.3   Understanding the roles of client team members

In the example above of a benchmarking document, there are three outside consultants but seven members of the client team directly involved in the project. There would also be many others in the client's organisation that would be involved to some extent. In addition to the benchmarking document, it might also be useful to think about the roles that these people play. A tool, called a responsibility assignment matrix (or 'RAM'), may be used to list the activities. It has four categories under which one or more members of the client organisation are listed. These categories are:

- Responsible – typically this is the person or group of people who will be performing the task. It may be useful to identify one person who is ultimately responsible.
- Accountable – here there can only be one person and the buck stops with them!
- Consulted – this may be for political reasons but, more critically, their advice will ensure that the activity is done properly.
- Informed – these have no direct impact on the project but need to be kept in touch due to the wider implications of a consulting project within a company.

You may also want to have an additional category:

- Supports – these can provide further resources to conduct the work or have a supportive role in the implementation of the project.

So, taking the benchmarking document in Table 8.1, we can construct a responsibility assignment matrix for the project (Table 8.2).

Table 8.2 Example of a responsibility assignment matrix

	Project goals	R	A	C	I	S
1	Market assessment	Ms X	Mr Y	Mrs P, Mr K, Miss L	Mrs G	Mr D, Mr U
2	Consumer assessment	Mrs P	Mr Y	Mrs J, Mr K, Miss L	Mrs G	Mr D, Mr U
3	Product assessment	Mr U	Mr Y	Mrs J, Mr K	Mrs G	Miss L
4	NPD review	Mr D	Mr Y	Mrs P, Mr K, Miss L	Mrs G	Mr U
5	Marketing strategy	Mr Y	Mrs G	Mrs P, Mr K, Miss L	Mr A	Mr D, Mr U
6	Product strategy	Mr K	Mr Y	Mrs P, Miss L	Mrs G	Mr D, Mr U
7	Promotional strategy	Mrs J	Mr Y	Mrs P, Mr K, Miss L	Mrs G	Mr D, Mr U
8	Sales strategy	Miss H	Mr Y	Mrs P, Mr K, Miss L	Mrs G	Mr D, Mr U
9	Pricing strategy	Miss L	Mr Y	Mrs P, Mr K	Mrs G	Mr D, Mr U
10	Review	Mr Y	Mrs G	Mrs P, Mr K, Miss L	Mr A	Mr D, Mr U

8.4   Relationship with the client during the project

In Chapter 7, we discussed the key interpersonal skills required to be a successful consultant and these are key in maintaining a good relationship with the client during the project. As David Maister points out in his chapter 'The Consultant's Role' in Fombrun and Nevins (2004) *The Advice Business*, a consultant has to be seen to be *helping* a client to be successful. Just providing the right answer is not enough; you have to deal with the client's emotions (and also the politics within the client company). Maister gives the common emotions your client might feel when using consultants:

1 *Insecure* – the employment of an outside person to address some of the issues the firm faces may be an indication of failure on the part of the client.

2 *Threatened* – a consultant is looking at my area of expertise; will this highlight my weaknesses?

3 *Personal risk* – the client could feel that they are losing control giving an outside person responsibility for looking at their business.

4 *Impatient* – a consultant is often called as a last resort when the corporate ship is often sinking, so the client may be more impatient for success.

5 *Worried* – what will these consultants discover and will it be to my detriment?

6 *Exposed* – outsiders will be able to look at the inner workings of the company and this can pose a risk if, for example, the company is subsequently up for sale.

7 *Ignorant* – the client does not fully understand what the consultant is proposing but finds it hard to articulate this without appearing incompetent.

8 *Sceptical* – often when clients have had unsatisfactory outcomes with previous consultants, they are naturally wary of others.

9 *Concerned* – clients worry that they often get a 'standard' package instead of a customised one for their business, as this is easier for the consultant.

10 *Suspicious* – consultants' (unfairly) poor reputation may precede them and for many clients they are worried that they are not being sold 'snake oil'!

Given this, the consultant has to tread very carefully. They have to maintain a professional distance to remain objective but must be sensitive to the client's needs. Mick Cope in his book *The Seven C's of Consulting* (2003) argues that trust is the key to building and maintaining a good relationship between client and consultant. He has developed the mnemonic TRUST to reinforce this:

■ **Truthful** – the consultant and the client must be truthful to one another. It would be very easy to tell the other person what you think they want to hear but this is a short-term gain. While the truth may be painful, it is a pre-requisite for a sound business relationship.

■ **Responsive** – this is about the consultant engaging totally in the client's world and being responsive to the client's needs.

■ **Uniform** – a consultant must be consistent in their ideas and attitudes towards the project. If they continually change their mind, the client will become confused and begin to doubt the abilities of the consultant to complete the task.

■ **Safe** – given some of the emotions a client may feel, as described above, it is important that the client can feel safe working with the consultant. This may be done formally through secrecy agreements or informally through constant dialogue and reassurance.

■ **Trained** – it may sound obvious but it is important that the client believes the consultant is competent in the area of expertise that they are being consulted about. This could come in the form of previous work experience for the individual or through the consulting firm's reputation.

8.5   The desire for change by the client organisation

Individuals normally resist change unless the need for that change is clearly recognised and accepted. This is often for good reasons. Change brings with it uncertainty and individuals are normally averse to uncertainty. Individuals may not always see the need for change. This can be particularly so when the management team is locked into groupthink, as discussed in Section 1.10. Recognising the need for change often represents what psychologists refer to as a *gestalt* shift: the sudden dawning of a whole, and integrated, new way of seeing things – like when we see the drawing of a cube lit from above become one of a different cube lit from below. Once the need for change has been recognised and becomes a desire for change by the organisation, it usually takes place with a predictable pattern of events. Kotter (1996) has developed an eight-stage process on successful change within organisations.

Step 1: Establishing a sense of urgency

The old motto 'if it ain't broke, don't fix it' often pervades businesses which delay change due to complacency. These sources of complacency are:

- the absence of a major and visible crisis;
- too many visible resources, e.g. expensive corporate headquarters;
- low overall performance standards;
- organisational structure that focuses employees on narrow performance goals;
- internal measurement systems that focus on the wrong performance indices;
- lack of sufficient performance feedback from external sources;
- a kill the messenger, low-candour, low-confrontation culture;
- human nature with its capacity for denial, especially if already busy;
- too much 'happy talk' from senior management.

These are part and parcel of the 'groupthink' mentality considered in Section 1.10. You will have succeeded if enough of the management feel that the status quo has to change.

Step 2: Creating a powerful coalition

Only with the right kind of team will you be successful with change, as this sends out powerful messages about the importance of this project. The key characteristics you should look for are:

- position – are enough key players on board, especially the main line managers, so that those left out cannot easily block progress?
- expertise – are the various points of view, disciplines, experience, nationality, etc. adequately represented?
- credibility – does the group have enough people with good reputations?

Stage 3: Developing a vision

As with any strategic planning, it is critical to have an effective vision. Kotter describes an effective vision as having the following characteristics:

- imaginable – conveys a picture of what the future will look like;
- desirable – appeals to the long-term interests of all those who have a stake in the enterprise;
- feasible – comprises realistic, attainable goals;
- focused – is clear enough to provide guidance in decision-making;
- flexible – is general enough to allow individual initiative and alternative responses in the light of changing conditions;
- communicable – is easy to communicate; can be successfully explained within five minutes.

Stage 4: Communicating the change vision

Never underestimate how much you need to communicate in business, and when you are going through a programme of change, this is vital. Kotter has shown that businesses *under*-communicate by a factor of ten! Some simple rules to bear in mind are:

- simplicity – all jargon and technobabble must be eliminated;
- metaphor, analogy and example – a verbal picture is worth a thousand words;
- multiple forums – big meetings and small, memos and newspapers, formal and informal action are all effective for spreading the word;
- repetition – ideas sink in deeply only after they have been heard many times;
- leadership by example – behaviour from important people that is inconsistent with the vision overwhelms other forms of communication;
- explanation of seeming inconsistencies – unaddressed inconsistencies undermine the credibility of all communication;
- give and take – two-way communication is always more powerful than one-way communication.

Stage 5: Empowering employees to act on the vision

After communicating the vision to employees, you need to make structures compatible with it, as unaligned structures block needed action. For example, more customer-focused visions often fail unless customer-unfocused organisational structures are adapted. Second, you need to provide the training employees need, as without the right skills and attitudes people feel disempowered. You need to consider what new behaviours, skills and attitudes will be needed when major changes are initiated, and decide how to deliver these in a cost-effective, meaningful way.

Lastly, you need to address managers who stifle needed change – there is no greater disincentive to an employee.

Stage 6: Generating short-term wins

A change process can take a long time, so it is important to have some short-term wins that are visible, unambiguous and related to the change effort. Although targeting short-term wins does increase the pressure on people, it can be a useful way of keeping up the urgency, especially when the end is a long way off in a major programme.

Stage 7: Consolidating improvements and producing more change

While celebrating early wins is important, these should add to the momentum rather than slowing it down by thinking that the job is nearly done. As the project progresses, additional people should be brought in to project manage and developed to cope with all the changes. The senior people should focus on keeping clarity of shared purpose for the overall project and maintaining urgency levels. Finally, unnecessary interdependencies should be eliminated.

Stage 8: Anchoring new approaches in the culture

The most critical part of the process is to ensure that the new ways of working are embedded in the culture of the organisation. However, new approaches sink into a culture only after it is very clear that they work for the individuals and are better than the old way. Communication continues to be vital, as without verbal instruction and support people are often reluctant to admit the validity of new processes. Perhaps the hardest part of all is that it may involve changing personnel to achieve a cultural change. Going forward, decisions on human resources will be critical. If HR processes are not changed to be compatible with the new practices, the old culture will re-emerge.

Why firms fail with change programmes

1 They allow too much complacency and forge ahead without establishing a high enough sense of urgency in employees.

2 They fail to create a sufficiently powerful guiding coalition.

3 They underestimate the power of a vision: it plays a key role by helping to direct, align and inspire actions on behalf of a large number of people.

4 They under-communicate the vision by a factor of ten or more.

5 They permit obstacles to block the vision. Whenever people avoid confronting obstacles they disempower employees and undermine change.

6 They fail to create short-term wins: without these, too many employees give up or join the resistance.

7 They declare victory too soon: until changes sink deeply into a culture, which can take between three and ten years, new approaches are fragile and subject to erosion.

8 They neglect to anchor changes firmly in the corporate culture: change sticks only when it becomes 'the way we do things around here'.

8.6   Change-enhancing interactions

The consultant can facilitate change at a variety of levels and by engaging in each of the stages described above. Important interventions include:

- providing information that highlights the need for change, i.e. information that rationalises one or more of the issues discussed in Section 5.6;

- ensuring that this information is integrated into the managers' decision-making roles, with special attention to the cognitive and political dimensions of the decision as well as its rational dimension;

- challenging groupthink by inviting the managerial team to share a new perspective, not least through challenging assumptions and the set of options under consideration;

- providing new options for consideration;

- evaluating and reconciling the different political positions of management factions;

- exploring the change process and taking away fear of it, not least through exploring, evaluating and reducing uncertainty about the future.

These different types of intervention are not separate. Rather they are elements that might be combined to produce a strategy for a particular intervention. At any one time one element may be more important than others. Cope (2003) has identified seven themes that a consultant should consider when trying to understand and address what he terms the 'human elements of change':

1 **System dynamics** – what are the deep systemic issues that will cause the change stage to hit problems?

2 **Organisation and disorganisation** – what factors related to the organisation of the system will impact on the success of the change?

3 **Understand the resistance** – how can people be encouraged to be involved in the transformation?

4 **Change spectrum** – what type of change interventions can be effected to help people through the change?

5 **Consumer segmentation** – how can the consumers be segmented into groups based on their desire for change?

6 **Methodology** – determine from the outset what methodology will be used to drive the engagement.

7 **Energy mapping** – understand where the forces are who can impact the change.

Overlaying this are 'unwritten rules' of the organisation that Peter Scott-Morgan has described in his books *The Unwritten Rules of the Game* (1994) and *The End of Change* (2001). These can often cause a change programme to fail if they are ignored. Unwritten rules are caused by the written rules of a company, the behaviour or actions of its leaders and the external environment. So, for example, a consulting programme that can determine the optimal spend for marketing would be seen as a 'good thing' by the Chief Executive and Finance Director but a 'bad thing' by all in the marketing department. This is because there is an 'unwritten rule' that the more the marketing department can spend on promotional activities, the more they can demonstrate their capabilities and thus further their careers. So the consulting project aimed at cutting marketing spending would be quietly 'killed off' by the marketers by them claiming it to be unworkable.

8.7   Types of project shock

Things go wrong! No matter how good the planning, there will always be things outside the consultant's control. No matter how good the anticipation, some events will be unpredicted. Planning is not just about defining a course of action. It is about building in the flexibility to respond to the unexpected. Some of the more common reasons why the project is knocked off course are as follows.

Changes in client's interests

One of the most common challenges to the project is that the client's interests suddenly change. This may be because he or she suddenly sees a new project more positively or as having higher priority than the one discussed initially. This can easily happen with a small, fast-growing business that faces constantly changing priorities.

Changes in the client's business situation

A consulting project is relevant only in that it helps the business achieve its goals. The project's aim must resonate with that of the business as a whole. If a major change in the business's situation takes place and causes it to change its overall goals, the relevance of the consulting project will change as well. The project may suddenly not be relevant at all! If the business faces particular difficulties, the priority of the managers may be to address immediate concerns. Short-term interests will come to the fore. Interest in longer-term goals and the consulting project's contribution to them may seem to evaporate.

Cuts in expenditure

Even if the consulting exercise is offered on a no-fee or success basis, resources may have to be dedicated to supporting activities such as market research. Budget cuts are a fact of managerial life. If resources are tight, the project may be targeted as having low priority. Clearly, a cut in the money available will limit the activities for which it was planned.

Loss of key people

If the people contributing to the project differentiate their tasks, they ensure the value of their contribution. If they leave the project their loss will be noticed. People can move on for a variety of reasons. Within the client business individuals can be promoted or leave to join another organisation. Members of the project team can leave to join other organisations (or, if students, to take other courses).

The impact of such a loss on the project will depend on the role played by the individual and the ability of the remaining members to undertake that role.

Misinterpretation of information

The course plotted by the consulting project, the direction in which it aims to take the business and the tasks needed to get it there are built on the interpretation of information about the business and its environment. If this information is misinterpreted the project may lead the business in the wrong direction. Recognition of misinterpretation will then call for the direction of the project to be changed. Typical areas of misinterpretation are overestimating the resource capabilities of the business, underestimating, or missing altogether, a competitor in the marketplace and overoptimism about the potential of a market or a product within it. Clearly, the impact of a misinterpretation on the project will depend on the information concerned and the nature of the misinterpretation. Its impact will depend on the initial assumptions made about the information misinterpreted. The potential consequences of misinterpretation can be minimised by recognising the limitations of the information available, modelling the scenarios that result from changing that information and building appropriate flexibility into the plan adopted. In short, develop a positive cynicism. Always ask: what will happen if this information is wrong? If the consequences are significant, the first step is to check the information. Second, be aware of contingency plans that can be implemented if it is incorrect.

8.8   Responding to project shocks

An effective response to a project shock is the sign of a good manager. Making an effective response to a crisis is evidence of true leadership. By their very nature, shocks are unpredictable. To manage them, consultants must call upon their experiences, insights and reserves of energy. Each shock must be tackled on its own terms. However, there are a series of ground rules that make the management of a crisis effective.

Be prepared

Although the details of a crisis may come as a surprise, crises themselves should not. They are a fact of managerial life. A good consultant expects the unexpected. He or she is prepared to move into action when a shock hits the project. What might go wrong will have been thought through. Scenarios will have been considered. Contingency plans will have been sketched. Critically, the effective consultant is prepared to do what is necessary to get the project back on track.

Avoid panic

Consultants have their own objectives in relation to a project. These are sympathetic to those of the client organisation, but they are different from them. The consulting team will have made an investment in the consulting exercise in order both to make it a good learning experience and to produce evidence (the proposal, the report, the log) that learning has taken place. If this is threatened, panic is a natural response. Team relationships are stretched. Recriminations take place; blame is apportioned. Such a response should be avoided. Panic achieves nothing. If the learning experience is to be salvaged, a cool, measured response is needed. Better than just avoiding panic in oneself is an attempt to control panic in others. An ability to do so is a key leadership trait.

Once the nature of the shock has been appreciated, effective crisis management demands that the following steps be taken.

Refer back to aims and objectives

The first response to a project shock should be to refer back to the aims and objectives of the project. Many events will affect the tasks of the project. They matter only if they have an impact on the achievement of *aims*. Check that they will do so. Ask whether the task profile of the project can be modified so that the original aims and objectives can still be achieved. If resources are cut, can a lower-resource approach offer the same, or at least satisfactory, results? If the objectives are affected, can they be renegotiated within the framework of the original aims? If resources are limited, can some objectives be given priority over others?

These questions should be asked about both the client's aims and your own. If either must be modified, it will be necessary to ensure that the modification retains its compatibility to the other.

Evaluate resource implication

If the shock affects the resources available for the project, the impact of this change needs to be considered. If the resource concerned is financial, the project budget must be reviewed. This is much easier to do if a budget has been prepared (*see* Section 11.3). Activities must be modified or dropped in a way that either least affects the original aims or fits best with new ones. If the resource is a person's skills within the team, the possibility of using other people to cover must be considered. If time and resources allow, an attempt may be made to replace that person. If the person is part of the client organisation, the loss of that relationship must be considered. Ask how that person fitted into the overall profile of relationships with the client. What information was he or she providing? Can new relationships be built with others in the client organisation to replace the person?

Modify plans

After consideration has been given to the impact of the shock on the project's aims and objectives and if necessary these have been modified and resource implications have been evaluated, the next stage is to consider the implications for the project plans. Ask what tasks will be affected. How will their undertaking be affected? What about the time scale of their delivery? What knock-on effects will there be on tasks further downstream? If the aims and/or objectives are altered, will new tasks be needed? Will planned tasks have to be dropped? These questions will be easier to answer if a formal plan has been developed.

Communicate

Ultimately, the management of a crisis depends on the effective management of communication. Don't be tempted to hide problems. Rather, draw people in and make them party to resolution of the problem. Consider who will be affected and how. Ask what ideas they might bring to bear on the problem and what resources they can offer towards its solution. Be prepared to brief affected parties. Take a measured approach. Avoid both understating and overstating problems. Ensure that others are informed of all the issues. But avoid panicking them. Above all, if there is one rule to effective crisis management, it is this: when communicating a problem try to communicate its solution as well. Or at least open up the possibility of a solution to which others might contribute.

Team discussion points

1 Hold a brainstorming session to identify the types of evidence that demonstrate progression of the consulting project through delivery of its subsidiary objectives. Once ideas dry up on the types of evidence, move on to classify them (say in quantitative–qualitative/documentary/non-documentary, etc.). Finally, consider how these different types of evidence will work given the spectrum of consultant–client interactions. Do some types of evidence work better with one type of interaction or another?

2 Consider the way in which your team is working. On an individual basis, consider how team working might be improved and develop a change strategy using the ideas in this chapter. Each present a one-page summary of the strategy to the other team members. Where are areas of agreement and disagreement? How might these be reconciled?

Summary of key ideas

- Understanding the relationship the consultant has with the client is important as it determines how a project is conducted.
- All those in the client company that the consultant interacts with should have a clearly defined role.
- Benchmarking involves anticipating and generating evidence that the journey is progressing to plan.
- Individuals within an organisation often resist change, especially if it is seen as 'change for change's sake'.
- Kotter has developed a generic eight-stage model for effective organisation change management.
- This model specifies a number of interactions that the consultant can call upon to effect successful organisational change dynamics.
- Consulting projects can be knocked off course for a variety of reasons. Usually shocks result from changes in client interest, external events or changes in resource availability.

■ An ability to respond effectively to a project shock is the sign of a good consultant. Key elements in a response strategy are preparedness for what might happen, a focus on the implications for the aims of the project, analysis of the resource implications and how this affects plans and communication of the issues.

■ Good leadership in a crisis situation is characterised by a measured response, control of panic in others and an emphasis on solutions rather than problems.

Key reading

Cope, M. (2003) *The Seven Cs of Consulting: The Definitive Guide to the Consulting Process* (2nd edn). Harlow, Essex: FT Prentice Hall (Chapters 3 and 6).

Fombrun, C.J. and Nevins, M.D. (2004) *The Advice Business: Essential Tools and Models for Management Consulting.* Upper Saddle River, NJ: Pearson Prentice-Hall (Chapters 12, 13, 17 and 23).

Further reading

Drennan, D. (1992) *Transforming Company Culture.* Maidenhead, Berkshire: McGraw-Hill Education Europe.

French, W.L. and Bell, C.H. Jr (1998) *Organization Development.* Upper Saddle River, NJ: Prentice Hall.

Hayes, J. (2002) *The Theory and Practice of Change Management.* Basingstoke, Hampshire: Palgrave.

Kotter, J.P. (1996) *Leading Change.* Boston, MA: Harvard Business School Press.

Moss Kanter, R. (1985) *Changemasters.* Chichester, West Sussex: Jossey-Bass Wiley.

Scott-Morgan, P. (1994) *The Unwritten Rules of the Game.* New York: McGraw-Hill.

Scott-Morgan, P., Hoving, E., Smit, H. and van der Slot, A. (2001) *The End of Change.* New York: McGraw-Hill.

Senge, P. (2006) *The Fifth Discipline.* London: Random House Business.

Schaffer, R. (2002) *High-Impact Consulting: How clients and consultants can work together to achieve extraordinary results.* Chichester, West Sussex: Jossey-Bass Wiley.

Springer, J. (2003) 'Shifting the unwritten rules of organizational behavior', *Systems Thinker,* 14 (3), 6–7.

Werr, A., Stjernberg, T. and Docherty, P. (1997) 'The functions of methods of change in management consulting', *Journal of Organizational Change Management,* 10 (4), 288–307.

Argyll Chemistry

Argyll Chemistry is a small chemical analysis laboratory providing mineral chemical analysis to the local mining industry. It has a staff of 19. The senior management team consists of three people: Dr John Argyll, the MD, Joan Argyll, his wife, who is the finance director, and Dr Paul Ohmes, who heads chemical services. The fourth member of the management team, Carl Allen, has a more junior role, is relatively new and is responsible for marketing and business development. Three staff deal with administrative and office support. The remaining 12 employees are technical staff. They are grouped into three teams. A development chemist who has three analytical technicians reporting to him or her heads each team.

Joan has called in a consulting team to look at the firm's business base. She is concerned about the decline in the local mining industry and believes the firm should broaden its customer base. She has put Paul Ohmes in charge of coordinating the project with the team. A proposal has been developed and agreed with Paul. The main thrust of the project is an investigation of the possibility of the firm offering its services to the textile, food and paints industries that operate in the area. A small sum of money has been put aside for telephone and postal surveys. The team intends to deliver its report to Paul.

The project has gone well. Paul has taken an interest and has supported the consulting team. He has introduced the team to other members of the management team. All seem to be keen on the project. The team has noted, however, that Carl is not particularly helpful. He has missed a meeting and has been slow in providing information. This has not hindered the progression of the project too much, though. Three months after the start of the project, however, the team discovers that Paul is leaving to join another firm. They contact Joan, who informs them that Carl will be assuming management of the project. The team try to contact Carl but find that he will not be available for some time.

Q1 What are the implications of this project shock?

Q2 What actions should the team take in order to make sure that the project progresses to its conclusion?

Q3 How might different team roles (*see* Section 11.1) contribute to the resolution of the shock? You may find it helpful to consider the different types of client involved (refer back to Section 1.5) and their roles (Section 8.3).

Creative approaches to analysis

Learning outcomes

The key learning outcomes from this chapter are to:

■ recognise the importance of a *creative approach* by the consultant;

■ understand the basis of different *analysis strategies*;

■ appreciate how information may be *visualised*;

■ understand the different *cognitive styles* managers use to make sense of the world and the cognitive strategies they bring to bear on problems;

■ be able to use a variety of *creativity-enhancing techniques*.

9.1 The importance of creativity and innovation

One of the most fundamental changes in the way managers approach their tasks has been the growth in the information available to them. At the touch of a button a manager can now call up an amount of information it would have taken a manager just one generation ago weeks, if not months, to collect. This information can take a variety of forms: it may be numerical information, facts, commentary, opinions or items in a list. Despite the growth in the availability of information, managers' jobs do not seem any easier. If anything they are harder. Managers must learn not only to make decisions but also to collect, manipulate and store ever more data upon which effective decision-making must be based.

Ultimately, most managers have access to the same information about the competitive world they work in. 'Secrets' are less important in business than many think. Information technology makes data on the business and its environment readily available. Numerous commercial and government organisations offer information and analysis on business sectors. Modern market research techniques can quickly identify new potential business opportunities. The Internet provides a stream of information on customers, suppliers and competitors.

Competitiveness is built not so much on *access* to data but on ability to *use it effectively*. Underpinning this is the ability to identify and adopt an appropriate analysis strategy so that data become information and information becomes the knowledge that leads to effective decision-making. Analysis may call upon straight-forward and familiar techniques. The simplest may be so trivial that they may not be recognised as analysis at all – the addition of sales from different product lines to produce an overall sales figure, for example. At the other end of the scale there are techniques that are extremely sophisticated and demand an intimate knowledge of their manipulation if they are to be used properly. Many statistical methodologies used in market research fall into this category.

Whatever the analysis technique adopted, analysis is an area where the consultant can add value. The consultant creates value by identifying the client's decision-making requirements, directing the client towards the right technique, assisting him or her in using it and helping to identify the insights it offers.

9.2   Analysis strategies

Fundamentally, analysis is about identifying the patterns and relationships that exist in data. An analysis strategy is a specific way of manipulating data so that such patterns and relationships can be revealed. Data in their raw form are not very informative. Our minds are the product of evolutionary pressure. Humans, like all the great apes, are primarily visual animals. Our evolution has not equipped us to make sense of rows and tables of figures. What it has done is make us good at making decisions when faced with clear verbal or visual codes. A good analysis strategy orders and organises data so that they are converted into verbal or visual codes that can inform decision-making. Most of the analysis strategies used by management consultants make use of one or a combination of the following basic approaches.

Categorisation

Categorisation is a process whereby data, facts or items are sorted into different groups by virtue of their features. This allows the significance of the information to be identified. Categorisation is different to classification. Categorisation uses internal criteria. Classification uses externally imposed criteria. Categorisation makes no demands on theoretical insights, whereas classification does. Important examples of categorisation used in management include the strengths-weaknesses-opportunities-threats ('SWOT') model and the political-economic-sociological-technological ('PEST') model used to analyse a business and its situation (as discussed in Section 6.1). Here factors that make an impact on the business are sorted on the basis of their type, making their implications clearer.

Classification

Classification is also a process whereby items are sorted into different groups. This time, however, the groups are defined by external criteria rather than by arbitrary features. An example of the use of classification is Porter's generic strategy model (1980). Here, a business's strategy is defined as cost leadership, differentiation or focus. These criteria are theoretically a priori. They are derived from theoretical insights as to how businesses compete. These strategies do not have simply an arbitrary relationship to each other (as do the categorisation examples). Rather, they are defined by the external criteria of competitive approach and business scope.

Porter's generic strategies are a specific example of *strategic group analysis*. This is a powerful technique, which can provide an insight into the structure of an industry and the competitive environment of an individual firm. The method involves identifying the factors that characterise players in an industry and determine how they compete. These factors are then used to classify the players into different strategic groups. This technique has been used extensively to help managers understand their competitive environments and position their firms within them. Peteraf and Shanley (1997) offer a good review of the technique. Strategic groups are explored from a cognitive perspective by Reger and Huff (1993).

Numerical analysis

Numerical analysis is any technique where numbers are combined in order to understand how they relate to each other. An *equation* or *function* is a 'recipe', which describes in definite terms how the numbers should be combined. Generalised instances of data are represented by symbols – called *variables* – in these equations. Another way of thinking about a function is that it is a *map* that relates one set of data to another.

The simplest form of equation is the *ratio*. In a ratio one number is divided by another so that the relative magnitudes of the numbers, rather than their absolute magnitudes, are revealed. Financial analysis uses a variety of profitability and liquidity ratios to assess the performance and stability of a firm. This is discussed further in Section 6.3. Statistical analysis uses more complex numerical relationships. It is used in a wide variety of business situations, including market research. Management science is a technical discipline that offers a highly sophisticated mathematical approach to support managerial decision-making. It is concerned with using mathematical techniques to model managerial decision-making situations and to calculate optimal solutions and strategies for management problems. It is not normally called upon by managers, but does have important applications in a number of areas, for example determining production capacity requirements and modelling the effect of advertising on sales. Given its mathematical nature, such consulting is usually undertaken by specialist consultants. For the student who would like to explore this avenue of decision-making support, a good introductory text on management science is the 1994 book by Donald Plane.

Association

Association is the recognition that two things are connected in some way. If two things are associated this suggests that the consideration of one thing might be made easier, or more revealing, if the other thing is considered at the same time. An example of association might be the fact that managers usually notice competitors within their own strategic group more than those in other strategic groups. Here the association is made between an organisation's presence in a strategic group and the cognitive picture of competition held by a manager from that organisation. Another example arises from qualitative market research where buyers associate different products and the degree to which they might be substituted with each other. Association might be noticed as a result of using the analysis techniques described. It may be emphasised and enhanced by the use of the visualisation techniques described in Section 9.3.

Correlation

Correlation is more precise than association. It is the recognition that the *variation* in one variable occurs in step with that of another. A correlation may be identified statistically by the measure of a correlation coefficient. A correlation of +1 indicates that the two variables follow each other perfectly and in the same direction. A correlation coefficient of 0 indicates that the two variables are totally independent. A correlation coefficient of −1 indicates that the two variables follow each other perfectly but in opposite directions. An example of correlation might be the fact that in many industry sectors costs are seen to be positively correlated to market share. This suggests that increasing market share might in turn increase profitability. This suggests that a strategy to increase market share will increase not only sales but also underlying profitability. (*See* the review by Bourantis and Mandes (1987) for discussion of this issue.) Correlation suggests that there *might* be a causal link between the two variables but it does not *prove* it. A good correlation is suggestive, though. It is an invitation to explore further for possible causal relationships.

Causation

Causation *explains* correlation. Causation suggests that two variables are correlated because there is a cause and effect link between them. It provides an important insight for management because, if a causal link exists, control of the cause will automatically lead to control of the effect. Care should be taken in assuming the order of causation, though. Suppose that factor A is found to be correlated to factor B. It is true that A might cause B. But it is also true that B could be causing A. It might also be true that both A and B might be caused by a third factor, C. C may or may not be known. If necessary, another concept may have to be introduced in addition to the two known correlates to provide a full picture of what is going on.

The relationship between 'planning' and 'performance' provides a very good example of the problem of assigning cause and effect in management. This is particularly pertinent to us as so many consultancy exercises advocate and involve planning activity. It is a theme discussed critically by Henry Mintzberg in his book *The Rise and Fall of Strategic Planning* (1994). In some sectors it has been observed that there is a link between planning activity and financial performance. This is an *association*. Further, if planning is quantified as the investment of time and effort in creating, documenting and communicating long-range strategies and plans, and performance is measured as return on capital employed, then planning activity and performance vary together in a positive way. This is a *correlation*. From this it is tempting to assume that *planning* results in *performance*. This would certainly be a justification for engaging in it.

However, this is only one possible interpretation of the correlation (which is of the 'A leads to B' type). It is also possible that good performance leads managers to plan (the 'B leads to A' type) or that planning and performance are the result of a third factor (the 'C leads to both A and B' type). Thus we must postulate further variables to understand the full causal picture. We can develop plausible arguments for all three scenarios.

- *Causal link A leads to B*. An example is 'planning is an aid to decision-making'. The argument might run as follows. Performance is improved if resource-allocation decisions are made better. Planning guides decisions about the allocation of scarce and valuable resources. Because these decisions are more effective when planned, the business's performance is enhanced. On this basis planning should be encouraged.

■ *Causal link B leads to A*. An example is 'planning activity is a way of using "spare" resources'. The argument might run as follows. A good performance by the firm brings in resources. Managers want to use those resources. They may see planning as a way of doing so. Planning adds nothing to performance. In fact, it may be positively wasteful; it may, for example, be just a way for managers to show their ability and importance to colleagues. Planning is, in effect, an *agency cost* expended when the firm's managers can afford it. On this basis planning should be discouraged. Reducing planning may even enhance performance further.

■ *Causal link C leads to A and B*. An example is 'planning and performance are both the result of information being available'. The argument might run as follows: if managers have access to a great deal of information, their decision-making will be better, so the firm's performance will be enhanced; they may also feel that, because the information is obviously valuable, they should make maximum use of it. A good way to use it is in planning. Planning not only demands that the information be used; it is a very visible way of using it. Both performance and planning result from the availability of information.

In this case care should be taken about advocating planning activity. Planning itself does not enhance performance (information does). But this is only a 'first order' interpretation of cause and effect. A deeper analysis might reveal that planning activity does in fact influence the type of information managers seek. It might also influence the way information is used to support decision-making. The caveat really shows that simple causal links are difficult to isolate in systems as complex as business organisations. McGuire (1997) considers creativity in relation to hypothesis explanation (broadly, explanations as to why things happen). The context is psychology, but the ideas are widely applicable. He suggests that there are five basis heuristics involved in being creative about hypotheses.

■ **Attention to odd occurrences**

The unusual calls attention to itself. It is easy to dismiss the odd as just that – unrepresentative of the normal. But in being dismissed, the opportunity to build richer hypotheses within which the odd becomes normal might be missed.

■ **Simple conceptual analysis**

Attempts to reclassify and recategorise observations and experiences in new ways so that new patterns and ideas emerge.

■ **Complex conceptual analysis**

Builds on the simple by using more formal deductive, diversifying and meta-theoretic ideas (theories that relate theories together).

■ **Reinterpreting the past**

Re-examining old experiences. Using single and multiple, cross-sectional and longitudinal case studies.

■ **Collecting new data**

Formal collection of new data and its analysis by quantitative and qualitative techniques.

These approaches range from simply thinking about things in fresh ways to using formal, and perhaps, technical techniques. Different consulting demands, and the approach and skills of different consultants, will lead to different levels. What matters to the client though is the original idea – not how it was generated!

9.3   Visualising information

Given our evolutionary heritage, we respond better to pictures than to numbers. Whereas we may not see the relationships present in a table of figures, we will immediately recognise the patterns in a visual depiction of those data. Visualisation offers an immediate representation of a field of data and the interrelationships within it. Visualisation can be used as a strategy on its own or as a supplement to the methods described above: the data may be 'raw' or they may have been generated by an analysis technique. Some of the more important means of visualisation include the following.

Diagrams

A diagram is a representation that has a one-to-one correspondence with the thing being represented. In a diagram, the individual *elements* of the thing represented are depicted. They also retain a depiction of their *relationship* to each other. An important type of diagram is a *map* depicting a geographic area, or a *plan* of a site. Another type of diagram is a *technical figure*, for example that of a machine such as a car engine.

Flow charts

A flow chart is a symbolic representation of a *process*. The stages in the process are represented by stages in the flow chart. The relationships between different stages can then be illustrated. An example is the flow chart depicted in Figure 2.3 to represent the consulting process.

Graphs

A graph is a visual representation of the relationship between two or more variables. Graphs are very good for demonstrating trends and relationships. There are many types of graph. Most personal computer packages offer bar charts, line graphs, pie charts, scatter graphs and three-dimensional surfaces. The selection of the correct graph demands a consideration of the data, the information that is to be communicated, the demands of the audience and the impact desired.

Matrices

A matrix is a visualisation, which uses a compartmentalised grid to depict relationships. Two axes define the grid. Typically, each axis is divided into two intervals

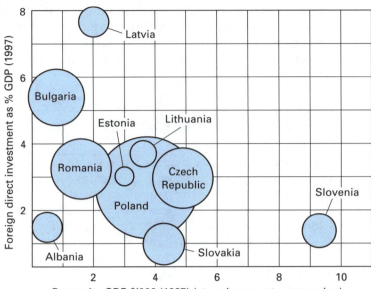

Figure 9.1 An example of information visualisation

Source: Based on data from *The Economist*.

(giving four compartments) or three intervals (giving nine compartments). Such grids are commonplace in management. Important examples include the *generic strategy model* of Michael Porter, the *business expansion matrix* of Igor Ansoff, the Boston Consulting Group's (BCG) *cash-flow matrix* (*see* Hedley, 1977) and the *directional policy matrix* (DPM) developed by Robinson, Hitchens and Wade (1978), three strategic planners with the oil company Shell. A grid is a very efficient means of presenting information in visual form. Up to four dimensions of data can be shown at once. The two axes define the first two dimensions. If a circle is used to depict an item on the matrix then the diameter (or area) of the circle can be used to depict a third. If the circle is replaced by a pie chart, a fourth dimension can be included. Tony McCann (1995) has discussed why matrices are such a powerful means of information display.

Figure 9.1 gives an example of a matrix. Here a matrix is used to present important economic statistics of some central European countries. Three dimensions are shown. The horizontal axis represents 'wealth' (per capita gross domestic product or GDP); the vertical axis represents foreign investment capital inflow; the size of the circle represents the country's population. The relatively large population of Poland, the high level of investment in Latvia and the relatively high wealth of Slovenia become immediately evident.

9.4 Supporting analysis with ad hoc visuals

Verbal communication can be enhanced by the ability to create visual images on an *ad hoc* – as and when needed – basis. Access to the means to create such images can enliven small group discussions. A formal presentation may be supplemented by visual images, perhaps created in response to later questions or to expand on points already made. The means for creating ad hoc visuals can be a simple paper and pen, black or white boards, flip charts or blank acetates and an overhead projector.

The visual information generated has a number of functions:

■ to act as a record of what is being discussed;

■ to explain and explore particular points and issues;

■ to provide a focus for and a guide to the group discussion;

■ to summarise ideas and points of agreement.

The information in the visual image can be built up in stages and can take account of feedback from the audience. Therefore, the creation of ad hoc pictures is a powerful means of explaining complex issues. Some guidelines for making ad hoc visual communication effective are as follows:

1 Plan the image before starting.

2 Start small and in the centre of the available area, so that the image can be freely extended.

3 Build it in stages, checking the audience's understanding at each stage.

4 Invite the audience to contribute to the image.

5 If possible, ensure that someone makes copies of the images and information gathered for later distribution.

Examples of the kind of visual devices that are particularly effective when created in this way are flow diagrams, mind maps, spider diagrams and position maps (discussed below).

9.5   Cognitive style and strategy

We all have our own approach to problem-solving. The way in which we see the world and manipulate, process and store data about it is called our cognitive style. A manager's cognitive style will be a critical factor in how that manager works. A cognitive *style* is different from a cognitive *strategy*. Cognitive style is the fixed set of preferences an individual has for organising information about the world. A cognitive strategy is an approach selected at a particular time to deal with a specific problem. Cognitive style and strategy are important in relation to many practical considerations when dealing with and influencing other people.

Studies of cognitive style provide rigorous insights into the commonsense questions we ask when we wish to communicate with another person. For example, is that person a 'big picture' or a 'small picture' person? Would he or she want to stick to the broad view or would he or she be interested in the details? Should only the 'core' facts be presented or are the facts better located in a wider context? Should the facts to be used in an argument be grouped to reinforce one another or should they be left distinct? How might the manager be positively influenced? By a detailed logical argument or by an emotional plea? Can the manager's existing experience be called upon or should a new way of seeing things be advocated? How will he or she perceive risk? As something to be relished or something to be avoided? Will the manager make a decision now or will he or she want to think about things for a while?

John Hayes and Christopher Allinson (1994) of the University of Leeds have written an excellent review of the work into cognitive style and its importance for management practice. These researchers identified 26 dimensions of cognitive style, which have been described in the literature. The following tabulations are indebted to their review. Necessarily, this summary must be limited. The interested student is referred to the suggestions for further reading at the end of this chapter for a full reference to this work. We have organised the cognitive dimensions described in their study into three categories: the way in which the world is perceived, approaches to problem-solving and approaches to tasks. We have done so for reasons of clarity. It must be recognised that, in practice, perception, problem analysis and task approach interrelate so such a distinction is to an extent arbitrary.

The way in which the world is perceived

Table 9.1 summarises the dimensions of perception.

Table 9.1 Perception

Dimension	Description
Cognitive complexity/simplicity	Cognitive complexity refers to the number of dimensions used to categorise the world. A complex cognitive style uses a large number of dimensions to make sense of the world. A simple cognitive style uses few or even just one dimension.
Analytical/non-analytical conceptualising	Conceptualising refers to the approach taken to distinguish items from each other. An analytical style uses distinct attributes as the basis for differentiating items. A non-analytical style uses broader relationships as the basis for differentiating them.
Levelling/sharpening	This dimension relates to the way new facts are incorporated into the cognitive scheme. A leveller tends to use existing cognitive categories to make sense of and store new experiences. A sharpener tends to set up new categories.
Incongruence tolerance/intolerance	Incongruence tolerance is a willingness to accept unusual events. Intolerance means incongruent events are not accepted. More data and confirmation may be sought in order to make sense of the incongruous.
Verbaliser/visualiser	The use of linear 'verbal' strategies for processing information as opposed to open 'visual' strategies.
Perceptive/receptive	A perceptive approach represents the tendency to process new data by adding to previously held concept categories. A receptive approach indicates a readiness to store the data in an unprocessed form.
Sensing/intuition	This dimension represents the priority given to 'actual' experience rather than feelings or intuition about it.
Thinking/feeling	This dimension has resonance with the one above. It reflects the priority given to the formal evaluation of data over emotional insights into it.
Active/reflective	This dimension reflects the preference for direct engagement in an experience rather than detached observation of it.
Splitters/lumpers	Splitters break down their experience of reality into its component parts. Lumpers group different aspects of their experience into an integrated picture.

Table 9.1 Continued

Dimension	Description
Concrete/abstract	This is the preference for tangible objects over abstract concepts when thinking about the world.
Field dependent/ independent	This categorisation deals with the way in which background information is taken in with pertinent information. Field dependent thinkers tend to take background information into account. Field independent people focus on the essential stimuli and do not take account of background information.

Source: Adapted from Hayes, J. and Allinson, C.W. (1994) 'Cognitive style and its relevance for management practice', *British Journal of Management*, 5, 53–71. © Blackwell Publishing, reproduced with permission.

Approaches to solving problems

Table 9.2 summarises the dimensions of approaches to problem-solving.

Table 9.2 Problem-solving

Dimension	Description
Scanning/focusing	This is the way in which information is selected as relevant to a particular problem. Scanners bring in a wide range of information. Focusers tend to concentrate on only the most immediately pertinent facts.
Converging/diverging	This refers to the approach to a problem. Converging thinking seeks a single, correct solution using formal search criteria. Diverging thinking is broad, open and comfortable in using several solution strategies at once.
Systematic/intuitive	A systematic approach represents the tendency to work through each part of the data in turn in a sequential way. An intuitive approach 'stands back' to get the whole picture from the data.
Serialist/holist	Similar to the above. A serialist approaches problems in a sequential way, working through them one stage at a time. A holist ignores the details and tries to get a global 'fix' on the problem.
Adaptors/innovators	When faced with a problem an adaptor utilises a conventional solution, modifying it if necessary. An innovator attempts to come up with a new type of solution.
Literal-analytic/ poetic-synthetic	This is a cognitive style that relates to the use of analogies in problem-solving. The literal-analytic prefer 'hard' analogies based on one-to-one correspondence. The poetic-synthetic are more comfortable with 'soft' analogies which draw on deeper and more metaphorical correspondences.
Logical/reference point reasoning	Logical reasoning demands a good survey of all available cases before conclusions are drawn. Reference point reasoning draws wider conclusions from limited experience or test cases.
Reasoning/intuitive	The preference for developing conclusions based on logical reasoning versus the preference for developing conclusions using insight and intuition.

Source: Adapted from Hayes, J. and Allinson, C.W. (1994) 'Cognitive style and its relevance for management practice', *British Journal of Management*, 5, 53–71. © Blackwell Publishing, reproduced with permission.

Approaches to tasks

Table 9.3 summarises the dimensions of approaches to tasks.

Table 9.3 Approaches to tasks

Dimension	Description
Automatisation/ restructuring	This dimension refers to task preference. Automatisation implies a preference for repetitive tasks, restructuring a preference for new and different tasks.
Constricted/ flexible control	This refers to the ease with which a manager can be distracted from dealing with a particular problem. Constricted control represents a susceptibility to distraction, flexible control a resistance.
Impulsiveness/ reflectiveness	Impulsive decision-makers make quick responses. Reflective decision-makers take longer to come to a decision. In general, the impulsive are quicker, but the reflective tend to make fewer errors.
Active/ contemplative	This refers to the preference for gaining insight into a problem by active involvement rather than detached contemplation and mental imaging.
Risk taking/ cautious	Risk takers favour options that offer a good reward, even when they have a low chance of success. The cautious avoid any options except those with a good chance of success.

Source: Adapted from Hayes, J. and Allinson, C.W. (1994) 'Cognitive style and its relevance for management practice', *British Journal of Management*, 5, 53–71. © Blackwell Publishing, reproduced with permission.

Cognitive style and strategy are important. They determine the way in which particular issues will come in and out of focus in the manager's attention and surface in the list of priorities. They underlie the way in which the manager might be convinced about a particular course of action. Effective communicators, negotiators and influencers develop an instinct for the cognitive styles used by others. They take them into account when developing relationships. Recognising another's cognitive style and resonating with it is inherent in building rapport (an idea developed in Chapter 7). Although this might look challenging, it is like any management skill, an ability that can readily be developed with practice.

9.6   Mind mapping

The first and most important person the consultant must communicate with is himself/herself. The idea of communicating with oneself may seem a rather strange one. After all, we might argue, we know what's inside our own heads. In fact, the contents of our minds are not transparently available. We do not have instant access to our subconscious. In order to access our thoughts, memories and ideas we must constantly communicate with ourselves. We mentally (or even actually) talk to ourselves. We are engaged in a constant personal dialogue. Recognising this personal dialogue and making use of it can improve analysis. We become more effective when we learn to actively bring up ideas from our subconscious and communicate with ourselves about them. One of the most powerful techniques for doing this is *mind mapping*.

If we write down ideas in an essay form we are constrained to a linear format. Because of the nature of writing (like speaking), one idea must follow another.

Ideas are, at best, connected to two others: the one in front and the one behind. At a fundamental level, our minds do not work like this. Mentally, one idea is connected to a host of others in the form of a *semantic network*. Mind mapping is a technique that explores this network. It does not constrain concepts to be arranged linearly. Tony Buzan in his book *Use Your Head* describes mind mapping very well, along with other creative techniques.

Mind mapping is a straightforward technique. An initial concept is written down in the middle of a blank sheet. This sheet can be as large as is practical. Using lines and/or arrows, the concept is then connected to the next one that comes to mind. The process is repeated. As the map builds, webs and branches of ideas form. Different colours or line styles may be used to relate ideas in different ways. The only rule is that there are no rules! Let your mind run away with itself. Connect ideas even if the connection does not, at first, seem sensible. Innovation comes from creating new relationships. If no new insight is obtained, it does not matter. Don't forget, a mind map is a *personal* communication. There is no need to show it to anyone else if you do not want to. Once a map has been created, further mind maps can be used to rationalise and organise the ideas that develop. By way of an example of the technique, Figure 9.2 illustrates the mind map I used to lay the foundations for this book.

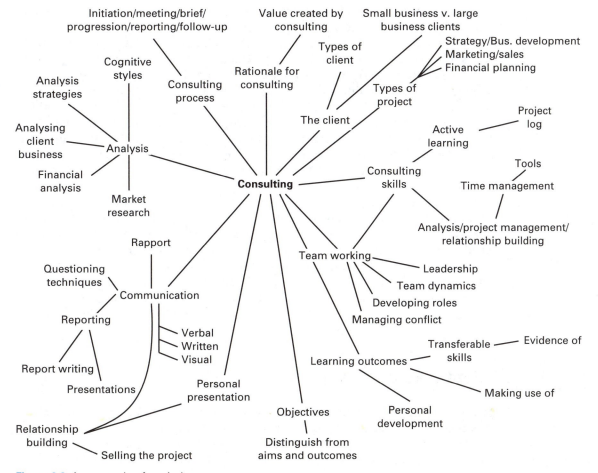

Figure 9.2 An example of a mind map

9.7 Brainstorming

Though it might be undertaken as a group effort, mind mapping is first and foremost a personal creativity technique. Brainstorming is a technique that facilitates group creativity. The creativity of a group is, potentially, more than the sum total of the creativity of the individuals who make it up. By acting in concert to enhance each other's creativity, a group can achieve more than individuals working alone.

To be effective, brainstorming must be organised properly. A facilitator should lead the brainstorming session. (Perhaps, but not essentially, the facilitator will be the group leader. The person in the group who has responsibility for analysis also makes a good facilitator.) Find a room where the session can be held. There should be no disturbances. The room should have presentation facilities such as an overhead projector and acetates or a flip chart. Seating should be comfortable and informal. Everyone should be able to see the overhead or flip chart. Ideally, five to seven people will be involved. Larger groups may be used – more people mean more ideas – but beware! The returns can diminish. The task of the facilitator becomes more difficult as the group becomes larger. If a large number of people can be involved it may be better to split the group into a series of subgroups that can address particular aspects of the issue under study. Ideas may be brought together at the end using a plenary session.

The facilitator should then announce the objective of the session. This might be a statement of the concept, idea or product that is to be explored and what the session aims to achieve. Stimulus material, such as illustrations and examples of products, can be introduced at this stage. The facilitator then invites comments, making it clear that only *positive* comments are allowed. Criticism of others' ideas is not accepted. *All* ideas are transferred to the overhead or flip chart. (The facilitator must resist the temptation to select ideas at this stage.) It is up to the facilitator to control debate, ensure that comments are positive and that the debate is relevant to the objectives. The facilitator should encourage all present to make a contribution.

When the ideas begin to dry up (usually after 20 to 30 minutes) the facilitator should start to draw the debate together. Key ideas are summarised. At this point criticism can be invited. Even at this stage it should be positive. Simple 'rubbishing' of ideas must be discouraged. When this criticism has been completed (some 15–30 minutes) the facilitator can draw the session to a close with a summary of what has been achieved. It is always good practice to produce a written summary of what has been found at the session. This can be distributed to those present. It is a record of the session and may encourage the submission of further ideas.

9.8 Features analysis

Features analysis is a method for encouraging innovation specifically about products and services. It can be built on both mind mapping and brainstorming methods. The first stage is to identify a product or service or a product or service category. The product or service is then stripped down into a list of features that define it in the eyes of its users. The next stage is to manipulate this list so that insights can be gained. Some ways of manipulating features include the following.

Prioritising

Ask the following questions:

■ Which features are most important to the user?
■ What are users willing to pay for?
■ How does this differ between different user groups?
■ To what extent are users willing to play off one feature against another?

Modifying

Ask what happens when features are removed, made larger, made smaller, made more obvious or less obvious, are made variable and so on.

Blending

Ask what happens if features of one product are combined with those of another. How attractive would the hybrid product look to a potential buyer? Figure 9.3 provides an example of features analysis in the form of a mind map.

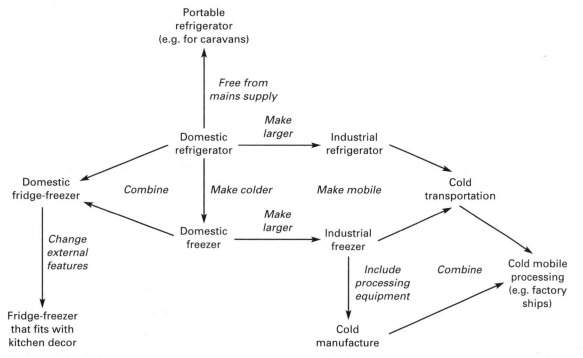

Figure 9.3 A mind map of features analysis on uses for a 'cold box'

9.9 Delphi auditing

Delphi auditing is a technique for gauging the opinion of experts on the development of some issue. It is named after the Oracle of Delphi, a famous classical Greek soothsayer to whom questions about the future could be put. Inspired by this, Oskar Helmer of the Rand Corporation developed the methodology in 1966. Typically the technique is used to explore a development that will have an impact on the way the client business operates but about which there is little consensus. It works well with highly speculative issues. At the time of writing, the development of the Internet as a means of advertising or the impact of a single European currency on business would be good examples.

The first stage is to identify the issue to be explored. This should be thought through in detail. Ensure that the issue is relevant for the client and that it is well defined. Delphi auditing is a form of market research and has the expenses associated with market research. Recognise resource limitations: avoid being too broad in scope and ambitious in detail. A good small study is usually better than a poor broad one.

The next stage is to identify a list of people who have expertise in the relevant area on a secondary research basis. This can be easily obtained by consulting appropriate articles, papers and books. The experts selected may be academics, consultants or industrialists. The third stage is to produce a questionnaire for the experts. The usual rules of postal questionnaire surveys apply. Make sure the questions are definite and unambiguous and will provide answers to the issues you wish to address. Be careful to distinguish between questions that demand a specific response (which can be quantified later) and those that invite general comment. General comments may need to be coded later as respondents may offer quite expansive suggestions.

For example, look at Exhibit 9.1 that presents two very different approaches to asking a question about the same issue. Don't make the survey too long. Your experts are likely to be busy people. While they will answer a short survey, a long one may put them off. Encourage them with a covering letter explaining the project and its objectives and an offer of a copy of the survey analysis. Include a post-paid reply envelope. Once the first survey is complete and has been analysed, a follow-up survey can be used. This will present the findings of the first survey and ask the experts to comment on it (*see* Exhibit 9.2).

If the issues are still unclear, a third cycle may be included. Don't forget that a Delphi audit does not give definite answers. It is merely the best consensus of the experts selected for their views. Don't assume that the 'average' response is the one that will occur. Look at the range of responses and evaluate the different scenarios that will result.

Exhibit 9.1 General and specific questions compared

General question

Some people have suggested that the Internet will be an important medium for advertising in the future. What are your views? Make your notes in the space provided. Please append a further sheet if necessary.

Specific question

How important do you think the Internet will be as an advertising medium, compared with other advertising media, in the future? Please indicate your views in the table below.

	Not important at all					Extremely important				
	1	2	3	4	5	6	7	8	9	10
Years from now										
1										
5										
10										
20										

Exhibit 9.2 An example of a follow-up survey question

We recently surveyed a number of experts on the impact of the European single currency on small business. It was suggested that three factors would benefit small businesses. These are:

1 reduced transaction costs;

2 predictable interest rates;

3 elimination of exchange rate fluctuations.

How important do you think each of these will be? How do you think their impact on (a) manufacturing and service firms and (b) domestic sales and export sales will differ in importance?

Team discussion points

Discuss whether or not you think these statements are true.

- 'Individuals are born creative; they cannot be taught to be creative.'
- 'Creativity is the responsibility of particular team members with particular roles. It is not the responsibility of the team as a whole.'
- 'Facilitating client creativity is fine. But it can leave the client feeling that the consultant has simply "sold them their own ideas back" and not added any real value.'

Summary of key ideas

- Business success is not dependent only on having access to information. It is also based on using it to create new insights and spot new opportunities.

- An analysis strategy is a means of manipulating data so that patterns and relationships can be revealed. Important elements of an analysis strategy include using categorisation, classification and numerical analysis followed by identifying associations, correlations and causal linkages.

- A good way to reveal patterns and relationships in data is to visualise them. Important visualisation techniques include diagrams, flow charts, graphs and matrices (grids).

- All managers have their own cognitive style, which influences the way they see the world, and their own cognitive strategy, which influences the way they identify with information, process it and use it to tackle problems and tasks. An understanding of cognitive style and strategy can help with the development of communication and can influence strategies.

- A number of techniques can facilitate individual and group creativity. Particularly useful to the consultant are mind mapping, brainstorming, features analysis and Delphi auditing. These may be supported by ad hoc visuals.

Key reading

McCann, A. (1995) 'The rule of 2 × 2', *Long Range Planning*, 28 (1), 112–15.
LeBlanc, Jill (1998) *Thinking Clearly: A Guide to Critical Reasoning*. New York: Norton (Introduction).

Further reading

Bourantis, D. and Mandes, Y. (1987) 'Does market share lead to profitability?' *Long Range Planning*, 20 (5), 102–8.
Buzan, T. (1995) *Use Your Head*. London: BBC Publications.
Hayes, J. and Allinson, C.W. (1994) 'Cognitive style and its relevance for management practice', *British Journal of Management*, 5, 53–71.
Hedley, B. (1977) 'Strategy and the business portfolio', *Long Range Planning*, 10 (2), 9–15.
Helmer, O. (1966) *Social Technology*. New York: Basic Books.
McGuire, W.J. (1997) 'Creative hypothesis generating in psychology', *Annual Review of Psychology*, 48, 1–30.
Mintzberg, H. (1994) *The Rise and Fall of Strategic Planning*. New York: Prentice-Hall.
Peteraf, M. and Shanley, M. (1997) 'Getting to know you: A theory of strategic group identity', *Strategic Management Journal*, 18 (SI), 165–86.
Plane, R.D. (1994) *Management Science: A Spreadsheet Approach*. Danvers, MA: The Scientific Press Series.
Porter, M.E. (1980) *Competitive Strategy: Techniques for Analysing Industries and Competitors*. New York: Free Press.

Reger, R.K. and Huff, A.S. (1993) 'Strategic groups: A cognitive perspective', *Strategic Management Journal*, 14, 103–4.

Robinson, S.J.Q., Hitchens, R.E. and Wade, D.P. (1978) 'The directional policy matrix – a tool for strategic planning', *Long Range Planning*, 11 (3), 8–15.

Segev, Eli (1995) *Corporate Strategy: Portfolio Methods*, London: Thomson Publishing.

Case exercise

Businesses in the chemicals sector

Table 9.4 Businesses in the chemicals sector

Firm	Annual sales (£m)	Growth (5 yr. av.) (ROCE %)	Profitability %	Product types	Sales base
Gigachem	5000	5	12	Wide range	International
Foodprod	30	10	10	Food additives	UK
Allchem	3500	6	7	Wide range	International
Bioadd	2	32	15	Specialist	Europe
Pharmchem	50	13	11	Pharmaceuticals	UK
Engomat	35	10	10	Engineering products	Europe
Specmat	5	30	20	High purity	Europe
Vorchem	1025	−4	5	Wide range/low cost	International
Marlube	507	−5	11	Lubricants	Europe
Monolay	54	3	21	Surface coatings	UK
Evero	5	10	16	Biotechnology	Europe
Danay	10	8	18	Biotechnology	UK
Emaprod	1502	6	5	Wide range/low cost	International
Vormadol	42	10	14	Lubricants	Europe
Gusta	15	−2	12	Food products	Europe
Drugserv	25	10	14	Pharmaceuticals	Europe
Coatex	150	7	12	Surface coatings	Europe
Megachem	4502	6	6	Wide range	International

The information in Table 9.4 relates to businesses in the chemicals sector. It has been collected using the Internet. Your team has been called in by a manager from Danay. She has asked how strategy in the sector affects performance.

Q1 Develop a visual representation to make the relationship apparent.

Q2 Consider how the presentation proposed might improve consultant and client understanding of key strategic issues.

Q3 Consider how the representation might be used creatively to generate ideas on strategic options.

Analysing decision-making in the client business and the decision context

The main learning outcomes for this chapter are to:

■ appreciate different approaches to understanding decision-making;

■ understand the basis of the traditional model of rational decision-making;

■ recognise the limitations of this model and be sensitive to how decisions are really made in organisations;

■ recognise the types of *decision-making roles* managers undertake;

■ recognise the ways managers *influence* each other's decisions;

■ understand the *dimensions* that can be used to define a particular decision;

■ be able to analyse the decision-making environment the client organisation presents: in particular to recognise how decision-making within the organisation is influenced by the following factors:

 – *organisational orientation* and the prioritisation of technical, selling and marketing activities;
 – different types of *organisational culture*; and
 – different styles of *strategy implementation* process;

■ appreciate the *naturalistic decision-making* approach and how this can inform the consultant's understanding of expert managerial decision-making.

10.1 Approaches to understanding decision-making

We all make decisions all the time. Some are significant, others trivial. Some seem hard, others easy. Some we are conscious of making, others are more intuitive. The study of decision-making is now an established subject in its own right that draws insights from both economics and sociology. Other social sciences, such as political sciences, also provide ideas that are relevant to the consulting context. The study of decision-making splits into three main areas:

■ **Normative:** Normative approaches are concerned with what a *rational* decision-maker will (or should) do. These target some definite objective such as utility (or, for a firm, profit) maximisation. Rational methods are favoured because they indicate decisions that are, in some way, *optimal*. This approach is usually quite mathematical. It features in a lot of finance theory and management science. It can be present in some decision support and planning tools. It is a specialist area, but is one some consultants have an involvement in, especially in financial management, operations planning and risk strategy development.

■ **Descriptive:** Human beings are rarely rational in the way that normative theory predicts or dictates. Deviations from rationality are rarely random, though. They are systematic and have a pattern in the way they deviate from rationality (referred to as biases). The study of actual human decision-making (under laboratory and real-world (so-called 'ecological') conditions) is referred to as the descriptive tradition. The descriptive tradition is important to consultants because they must work with what managers actually do, not what they should do.

■ **Prescriptive:** The third tradition, the prescriptive, is concerned with advising and supporting people (managers, or experts generally) in improving their decision-making skills. Clearly, this is the approach that is of central concern to consultants.

One prescriptive philosophy is that rationality is (always) best, and so the objective of prescriptive interventions is to make managers more rational. There are, however, a number of issues with this. First, who is to say that rational is best? Rational (normative) models are only best if they take into account all managers' concerns. There is no guarantee that they do so. Second, even if rational is best, to find the rational decision may require a high degree of technical knowledge (or support), be involved, time consuming and difficult. Rationality may not always be conducive with decisiveness. Third, even when they know the rational answer, managers may not actually feel comfortable with what it is telling them to do.

So, all in all, a manager may prefer a rough and ready – or 'fast-and-frugal' – approach to decision-making that is straightforward and rapid that gives 'good enough' (if not strictly optimal) answers to a slow, overly analytical approach. Comfort is found in the space between 'paralysis by analysis' and 'extinction by instinct'. Modern approaches to prescriptive advice and technologies take these concerns into account. Prominent here is the naturalistic decision-making approach discussed further in Section 10.11.

10.2 Decision-making in organisations

For an individual, a decision is a choice between two or more courses of action. Complex psychological processes involving recognition of personal need, cognitive style, cognitive strategy and motivation influence individual decision-making. Organisations must also make choices between different courses of action. Organisational decision-making goes beyond the concerns of the individual, however. It involves interactions between individuals. These interactions include the passing of information, discussion about analysis and the negotiation of outcomes. Individual choices are only part of the process of organisational decision-making; organisational decision-making occurs at a level above that of individual decision-making.

The 'traditional' picture of decision-making in organisations sees it as an open process in which the manager seeks information, analyses it in a rational way and then implements the decision through the organisation. Such a picture is represented in the general model of organisational decision-making. The origins of such a model go back to the work of T.T. Patterson (1969). Models of this type, as illustrated in Figure 10.1, highlight six stages in the organisational decision-making process.

Such models are valuable in that they suggest ways in which decision-making may be accessed and influenced. However, they present a somewhat idealised picture of how decision-making really occurs in organisations. As with many models of organisational life they depict the 'essence' of a process rather than its reality. The details of decision-making are often much more complex than such models suggest. Human issues complicate the matter. For instance, managers do not always sit and plan decisions in detail. Information may be limited. Advice, even good advice, may not be appreciated. The manager does not instigate all decisions; some are forced upon him or her. Not all decisions are rationalised through a formal interpretation of choices. Some are impulsive and based on intuitive understanding. Authorisation may not always be 'official'. Execution may be hindered by political concerns and internal infighting.

The consultant aims to influence decision-making in the organisations with which he or she works. It is important that the consultant understands how decisions are made in practice. Every organisation has its own style of decision-making. If the consultant is to be effective in supporting the client organisation in achieving its objectives then he or she must be sensitive to this style: the way in

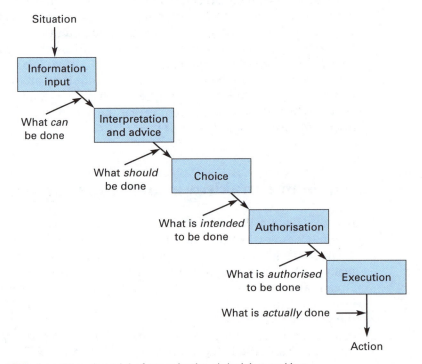

Figure 10.1 A traditional model of organisational decision-making

which decisions are *actually* made, justified and implemented within a business. To do this, four levels of insight are valuable:

- an appreciation of the *types* of decision a manager is called on to make;
- an understanding of *who* is involved in decision-making;
- an understanding of the way in which a decision may be *defined*;
- an ability to define the *styles* of decision-making an organisation can adopt.

This chapter develops models that provide a guide to gaining these insights and using them to influence decision-making in the client business.

10.3   Types of management decision-making roles

Not all decisions are the same. As we discussed in Chapter 1, Henry Mintzberg (1973, p. 77) has defined four distinct types of decision-making role for managers. These are the *entrepreneurial*, the *disturbance handler*, the *resource allocator* and the *negotiator*. We can now reflect on the type of decisions these roles entail.

The entrepreneurial

Entrepreneurial decisions are those aimed at generating controlled change for the organisation. They involve the manager in actively seeking out new opportunities and identifying problems that, although not pressing at present, may limit the organisation in the long term. The manager who initiates entrepreneurial decisions and actively promotes them in the organisation is often called an intrapreneur, a term introduced by Gifford Pinchot in his 1985 book, *Intrapreneuring*. Formal evaluation techniques may or may not be used to evaluate and justify entrepreneurial options.

The disturbance handler

Disturbance-handling decisions are those that are forced on the manager by some crisis or organisational 'disturbance'. Such disturbances take three broad forms. They may result from (a) conflicts between individuals within the organisation; (b) some change in the external environment which affects the way the organisation operates; or (c) a sudden loss in some important resource. Real organisational crises often result from a combination of these three things. Disturbances must be handled quickly and often in a situation of panic and political intriguing. The manager must often act on impulse and insight and may not have time for much formal evaluation of the decision. Decision-making in a crisis is often based on a manager's intuitive knowledge and understanding.

The resource allocator

Resource allocation decisions are those that involve the dedication of resources to specific projects on behalf of the organisation. These decisions may relate to capital investment, the purchasing of the factors the organisation uses or the delegation of particular tasks and work programmes to individuals and groups. The ways in which such decisions are made and justified depend on the significance of the decision to the organisation and its culture.

The negotiator

Negotiation decisions involve debate about and the agreement of outcomes on behalf of the organisation with the other organisations and individuals with which it comes into contact. Important outcomes include the commitment of resources to and the sharing of rewards gained from joint projects. Negotiations take many forms. Some are seen as 'zero-sum' games in which one party must lose if another wins. The negotiator sees a 'pie' of fixed size that can go only so far. The aim is to get the biggest share. Alternatively, they may be more positive and be driven by a win–win attitude. In this case the negotiator sees the parties to the negotiation as able to work together to make the pie bigger for all.

10.4 The decision-making unit

Mintzberg's four roles relate to individual managers. They represent only one dimension of decision-making. A business decision also involves the interaction of managers in groups within the organisation as a whole. The group involved in making a decision is called the decision-making unit (DMU). The key players in the DMU are the decision-maker, the authoriser, information providers, the resource provider, influencers, implementers and gatekeepers.

The decision-maker

The decision-maker is the person called upon to actually make a decision. He or she will be the person who is seen as responsible for the *outcomes* of the decision.

The authoriser

The authoriser is the person who is called on to authorise, modify or sanction the decision made by the decision-maker. In hierarchical organisations the authoriser is often the decision-maker's line manager. In team-based organisations it will be the project leader.

Information providers

Information providers give the decision-maker the information that he or she will use to analyse possible courses of action and then to justify the decision eventually made. Information providers may be part of the organisation but are often external experts called in when needed. Consultants are often information providers.

The resource provider

The resource provider is the person who authorises the use of any resources that are required before the decision can be implemented. The resource provider can be the same person as the authoriser but this is not inevitable.

Influencers

Influencers are individuals who are in a position to change the opinion of other members of the decision-making unit and develop their attitude towards particular decisions. The influencer's role may be formally defined or it might be informal.

Implementers

Implementers are those individuals who must put the decision into effect. Important implementers are production staff, research and development specialists and sales staff.

Gatekeepers

Gatekeepers are those people who control access to other members of the DMU. Personal assistants, secretaries and receptionists are often important gatekeepers. Different decisions call on different DMUs within the organisation. The extent of the DMU will depend on the scope and significance of the decision being made. Routine decisions may be controlled by long-standing DMUs. Non-routine decisions may require the setting up of an ad hoc DMU. Some DMUs are recognised formally – the board of directors, special committees and project teams, for example. Others may be quite informal – the clique of managers who meet for a drink after work, for example. It is possible that the organisation may not even recognise that some informal DMUs are functioning, though their impact on the business may be considerable.

10.5   The dimensions of a decision

The decision-making roles outlined above suggest that all decisions can be described in terms of a small number of features, in particular the significance of the decision, who is involved in making it, how it is justified within the organisation and how it is communicated to the organisation.

The significance of the decision

What impact will the decision have on the business? Is it a major decision defining the future of the business or is it a relatively minor one? What proportion of the organisation's resources will be affected by the decision? How many people within the organisation will be affected by the decision? In general, the more important the decision, the more extensive, and formal, will be the involvement of a DMU.

Who is involved in the decision?

Who is involved in making, authorising and implementing the decision? In other words, what are the structure, function and membership of the DMU that will judge the decision? (*See* Sections 10.3 and 10.4.)

How the decision is justified

How does the decision-maker go about justifying the decision he or she is advocating? There are a number of ways a decision can be promoted within the organisation. For example, it can be through a process of logical analysis (presenting detailed market data, cost analysis and option evaluation, for instance); it can be advocated on the basis of the decision-maker's expertise and past successes ('Trust me – I know what I'm doing!'); it can be insisted upon on the basis of the decision-maker's authority ('I'm the boss and I say it's going to happen!'); it can be made to happen through political manoeuvring ('Help me on this and you'll get my support later!'). In practice, many decisions are promoted in different ways to different members of the DMU. Typically, the consultant will be more formal in his or her decision justification than the organisation would expect its internal managers to be. This is for two reasons. As an outside expert the consultant will be expected to work as an expert – and for many people this means formality. Second, the consultant, lacking experience of the internal situation and formal authority, must rely more on overtly logical justification. Process consulting, though, may deliberately avoid an excessively formal approach.

How the decision is communicated

How will the members of the DMU be informed about the decision? It might be through a formal meeting or presentation. The decision might be communicated in a written format, perhaps by way of a memorandum, or be part of the recommendations in a report. Alternatively the decision-maker may talk it through on an informal one-to-one basis with members of the DMU. It may also travel through the informal grapevine in the organisation. Normally, a consultant will be called on to communicate his or her ideas in a formal way, through a report or presentation, though effective consultants also know how to use informal channels of communication. We can picture a particular decision as located in a three-dimensional space, with the axes defined by the decision-making role, the functioning of the DMU and the features of the decision. This decision-making space is depicted in Figure 10.2.

10.6   Decision-making style and influence

Every organisation has its own style of decision-making. The consultant must recognise this and be ready to use it. Consultants should not challenge the organisation's style of decision-making (not in the first instance anyway, though this may be the objective of change management programmes). They are most influential when they present their arguments in a way that is sympathetic to

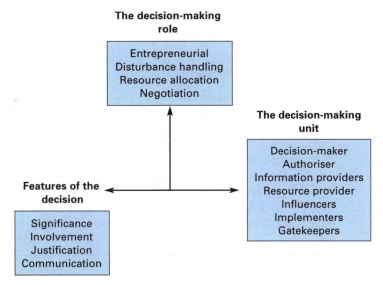

Figure 10.2 The dimensions of a business decision

the organisation's decision-making style. Even if they are involved in a change management project dedicated to developing organisational decision-making skills, they must still work with the organisation's initial style, not against it. In short, a consultant should go with the flow! This presents the consultant with a challenge. How is he or she to understand the decision-making style in the client organisation and then use it? There are a number of models that help provide such an understanding. Three which are particularly valuable are the ideas of *organisational orientation, organisational culture* and *strategy process*. The following three sections explore these.

10.7   Organisational orientation

Businesses are sometimes described as having an orientation. This orientation defines the priorities the organisation sees itself as having and the kind of issues it must address. Three orientations are described: the *production orientation*, the *sales orientation* and the *marketing orientation*.

The production orientation

The production-orientated organisation is primarily concerned with how it makes the things it sells, or delivers the service it offers. The business will prioritise decisions that relate to the developing of products, the setting up of production and the solving of operation problems. These things will be seen to be more important to the organisation than actually creating demand for what it offers. For a business with a production orientation, generating demand for products is secondary to actually making them. The production orientation is often found in new businesses and those that are adopting an innovative approach to production and service delivery. Technologists and operational specialists tend to be important players in decision-making units (DMUs).

The sales orientation

The sales-orientated organisation is primarily concerned with actually *selling* its goods or services to customers. It is interested in creating short-term demand and gaining immediate sales revenues. The business is usually very confident in its belief that what it sells is attractive to its customers – it just needs to get them to buy it! The sales-orientated business can sometimes give the impression that it is seeking power over the customer. Priority is given to decisions focused on sales strategy and (short-term) promotional tactics. The sales orientation is often found in businesses that are in highly competitive markets and those which are underperforming financially. Sales managers are usually key players in the business's DMUs.

The marketing orientation

The marketing-orientated business gives priority to understanding customer demand and developing a means to satisfy it. The business will profess that the customer lies at the centre of the business and that addressing the customer's real needs is the key to performance. It will eschew what it sees as 'hard selling' techniques as unnecessary. The business is usually concerned with developing a strategic approach to its marketing and to product development. These factors will feature strongly in the decisions it makes. Marketing and development people play key roles in DMUs. Many management thinkers advocate the marketing orientation as the 'highest' or 'best' orientation and the key to long-term success. It has been suggested that a business evolves from the production to the sales to the marketing orientation as it grows, matures and learns.

This may be so, but the marketing orientation can only really establish itself in a business that can free its managers to take on the entrepreneurial decision-making role and engage in long-term, self-instigated projects. Hence, the marketing orientation is often found in innovative businesses that have enjoyed a degree of success and in which there are no immediate crises. If a critical issue arises and the disturbance decision-making role is demanded, the marketing orientation can often be dropped in favour of one of the other two. The marketing orientation may be seen as 'unrealistic' or too 'long term' whereas the sales orientation will seem to offer an immediate solution to demand-based problems and the production orientation solutions to supply-based problems that challenge the business. It is a valuable exercise for the consultant to assess the business and determine its orientation. Different parts of the business may have different orientations. This is often the case in larger organisations that have separate production, sales and marketing functions.

10.8 Organisational culture

The idea of organisational culture is one of the most important to enter the management lexicon in recent years. It has been advocated (most notably by Tom Peters and Robert Waterman in their 1982 book *In Search of Excellence*) as *the* most important facet of the business, which can be used to differentiate it from competitors and establish a base for success. Others, it must be added, challenge the way the concept is used by management thinkers and suggest it cannot provide a meaningful management tool. It is not possible to engage in this debate here. All that will be said is that the idea of culture as a description of the 'way a business does things' can be used to give a good picture of the decision-making environment in a business. Charles Handy has described four types of organisational culture in his book *Understanding Organisations* (1993). These are the power culture, the role culture, the task culture and the person culture (or people culture). Consideration of culture in this way can provide a particularly useful insight to the consultant.

The power culture

The power culture is characterised by a strong, central figurehead who dominates the business. He or she is the source of all authority in the organisation. Often the authority is based on ownership of the business combined with personal charisma and leadership. Tasks other than the most routine are delegated by this central figure on a 'need to do' basis. Planning is ad hoc and largely concerned with short-term issues. There is little formality in the business. Procedures are ill-defined and bureaucracy low. It is likely that communication will, in the main, take the form of informal discussions. The central figurehead will dominate any DMUs in the business. He or she may even be the DMU. Power cultures often occur in small, privately owned and entrepreneurial businesses. Power cultures work only in an organisation that is small enough for one person to make all the important decisions.

The role culture

The role culture is characterised by structure and procedures. Individual roles are defined through job descriptions and specifications. An individual's position in the organisation is defined in an organogram. Position bestows authority. The business is likely to be broken up into well-defined departments or functions such as finance, marketing, production and so on. The organisation may engage in formal planning and use it to specify definite goals and future situations. Officially, communication is formalised by the use of regular meetings, reports and memoranda. Informal grapevines are often important as well, though. Decision-making in such organisations is routinised as far as possible. DMUs are extensive, with individuals taking on recognised, official roles. Organisations with role cultures are often quite bureaucratic. They are typically well-established medium to large firms operating in a stable environment.

The task culture

A task culture is characterised by the need to get certain jobs done. Achieving objectives is seen as more important than defining what one's job is. The business is often structured around multidisciplinary teams rather than departments. Authority is based on expertise rather than formal position. Teams may be permanent fixtures or may be set up when needed to undertake a particular project.

Long-term planning may be engaged in but it is likely to be seen as offering a way of gaining insights rather than specifying a definite path. The organisation attempts to keep bureaucracy to a minimum though formal procedures may be established to monitor and provide resources for the activity of the task teams.

Decision-making is centred on the project team who largely constitute the DMU. The authorisers and resource allocators may nominally stand outside the group, but they will be susceptible to advocacy by the group. Businesses with task cultures are often innovative and fast-growing entrepreneurial businesses that are too large for a power culture. They are effective in unstable and rapidly changing environments where decision-making must be 'pushed down'.

The person culture

The person culture is characterised by a prioritising of the needs of the individual over those of the organisation as a whole. Organisations with a person culture resist the imposition of formal structures and procedures though informal ones may emerge. The main concern is with the internal environment rather than with the organisation's relationship with the wider world. Decision-making is informal. DMUs tend to cluster round influential individuals who may exercise unofficial authority based on expertise and/or personal charisma.

This type of culture is hard to sustain, as it can be difficult to reconcile the needs of the organisation as a whole with those of the individual. Organisations with person cultures can find it hard to focus on well-defined objectives and may tend to fragment. They often need support in obtaining resources. Person cultures can be found in some non-profit organisations (public health care, charities and so on) and in religious groupings. Some unorthodox profit-making organisations such as co-operatives may profess or aspire to a person culture. A person culture may also be found in some 'professional' organisations that have a small number of 'highly valuable' people who must be handled with care. Important examples include business support agencies such as advertising agencies, legal firms and management consultants.

10.9   Strategy processes

A business strategy has two sides. One is the *content* of the strategy – this is what the business actually does. The other is the strategy *process* – this is the way in which a business decides what to do. Strategy process is the way a business organises its decision-making. Henry Mintzberg (1973) has described three basic modes of strategy process: the *entrepreneurial*, the *adaptive* and *planning*.

The entrepreneurial mode

Four main features typify the *entrepreneurial* mode of strategy process. First, it is focused on identifying and exploiting new opportunities. Second, entrepreneurial decision-making is concentrated into the hands of a powerful individual. Third, it is concerned with major moves forward rather than incremental or gradual change. Fourth, it concentrates on decisions which offer the possibility of business growth. An entrepreneurial mode of decision-making has resonance with a power culture.

The adaptive mode

The adaptive mode of strategy process is reactive rather than proactive. It represents a response to short-term and immediate opportunities and threats. Four characteristics arise as a consequence of this. First, adaptive decision-making is made by individuals and small groups and is not coordinated by the organisation as a whole. Second, it is not aimed at achieving well-defined long-term organisational goals. Third, adaptive decision-making is incremental. It is concerned with small changes, not with major leaps forward. Fourth, it is disjointed – it may be difficult to relate the logic behind one adaptive decision to that behind another.

The planning mode

The planning mode of strategy making is characterised by systematic analysis and formality. Three features of decision-making arise from this. First and foremost, individual decisions are integrated into and related to an overarching strategy for the business. Second, alternatives are carefully evaluated to assess costs, benefits and risks. Formal techniques may be brought in to do this. Third, not least as a result of the need for the application of formal planning and decision analysis techniques, expert strategic analysts play an important role in the organisation's DMUs.

P.J. Idenberg (1993) has built on these insights by Mintzberg and others and proposed a two-dimensional matrix that defines four types of strategy development process. The axes of this matrix are defined by goal orientation and process orientation. These are defined as follows.

Goal orientation

Goal orientation is the *what* of strategy development. It is concerned with the definition of goals, targets and desired future states for the business. It considers the actuality of decisions and their outcomes. Goal orientation decisions are of the 'where do we want to go?' type.

Process orientation

Process orientation is the *how* of strategy development. It is concerned with the rules and procedures by which strategy making is guided, evaluated and monitored by the organisation. It considers how decision-making will be controlled, rather than what the actual decisions are. Process orientation decisions are of the 'how are we going to get there?' type. Each orientation may be strong or weak in the way it influences organisational decision-making. The options define the 2 × 2 matrix illustrated in Figure 10.3. This matrix has four quadrants, each of which represents a distinct strategy-making style.

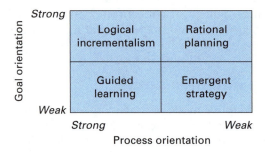

Figure 10.3 The Idenberg matrix for strategy process

Source: Reprinted from P.J. Idenberg, 'Four styles of strategic planning', *Long Range Planning*, 26 (6), 132–7. Copyright © 1993, with permission from Elsevier.

Logical incrementalism

The logical incrementalism style results from the organisation having both a strong goal orientation and a strong process orientation. There is a concern both with *where* the organisation is going and with *how* it will get there. Decisions are monitored and evaluated by pervasive control functions in the organisation. The justification of decisions may be formalised by both systematic analysis and review procedures. Critically, decisions are related to each other. The organisation moves forward in a pattern characterised by small (incremental) and logical (rational) steps. The business may well mistrust 'entrepreneurial' decisions that demand significant leaps into the unknown.

Guided learning

A guided learning style results from an emphasis on the process of making strategy at the expense of what the strategy is meant to achieve. The business may be active in delegating decision-making to local managers. Rather than give them targets, the business expects them to set their own and perhaps to engage in planning activity. However, this will be seen as a way of getting managers to explore their environments and the possibilities the business faces and perhaps even their own thinking modes rather than as a procedure for simply defining objectives.

A guided learning style does not mean managers are free to make any decision they wish. Controls still exist. The organisation will be active in developing managers so that they make the 'right' decisions. This control can be explicit, say through training programmes. It can also be implicit. The organisation may rely on its culture – its 'how we do things around here' – to define and limit management decision-making.

Rational planning

The rational planning style is characterised by an emphasis on meeting definite goals rather than worrying about how managers go about achieving them. In many respects it parallels Mintzberg's planning mode. Definite commercial targets imposed on managers from the top define it. Planners adopt systematic decision-evaluation techniques and decisions are reviewed using formal procedures. Top management carefully monitors the achievement of objectives.

Emergent strategy

In the final quadrant of the Idenberg matrix strategy development occurs in the absence of both strong goal and process orientations. The business's strategy 'emerges' rather than being explicitly developed. As discussed in Section 10.2, managers do not always have the luxury of being able to sit down and plan every decision. Some must be made on the spur of the moment in response to a crisis. Some decision-making may not be guided by consideration either of the organisation's goals or of how it should best go about making decisions. Managers just use their intuition and make them. Entrepreneurs starting a new business rarely consider their decision-making in an abstract sense. They are likely to be more interested in using their decision-making skills to chase opportunities and get the venture off the ground. If they are successful and the business grows (perhaps through a power culture, then a task culture phase), they may never explore, in isolation from the actual running of the business, the way in which the business makes decisions about where it is going and how it is to get there.

This is not to say that emergent decision-making is a free-for-all. It is just that decision-making is controlled by being embedded in the experiences, knowledge and culture of the business rather than by location with reference to externally considered goals and processes. Organisational life is rich and complex. Decision-making is an integral part of the organisational tapestry. These three approaches to understanding organisational decision-making – organisational orientation, organisational culture and strategy process – simplify the complex picture of decision-making. By simplifying it, they make it easier to understand. However, they also present the risk of caricaturing it. They are best used as frameworks that can guide the consultant's experience of the client organisation, rather than as rigid boxes into which 'facts' about the organisation must be forced. Used in this way they can be a valuable tool that can help a consultant convince the client organisation that his or her ideas are worth putting into practice. Evaluation of decision-making style is a critical first step to developing a strategy to communicate ideas to the client organisation.

10.10 External influences on organisational decision-making

Management thinking often, and quite metaphorically, pictures organisations as somehow bounded and separated from the outside world. We talk of an 'internal' environment and an 'external' environment. In reality, of course, organisations are not separated from the 'outside' world by any boundary. Organisations are made up of individuals and individuals come into contact with, and share information with, people who work both within the organisation and outside it. In fact, it is better to think of individuals as having a spectrum of relationships with the organisation from intimate to distant rather than think of those who (formally) work for it and those who do not.

This means that the outside world can influence internal decision-making in a variety of ways, not all of them formal. The overall PEST environment impacts on individual decision-makers in their private lives as well as in their profession. An increase in interest rates, for example, may mean an individual's mortgage will go up. This may influence his or her attitude to risk for the business in addition to the increase's effect on the firm's cost of capital. A bad experience when travelling in a country while on holiday may impact on a decision-maker's attitude towards his firm developing export markets in that country. Comments about a particular supplier made by a friend at a dinner party may have as much, if not more, influence on a decision-maker than those made by a professional colleague within the firm. In short, individuals do not compartmentalise their lives, separating their 'professional' from their 'private' experiences. They make decisions based on their overall, and integrated, life experiences. Good consultants must be aware of this and, at times, draw out decision-makers' general life experiences as well as their professional ones if their decision-making is to be fully understood.

10.11   The naturalistic decision-making approach

Traditional approaches to understanding decision-making, whether normative, descriptive or prescriptive share a number of things in common. They often assume, often implicitly, that a decision problem can be broken down into a series of features – outcomes – that the decision-maker will value in some way (like or dislike) and that the decision-maker will consider options on the basis of whether they will deliver these features or not (perhaps by chance). Orasanu and Connolly (1993) suggest that this approach does not capture many aspects of decision tasks that managers find relevant and take into account. For example, a managerial decision problem is often characterised by having high stakes, being ill-structured, directed at achieving shifting, uncertain and perhaps competing goals, as playing with the interests of people other than self, with the manager paying attention to feedback from earlier decisions and constrained by organisational and social norms in an uncertain and poorly defined environment. As such, an approach that takes these things into account, even if it means dropping formal ideas such as outcomes and probabilities, is valuable. This has become known as the *naturalistic decision-making approach*.

The naturalistic decision-making approach puts emphasis on the following:

- Mental simulations of decision problems (not necessarily concerned with just problem attributes).
- Prioritising assessment of the decision situation, rather than decision options.
- Calling upon (perhaps intuitive and ill-defined) expertise rather than decision models.
- Finding 'good-enough' solutions rather than strictly optimal ones.
- Trying one option, then another, until one that is good enough is found, rather than simultaneously considering all options.
- Being prepared to act before a decision is made, rather than waiting until after the decision to act.

One idea developed by Orasanu and Connolly is that a manager's decision-making will depend on familiarity of the decision situation. The recognition primed decision

(RPD) model suggests that managers judge situations according to whether they demand:

- **A simple match:** Situational cues mean a situation is perceived as typical (prototypical or analogous). This creates expectancies (about what will happen if previously tried actions are taken). Goals are understood and plausible.

- **Developing a course of action**: Situation is not typical, but aspects of it can be integrated with previous goals, actions and expectancies to produce the innovation of a novel approach.

- **A complex approach**: Situation is quite new and has few features that mean past experience can be (directly) called upon. Demand is that decision-maker simulate (tell stories to self and others) about possible decision and outcomes and actively evaluate new possibilities.

The RPD model is useful because managers will use familiarity as a platform for decision effort and inventiveness. Familiar situations will favour tried and trusted decisions and choices. Novel situations will demand a new and inventive approach. The consultant is likely to be engaged with managers involved in all three decision modes, but their expertise is most likely to be demanded when the manager recognises that simple match (and probably developing a course of action) are seen as insufficient. Learning to work at the complex level (both with one's own decisions and supporting the decisions of managers) is a critical aspect of consultants' skill, knowledge and experience.

Managers often have to deal with risk. Calling in a consultant may be motivated by recognition of risk situations. Whatever the objectives of the consulting project, it is likely that risk will enter into considerations in some way and it is inevitable that the consultant will have to consider the risk implications of his or her recommendations. Much normative modelling is concerned with how risk should be valued. In these models, risk is regarded straightforwardly in terms of the probability (chance) that something valued (good or bad) might, or might not, happen. Descriptive research is clear that we do not see risk in this simple way. Lipshitz and Strauss (1997) suggest that when faced with risk, rather than assess outcomes and their probabilities, managers will engage what they refer to as the RAWFS heuristic. This acronym summarises the following ideas:

Reduction	Simplify the situation by concentrating on its critical aspects. The consultant might assist by identifying which aspects are critical and which are (less) relevant.
Assumption-based reasoning	Where information is missing, make assumptions. The consultant can help by providing missing information and challenging (often hidden) assumptions.
Weighing pros and cons	Broad-based evaluation of options in terms of good and bad aspects. The consultant might help by clarifying options and criteria on which they might be evaluated.
Forestalling	Where no clear decision is apparent, make moves that buy time. The consultant might offer creative insights into how this might be done.

Suppression

Where information is complex, or uncertain. Neglect or ignore (suppress) information that confuses and hinders decision-making. The consultant can help by prioritising information and challenging where important information is improperly suppressed.

The naturalistic approach clearly offers a more convincing narrative of managerial decision-making than traditional models (but this does not, in itself, make the naturalistic approach more true or valuable). It does, however, provide the consultant with a 'language' of decision-making that managers can relate to and a perspective on decision-making that invites supportive intervention. The consultant may advocate a naturalistic approach to their own and others' decision-making and use the naturalistic approach as a framework for analysing client decision-making.

Team discussion points

1 Discuss the following statements. Do you believe them to be true or not?
   ■ 'It is the consultant's responsibility to facilitiate client decision-making, not change the decisions the client would have made anyway.'
   ■ 'The naturalistic account sounds more like the way in which managers *really* make decisions than other descriptive approaches. It is therefore a better *theory* of management decision-making.'
2 Consider the project your team is undertaking. Evaluate the risks the project faces (from both your own and the client's perspective). Analyse the way in which your team has interpreted and reacted to those risks using the RAWFS heuristic.

Summary of key ideas

■ The study of decision-making is a mature discipline within the social sciences, drawing from insights in psychology, economics and other areas.

■ It is split into three avenues:
   – Normative: Development of formal, optimising (e.g. profit maximising) solutions to decision problems. This is usually quite mathematical.
   – Descriptive: Concerned with observing and analysing what managers actually do, rather than what they should do.
   – Prescriptive: Developing ideas and approaches and intervening to enhance management decision-making. Nowadays this goes beyond simply telling them to be more rational!

■ Decision-making in organisations can take a number of forms. It may be explicit, open and rational or it can be implicit and based on management intuition.

■ Businesses adopt a variety of styles of decision-making. If the consultant is to see his or her ideas take shape, he or she must work with the client's decision-making style.

■ Managers take on four distinct decision-making roles:
   – the entrepreneurial;
   – the disturbance handler;
   – the resource allocator;
   – the negotiator.

- Decisions in an organisation are controlled by decision-making units (DMUs). The key roles in a DMU are:
  - the decision-maker;
  - information providers;
  - influencers;
  - gatekeepers;
  - the authoriser;
  - resource provider;
  - implementers.

- The four features of a particular decision are:
  - its significance;
  - who is involved in making it;
  - how it will be justified;
  - how it will be communicated.

  Together, the last three dimensions above form the basis of decision analysis.

- A number of frameworks can be used to analyse organisational decision-making style. Three particularly useful ones are:

- *Organisational orientation*: important types include:
  - production orientation;
  - marketing orientation;
  - sales orientation.

- *Organisational culture*: important types include:
  - power culture;
  - task culture;
  - role culture;
  - person culture.

- *Strategy process*: important types include (after Mintzberg):
  - entrepreneurial mode;
  - planning mode;
  - adaptive mode;

  and (after Idenberg):
  - logical incrementalism;
  - rational planning;
  - guided learning;
  - emergent strategy.

- Managerial decision-making is influenced by factors outside the organisation, as well as inside.

- The naturalistic decision-making approach draws away from traditional optimisation approaches to understanding and prescribing effective decision-making.

- It emphasises the ill-defined, uncertain and unstable of both decision situations and decision goals.

- Key ideas are:
  - Classification of decision situations in terms of familiarity (recognition primed decision-making – RPD).
  - Understanding of risk via the RAWFS heuristic.

Key reading

Idenberg, P.J. (1993) 'Four styles of strategic planning', *Long Range Planning*, 26 (6), 132–7.

Lipshitz, R. and Strauss, O. (1997) 'Coping with uncertainty: A naturalistic decision-making analysis', *Organizational Behavior and Human Decision Processes*, 69, 149–163.

Further reading

Gigerenzer, G. (2002) *Reckoning with Risk: Learning to Live with Uncertainty*. London: Allen Lane.

Handy, C. (1993) *Understanding Organisations* (4th edn). London: Penguin.

LeBlanc, J. (1998) *Thinking Clearly: A Guide to Critical Reasoning*. New York: W.W. Norton & Company Inc.

Lipshitz, R., Klein, G., Orasanu, J. and Salas, E. (2001) 'Taking stock of naturalistic decision making', *Journal of Behavioural Decision Making*, 14, 331–352.

Mintzberg, H. (1973) *The Nature of Managerial Work*. New York: Harper & Row.

Mintzberg, H. (1989) *Mintzberg on Management*. New York: Free Press.

Orasanu, J. and Connolly, T. (1993) 'The reinvention of decision making', in G.A. Klein, J. Orasanu, R. Calderwood and C.E. Zsambok (eds) *Decision Making in Action: Models and Methods*. Norwood, NJ: Ablex Publishing Corporation, pp. 3–21.

Patterson, T.T. (1969) *Management Theory*. London: Business Publications.

Peters, T. and Waterman, R. (1982) *In Search of Excellence*. New York: Harper & Row.

Pinchot, G. III (1985) *Intrapreneuring*. New York: Harper & Row.

Plous, S. (1993) *The Psychology of Judgement and Decision Making*. New York: McGraw-Hill.

Zsambok, C.E. and Klein, G. (eds) (1997) *Naturalistic Decision-Making*. Mahway, NJ: Erlbaum.

Case exercise

Inflight entertainment

Sarah had worked with a small manufacturing company as part of a team on an undergraduate consulting project. The firm produced inflight entertainment systems which it supplied to the aircraft-manufacturing industry. The project Sarah had worked on had been instigated and then coordinated by Isobel, the firm's business development manager. Isobel held a middle-ranking position in the firm. Sarah's project involved assessing the potential for developing the firm's presence in the Chinese market. Based on what she had heard about the country, Isobel had a feeling it might offer a lot of potential in the future.

Sarah's team had investigated this. Their final report confirmed Isobel's feelings. They had found that, though at a low base, the average number of air miles flown by a Chinese citizen was doubling every year. The government was also committed to developing China's own aircraft-manufacturing business. This meant a great many new aircraft would be built in China. And, as China grew wealthier through economic growth, the demand for luxuries such as inflight entertainment would grow. It seemed a golden opportunity for the business.

The team established some contacts via the Chinese Embassy and found that a trade fair concerning the right sort of product areas was to be held in Beijing in the near future. In the final report they recommended that Isobel's business give priority to development of the Chinese market and start by making representation at the trade fair. Isobel had been pleased by the report and agreed that a good opportunity had been identified. After Sarah had been invited back by Isobel to do some vacation work one of her first questions was how the Chinese project had gone. Isobel just smiled and said that it had stalled. Sarah asked why.

Isobel explained what had happened. Her manager had been enthusiastic at first. He agreed that China looked like a good opportunity. He asked Isobel to cost out going to the trade fair in China. It proved to be quite expensive, more than her manager was authorised to spend on a single project, and so it had to be taken to a full board meeting for a decision.

Isobel was invited to present the project and what it had to offer to the board of directors. The board was impressed with the analysis Isobel had done but a number of issues were raised. First, the finance director made the point that he had attended a seminar on developing markets where it had been said that the Chinese market, though attractive because of economic growth, was proving more difficult for Western businesses to break into than many had predicted. 'If you want to develop a real presence in China, it's a long haul and takes a lot of investment,' he had said. Then the sales director had insisted that any trade fair must be attended by a trained sales representative ('so we can be sure the right image of the firm is given'). When the dates of the fair were announced he had said that this was during the main campaigns of the year for the launch of a new entertainment system and that he couldn't possibly spare anyone.

Isobel concluded by relating that, in the end, the MD decided that China should wait until the proper level of resources could be made available to invest properly. The project was 'on hold'. Sarah said she thought this was a pity because China had seemed like a real opportunity for the business. Isobel agreed.

Consider the following:

Q1 The type of management decision-making role that Isobel was undertaking when she instigated Sarah's project. (Use Mintzberg's framework described in Section 10.3 as a guide.)

Q2 The DMU roles of each person mentioned in the case study. (Use the framework described in Section 10.4 as a guide.)

Q3 The nature of the decision to move into the Chinese market. (Use the framework described in Section 10.5 as a guide.)

Q4 The orientation and culture in the firm.

Q5 The nature of the strategy process operating in the firm.

Q6 How Isobel's decision falls into the RPD categories (Section 10.11).

Q7 How a RAWFS analysis might be used to explore and enhance Isobel's decision-making.

Consulting project planning and time management

Learning outcomes

The learning outcomes from this chapter are to:

- recognise the *key tasks* which contribute to the consulting project;
- recognise how tasks might be *allocated* between team members;
- develop a *plan* for the project with an allocated budget;
- understand how *meetings* with the client can be made effective;
- be able to *monitor* the project and its progression;
- recognise the value of effective time management;
- understand the simple rules which make time management effective;
- be able to use simple systems to support time management;
- recognise how a *project log* can help the effective delivery of the consulting project;
- know what to *include* in the log;
- be able to select a log *format* that is right for you and your project.

11.1 Individual roles for team members

The advantage of working in a team is that it allows individuals to specialise their contributions. Differentiating and coordinating activities is a way to make the team more effective. It also allows individuals to specialise in the way in which they want and to develop the skills they prefer to use. Some of the types of role the consulting project will demand are as follows. However, one individual may take on a number of these roles in the consulting exercise.

A team coordinator and leader

The team coordinator is the individual who organises the team as a whole, who allocates tasks and ensures that deadlines and targets are met. In short, this person is the project leader. The leadership role will demand assessment and motivation of other team members.

A client contact

As the project progresses it will be important to keep in contact with the client. This requirement will be driven by a need to get information from the client. It will also act to keep the client informed and reassured that the project is progressing. It is better if the client gets to know a particular member of the team and knows that it is he or she whom they can contact. This enables a definite one-to-one relationship to be built. This relationship is the one around which the project rotates. It will be particularly valuable if there is a crisis in the project and objectives need to be renegotiated.

An information gatherer or researcher

The information gatherer is the person who identifies what information is needed for the project, or who receives information requests from other team members and then finds sources of that information. When secondary research cannot provide answers the information gatherer may undertake or initiate primary research.

An information analyst

The information analyst is that member of the team who takes information from the information gatherer and makes sense of it so that it can be used to support decision-making. The analysis may call upon formal techniques that demand numerical manipulation (for example, financial ratio analysis). The analyst can require the use of industry analysis methods (for example, those described by Professor Michael Porter in his 1985 book *Competitive Advantage*). At other times, more intuitive techniques will be used such as mind mapping and brainstorming (discussed in Chapter 9). In these cases the information analyst may facilitate the analytical creativity of the consulting team as a whole.

A report writer

The final report is the physical manifestation of the project as a whole. It is the tangible thing the client is getting from the consulting team. The final report is important. It is not only a communication; it is a representation of the team as a whole. Modern word-processing technology allows the report to evolve. It is not necessary to write and rewrite drafts. A framework can be laid down early in the project and the details can be filled in as the project progresses. It is useful to assign responsibility for this to a particular team member. This person will have responsibility not only for producing the report but also for circulating interim drafts at intervals to get the opinion of other team members. This approach to developing the final report is expanded upon in Section 12.6.

A report presenter

The final report must be delivered to the client. A good report speaks for itself. However, it can be useful for a member of the team to talk the client through it and be available to answer any questions the client may have. The report may be supported with a formal presentation. If so, a member of the team will have to prepare a presentation and lead its delivery.

A team coach

Teams are made up of individuals. And individuals occasionally come into conflict with each other. Disagreements can arise over a wide variety of issues. They may relate to the definition of objects or the management of the project. Often a conflict can arise if more than one person sees himself or herself as the leader of the project. Personal issues outside the bounds of the project may complicate matters. Such conflicts are a normal part of team dynamics (and are discussed further in Chapter 7). However, such disputes need rapid resolution if the team is to work effectively. The team coach is the person who acts as an arbiter and helps reconcile conflicts between members. In a more general sense, the team coach will keep the whole team motivated and interested in the project, especially when the project is going through a difficult patch. Often, but not inevitably, the team coach will be the person who has taken on the leader's role.

There is a great degree of latitude in the way in which these tasks are distinguished, formalised and allocated. Some teams will be quite homogeneous, with all members engaging in all tasks and perhaps only occasionally dedicating specific types of task. Others will operate with a high degree of formality, even to the point of having individual job descriptions within the team. A number of factors drive specialisation. Some of the more important are the size of the team, the nature of the task the team is taking on, the expertise of team members, the longevity of the team, the team leader's style and external influences. These factors are explored in more depth in Sections 7.7 and 7.8.

11.2 Setting a timetable and critical path analysis

Objectives have little meaning unless it is known when they can be delivered. Setting a timetable for the project lets the client know when he or she can expect the outcomes to become available. It is also a way to set signposts so that it can be seen that the project is on track and to highlight when slippage is occurring. A timetable is the basis of effective time management (*see* Section 11.7). A good timetable also ensures that resources are used in an optimal way. The level of detail in the timetable will reflect the complexity of the project. A simple project may need a list of only a few key events. An extensive project will require a detailed list of activities and their interconnections. At its simplest a timetable will be a list of important events and when they will be achieved. It is important to include things like an initial meeting with the client, the preparation of a formal proposal, a period for information gathering, analysis sessions with individuals and perhaps the team as a whole, regular contacts with the client and a period for preparing the final report.

Critical path analysis is a technique that has been developed to aid the management of complex projects. In essence, the technique involves identifying the critical path, the sequence of tasks that will define the schedule for the project as a whole. These tasks must be undertaken in order, and the time needed for undertaking them determines the rate at which the project progresses. Other tasks can be fitted around the critical path. Two American industrialists, J.E. Kelly and M.R. Walker, developed the method to aid plant maintenance in the chemicals

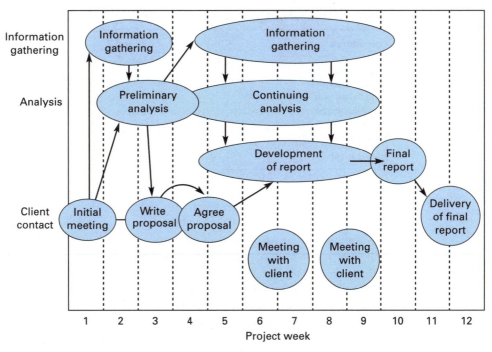

Figure 11.1 A simplified critical path analysis for a consulting project

industry. Critical path analysis has found particular favour in the management of very complex, new product development programmes, designing a new aircraft for example. In such projects, a large number of tasks must be integrated if the project is to be achieved on time and on budget. The method is quite straight-forward. The individual tasks that make up the project are listed. The time needed to undertake the task (and, if appropriate, its cost) is then assigned. The way tasks connect to each other is analysed. Particularly important is recognising when one task cannot be undertaken until another has been completed. Many tasks will not have a unique time period/cost relationship. One can be played off against another. Many tasks can be done quicker – the term is 'crashed' – if more is spent. The relationship between cost and time is called the time–cost curve. Computer software is available to help with critical path planning. Most consulting projects will not have the level of complexity that demands use of sophisticated planning techniques. However, a simplified version of critical path analysis can help organise the project. Figure 11.1 shows how the stages of the consulting project described in Chapter 2 are organised into a critical path. The times shown are typical.

11.3 Project budgeting

Most student consulting projects are undertaken for the experience they offer rather than as a way of generating funds. However, there will still be expenses. The client manager may make some money available to support the project, to

Table 11.1 A typical budget sheet for a consulting project

Expenditure	Period 1	Period 2	...	Period N	Category total
Consultant's fees*					
Travel expenses					
Periodicals and reports					
Commissioned market research					
Telephone and postage					
Report preparation					
Period total					**Grand total**

* (Daily rates × number of days worked)

pay for market research. Being able to cost and budget the project is a useful skill. Even if it is not part of the student project, it is a transferable skill that will be useful in the future. Broadly, budgeting means assigning expenditure in two dimensions: *over time* and by *type of expenditure*. The timescale will depend on the length of the project. Typically, weeks or months are used as the basis. The type of expenditure will depend on the nature of the project. Some of the most common categories of expenditure on consulting projects are detailed in Table 11.1.

The budget has two parts. Expected expenditure is a forecast of what will be spent. This is money that must be reserved for the project. This is replaced by actual expenditure as the project progresses. Comparison can then be made. Actual expenditure is often different from what was budgeted. However, both under- and over-expenditure should be avoided. Over-expenditure means additional funds must be found while under-expenditure means money that could have been used elsewhere is tied up.

11.4   Organising meetings and reviews

Meetings are among the most common of business communication forums. The formality of a meeting with the client will depend on the situation, the relationship with the client, the objectives and significance of the meeting and those present. Meetings are so pervasive as a form of organisational communication that the advantages of actively managing them can be overlooked. Meetings are resource intensive. They are time consuming and can be a distraction. But dividends are available if thought and preparation are put into setting up and running meetings properly. Some key considerations are as follows.

The meeting's objectives

Consider the objective of the meeting. What is it setting out to do? What will be achieved as a result of holding it? How do the objectives of the meeting fit with the objectives of the project as a whole? Are all present aware of the objectives? The project log is a good place to review these issues.

Is the meeting really necessary?

This is an obvious question but one which is well worth asking. Might a less dis-
ruptive and time-consuming form of communication be better? Being called to a
meeting he or she does not feel to be necessary will not impress the client.

Consider who needs to be present at the meeting

Clearly, the members of the consulting team should usually be present at an
important meeting. In principle, the client is free to invite whoever in their organisation should be present. In practice, however, they will often ask the advice of
the consultant. A balance needs to be struck. On the one hand, people are easily
offended if they are not invited to meetings to which they feel they should have
been invited. However, being asked to attend a meeting that is not relevant makes
people feel that their time has been wasted. The solution is to advise the client
to inform people about the meeting and explain its objectives. They can then ask
those informed whether they would like to attend. There will be more commitment to making the meeting successful if everybody attending has requested to
be present.

Plan ahead

Recognise that people are busy and diaries fill quickly. Try to give as much notice
of the meeting as possible to give people a chance to plan their schedules.

Consider what information will be needed at the meeting

Inform people of the information they are expected to bring to the meeting. If
information is to be shared and discussed at the meeting, prepare and copy it in
advance. Consider the way the information might be presented to make it easier
to understand and more likely to have an impact.

Prepare an agenda for the meeting

An agenda should detail the points that the meeting needs to discuss. It should
be distributed in advance, along with the objectives of the meeting and indications of special information that will be required. Make sure that the key roles
have been allocated for the meeting. These include:

1 A *chairperson* who has overall responsibility for coordinating and guiding the
  meeting. This may or may not be the project leader.

2 An *opener* who has responsibility for opening the meeting and giving a short
  verbal presentation (which may be supported with visual stimuli) on what the
  objective of the meeting is and what the background issues are. This person is
  usually the chairperson but having the same person in both roles is certainly
  not compulsory.

3 Someone to take the *minutes* of the meeting. Formal minutes detailing everything that has been said are rarely necessary unless the meeting is particularly

formal. However, a short statement of the objectives of the meeting and details of the key action points decided upon (and who it has been agreed will follow them up) are useful. The minutes should be distributed to all who attend (plus other interested parties) as soon as possible after the meeting. Even if formal minutes are not required, the project log is a good place to keep personal notes on the meeting.

4 Someone to *facilitate* the meeting. This person acts in a neutral capacity and can either arbitrate in conflicts or move things forward if the meeting has become stuck in irrelevant details. External consultants are often called in to perform this role as they are seen as unbiased.

Plan the venue

Planning the venue is the responsibility of the consulting team if they are calling the meeting at their own venue. Make sure the room is adequate for all who wish to attend. Consider seating arrangements. Get into the habit of allocating places rather than just letting people sit where they want. If you know that two people are particularly likely to come into conflict, sit them next to one another rather than opposite one another. (It is much harder to argue with someone who is sitting next to you!) Before the meeting starts ensure that any communication tools (overhead projectors, laptops, beamers, flip charts, etc.) are available, set up and working. Are people seated so they can see them properly?

Maintain focus on the key issues

Meetings are a great chance for people to get together and discuss the host of issues they have on their mind. It is easy for the original objective of the meeting to be lost and the conversation to be diverted into discussion of a variety of unrelated issues. It is the job of the chairperson to maintain the focus of the meeting and ensure that it keeps to its objectives, though a good facilitator can also do this. Learn to recognise when productive discussion on one agenda point has come to an end. When this happens, close discussions on it with a summary of the key points raised and move on to the next point. It is useful to have an idea of the time available for each agenda point to keep the meeting on schedule. If the discussion has drifted on to an issue unrelated to the core business, a good way to redirect the discussion is to summarise the point being discussed and offer to take it to a separate forum. Get those involved in the discussion to agree to this. This simple device can prevent people feeling they have not been allowed to have their say. Pre-agreement on particular contributions may also help keep the meeting on track. For example: 'Right, that brings us to the marketing issues. A, I think you had a number of points to make on that.'

Involve everybody

People vary greatly in their confidence. Some people are open and extrovert. They will contribute easily and with little prompting. Other people are more introverted. They will not feel comfortable about pushing in to make their contribution. This doesn't mean to say that they have nothing to say. Far from it!

The quietest people often have the best ideas. Another important role for the chairperson is to ensure that space is created for everybody to contribute. Doing this involves two things – first, controlling the contribution of extroverts; second, encouraging the contribution of introverts. These two things go hand in hand. If someone is dominating the debate, you cannot just tell that person to be quiet, not without creating a lot of ill feeling anyway! There are a number of useful devices for handling this, such as interrupting with, for example, 'That's actually a very interesting point – how does everybody else feel about this?' or 'Thanks for raising that, A. How will it affect you, B?' The point of these interventions is to move the conversation on while leaving the dominating speaker with the feeling that he or she has made a useful contribution.

Encouraging quiet people to speak is often just a case of redirecting the conversation towards them. For example, 'What's your opinion, A?' or 'How will that affect your approach, B?' If someone is particularly nervous about contributing in meetings it may help to discuss their contribution with them before the meeting and set aside a slot within the meeting for them to make it. It is useful here to recognise how people have differentiated their tasks within the team. If an issue comes up which will benefit from the comments of one who has taken a particular role, use this to draw that person into the discussion.

11.5 The importance of time management and effective time management

Time is one of the most valuable commodities a manager has. Most managers are not limited by knowledge, inspiration or even energy – they are limited by the time they have available to do things. Effectively managing time is rewarding and it is not difficult. It is largely a matter of common sense and practice. It is a good investment. Freeing up time frees up the manager to achieve more. Effective time management is not just about doing more, it is also about *enjoying* doing things more. Managers who manage their time well are in control. They approach their jobs in a more relaxed way. They avoid panics. Indeed, they are in a good position to deal with panics created by others. Appearing relaxed and in control is an important part of demonstrating leadership. Time management is more a matter of good management practice than complex systems. Effective time managers follow a series of simple rules so that they make best use of their time. With a little practice these rules can become second nature. The most important rules are as follows.

Be aware of time

Don't let time catch you out! Deadlines loom up. Recognise that time is passing by. A task may seem a long way off. However, it can quite suddenly become current, especially if the project is a busy one and you are distracted. Be aware of the tasks that are coming up. If you don't have the kind of memory that is good at keeping track of what needs to be done when, a time management system that reminds you (discussed below) can be of great help.

Prioritise tasks

The consulting project will demand that some tasks are undertaken before others. Some tasks will be 'bottlenecks'. If they are not done, many other things will be held up. A critical time management skill is to recognise which tasks are more important at a particular time. Importance is not an absolute. The priority of a task will change as the project progresses. A task that is of low priority can suddenly become high priority, especially if it is delaying the rest of the project.

Anticipate tasks

In short, do tasks when you *can* – not when they *need* to be done. No manager can fill every moment of his or her working life. There are always periods when no job is demanding immediate attention. This is the way it should be. Having periods of low activity is part of the reward for good time management. Such periods are an opportunity. They offer a chance to anticipate and tackle jobs for the future. Assess what jobs can be undertaken now even if they are not an immediate priority. Because they are not being tackled under pressure you will do them better. You will find you enjoy doing them more. Anticipating tasks is an investment. A task that is completed early cannot suddenly present itself as a priority. More low-activity periods are created for the future. More tasks can be anticipated. The process builds itself in a virtuous cycle.

Avoid putting off jobs

We all enjoy doing some things more than others. Team working allows people to undertake a specialised role. Even so, there will still be some jobs we don't feel like doing. It is very tempting to concentrate on those jobs we like and put off those we are not so fond of. This temptation should be resisted. A job which is not enjoyable, when undertaken at ease in one's own time, will be even less enjoyable if it is done under pressure because it is a priority and cannot be put off any further. The job certainly will not be done well under these circumstances. In fact, the best tasks to anticipate are the ones you find least enjoyable. This gets them out of the way and leaves you free to take on those tasks you do enjoy doing. It will also give you time to reflect on the task. Ask why you don't like doing it. What is it about the task that you don't enjoy? Can the task be undertaken in a different way so that it is less onerous?

Break down tasks

Many tasks on a consulting project can be broken down into a series of subsidiary tasks. The final report, for example, involves a series of activities. A structure must be decided for the report. This will be reflected in the contents. A management summary must be written. Diagrams must be prepared. Each of these tasks is to some extent independent of the others. If a complex task is broken down into smaller parts, it may be possible to approach that task in stages. There might not even be a need to write the final report in one go. Modern word-processing technology will allow it to evolve as the project progresses. A structure can be laid down. The body of the report can be filled in as ideas emerge. Sections can be written, and then rewritten. This will ensure that the report communicates the project findings in a professional manner.

Ensure deadlines are understood

Make sure that all involved in the project are clear on deadlines. If in doubt, raise the issue. If you think others are not aware of a deadline, communicate it. Be ready to plan, discuss and negotiate deadlines, especially for non-critical tasks. Make sure that agreement is finally reached and that all are aware of that agreement.

Be prepared

Time when members of the project team meet with each other, or with the client, is particularly valuable. You and other team members will have other projects in progress. The client will be busy with his or her role in the organisation. In fact, the time needed to support the consulting team may be one of the factors leading to the client's resistance to using consultants in the first place. In many cases, this will be a more important factor than the consultant's direct cost. Preparation for meetings not only means contact time is used effectively, it will also project an overall professionalism that will reassure the client. As advocated in the above section, manage meetings effectively. Before a meeting, decide on the objectives of the meeting. What outcomes are desired from it? Define an agenda for the discussion and stick to it. If information is needed, ask whether the client should be given notice so that it can be collated. If the client will need information, make sure it is taken to the meeting. If a detailed response is needed, send the information in advance.

Support others with time management

A consulting project demands that people work together. Someone whose time management is not good can let the whole team down. Effective time managers do not just manage their own time, they help others manage theirs as well. Supporting others in this way is an important leadership responsibility. Always make sure others are aware of deadlines. If someone is having problems with time management, advise them on how they can improve. Set objectives for learning on time management. Don't make the project hostage to poor time managers. Build in interim deadlines so that outputs can be checked before they become critical.

11.6   Time management systems

A time management system has two essential parts. First, a guide to breaking down projects into their component tasks. Second, a means of reminding when the task is due to be completed. A third part, a guide to reviewing the task, may also be included. A time management system is easy to set up. A number of systems are commercially available. However, all that is really needed are a few ordinary items of stationery.

One-page plans

A one-page plan is a flow chart that illustrates the stages of the project. Time is usually depicted along the horizontal axis. Different types of activity are defined on the vertical axis. For a small project an A4 or A5 sheet will suffice. For a complex project a larger sheet may be needed. This may take the form of the critical path analysis discussed in Section 11.2. The project can be monitored as it progresses along the horizontal axis. The jobs coming up, and how they connect to other jobs, can easily be reviewed. The consequences of pushing a task back can also be seen.

Tasks-to-do list

A list of tasks to do is a system that divides the project into intervals (usually weeks or days). Each interval is given a page of its own and on this page the tasks that need to be done can be listed. Some prefer to list only the major task headings. Others like to put in a great deal of detail. It is a matter of how much reminding you need. A bound diary or a loose-leaf folder can be used.

Job cards

A job card system splits the project into task types rather than time intervals. Each task is given its own card with a note as to when it should be completed. The cards can then be sorted into completed, current and to-be-done files. Blank postcards with a file box make a good job card system.

The project log

The project log can be used as the basis of or to support effective time management. A tasks-to-do list can easily be added to the log. A one-page plan can be added at the front. Loose jobs-to-do cards can be stored in insertable plastic sleeves. The project log not only allows you to keep track of tasks and make time management more effective, it also provides a forum for their review, thus making time management part of the active learning programme.

11.7 The function of the project log

A log is a day-by-day record of the consulting project. It summarises the activities, analysis, observations and experiences that occur as the project unfolds. Most professional consultants keep a private log of the consulting projects they undertake. Keeping a log may be part of the assessment procedure for a student consulting exercise. Even if it is not, the fact that professional consultants use one suggests there may be advantages in keeping a personal log in any case. Why should this be so? Keeping a log takes time. It requires a commitment on the part of the consultant. We should always ask the same questions about any activity that demands a significant input on the part of the manager. First: what value is this activity adding?

Second: is the value added worth the effort? These questions must be demanded of the keeping of a consulting project log. This section will make the case that the value created through the keeping of a project log more than justifies the effort needed for its upkeep. This does, of course, depend on exactly how much information goes into keeping the log. This is subject to its format. We will deal with the question of what format to use in detail later in this chapter. The main benefits the log offers are as follows.

It aids project planning activities

A consulting project, like any other project, needs managing in its own terms. Formal project management techniques are valuable (these are discussed in detail above). The consultant must have a detailed and up-to-date schedule of the tasks that need to be undertaken. This demands an understanding of how activities support each other and depend on each other. Once this schedule is in place it provides a series of milestones or benchmarks against which the delivery of the project can be monitored. These benchmarks have a 'what' and 'when' aspect: *what* must have been done and *when* it must have been done by. The log offers a ready device for monitoring the *what* and *when* of these outcomes and for triggering remedial action if an expected outcome does not happen.

It provides a summary of information collected

In order to deliver the consulting exercise effectively it will be necessary to collect information. The amount of information needed will depend on the nature of the project. This information can often be quite extensive. It is not likely that it will be in the form of a neat summary. Articles and reports will be sourced. Statistics and facts will be identified. The log provides a good place to keep key data, a summary of the information collected and references back to primary sources. Ready access to this will make analysis and compiling the final report much easier.

It provides a secure location for notes taken when communicating

A consulting exercise demands both extensive and wide-ranging communications. As the exercise is undertaken a large number of notes will need to be taken as a result of these communications. These will arise from taking minutes in meetings, taking details from telephone conversations and recording the details of interviews. It is tempting not to take detailed notes when engaging in communication with others. It is quite natural to assume that we will retain all the points made during communication in our memory. This is illusory. Our memories are not particularly good. Although we think we can retain everything, details are quickly forgotten. Important and valuable points slip from our grasp. Taking written notes helps in two ways. First, the very act of writing something down helps reinforce it in our memory. Second, it provides a hard source to refer back to when our memories need refreshing. Using the log as a place to keep these notes means they can be found later (odd scraps of paper are always lost). It should also be added that taking notes is a good way to assist in *active listening*.

It provides a forum for analysis

Analysis is an important part of decision-making. Approaches to analysis are discussed in Chapter 9. Analysis acts on information. Information must be processed before it becomes meaningful. Analysis takes a number of forms. It can be calculations performed on numerical data. It might be statistical manipulation aimed at identifying trends. It could be developing a visual representation, such as a graph, so that relationships become clear. It might be generation of a mind map to aid inventiveness and encourage innovation. Whatever its form, analysis must be an active process. Active analysis is best undertaken in a written or visual form. The project log provides a good place to undertake analysis notes. First, using the log encourages analysis to be undertaken where and when it is necessary. This is better than leaving it until later. Doing analysis as the opportunity arises means that its insights are immediately available to guide the project and direct the need for more information. Analysis is usually more productive if the information to be processed is fresh in the mind and the motives for performing the analysis are clear and pressing. The motive for undertaking is the need to know something. If the analysis is sophisticated and is better left to a later time, the log can still be used to make a note about the need to do the analysis. If a piece of analysis is undertaken by the group as a whole, or by one group member on behalf of the group as a whole, copies may be included in other group members' logs. You should not forget that any analysis performed may well be included in the final report to the client. If it is included in the log it will act as at least a first draft that can be accessed easily. This will mean that you will not need to redraft it when writing the final report.

It encourages reflection on the consulting experience

The consulting project is an opportunity to learn. Learning is most effective (and easiest) if it is undertaken actively. Active learning involves a cycle of analysis, practice and reflection. The log, if used properly, can help the development of an active learning strategy. It does this by encouraging reflection and facilitating analysis.

A few questions that you might consider reflecting on within the log include the following:

- What outcomes have been achieved at this stage of the project?
- How do these compare to the project plan?
- How did they compare with my own expectations? (The answer to this question may not be the same as that to the previous one!)
- How might they compare with other people's expectations? (In particular: other members of the group; the client; the project assessors.)
- What has gone well to this stage?
- What made it a positive experience?
- What might have gone better?
- Why were these aspects not such a positive experience?
- How might this experience be improved in the future?

It acts as a permanent record of the consulting exercise

Our memories are not perfect. In some instances it is useful to be able to refer back and find out when something happened, what was undertaken or what was said or agreed at a particular point. The log can be used to store this information. This enables quick and productive review of the project as an aid to reflection on it. The log can be used to establish how much time was spent on a particular activity undertaken on behalf of the project. This can be useful for planning new projects. Information in the log can be used to resolve some of the disputes that inevitably occur when working in teams.

It provides a long-term learning resource

Active learning never ends. The future tends to throw new situations at us. But this does not, of course, mean that our learning from previous situations is of no value. We can only build on the experience we have. The project log can provide us with information that we might use to plan our responses to new challenges. It can offer a guide to personal strengths and the areas that might be developed in the future. It can offer insights into what types of task we enjoy doing (and why). In this respect, many students, for example, find it very useful as a source of points to discuss at job interviews.

11.8 What to include in the project log and suggested formats

The discussion in the previous section gives an indication of the kind of information that can feature in the log. At this stage it is useful to summarise what might be included. Key headings include:

- the date;
- the stage of the project;
- the status of the project (actual outcomes relative to objectives);
- a summary of activities undertaken since the last entry;
- the objectives of those activities;
- minutes of meetings held;
- details of information gathered;
- notes from communications;
- details of analysis undertaken.

And, in addition to these 'routine' headings:

- active learning reflections on the consulting experience.

Of course, the length of the inclusions under each heading will vary. Not every heading will be needed for every day's entry. Detailed reflection on active learning may not be a priority for *every* entry, especially if the project is at a very busy

Project Log – Date: 13 June 2007

Key achievements to date:
- *first meeting with client;*
- *initial analysis undertaken;*
- *team have met to develop first draft of proposal.*

Objectives for next stage:
- *agree proposal with client;*
- *move on to next stage of analysis.*

Note: Meeting to be held next Wednesday – make sure all team know about it. Especially John, who missed last meeting!

Analysis
Client does not seem clear on what he wants. We must get a clear idea by the end of the meeting. Two strategies: (1) we explore options fully and hope that a decision comes out of the meeting; (2) we need to put forward clear proposals – tell him what he needs. It seems we must choose between the expert and doctor–patient modes described by Edgar Schein – task for self: get book out of library tonight to review. After this we must decide who will be doing what.

John
John is starting to be a bit of a problem. He has missed meetings and when he has attended he has not been prepared. I think I need to apply a bit of leadership!

Mind map on how to deal with John

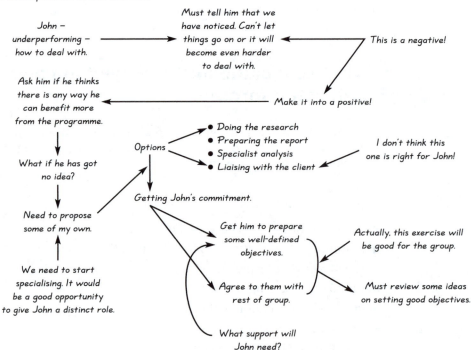

Figure 11.2 An example of a page from a project log

stage and entries are being made every day. Time should be taken at a convenient point to reflect on what has been learned. Text is the main form of written communication and is very useful. However, many people also like to explore ideas using mind maps and other creative devices. The log is a good place to develop and keep these.

The project log is a working tool that the consultant uses to assist in delivering the consulting project. It is a private document. It is not intended to be shown to the client. It is a flow of ideas, comments, notes and reflections. It does not matter if it is rough and untidy in appearance. What matters is that it works as a store of notes on the project and a stimulus to reflection, not that it be polished and presentable. The project log should not be completely lacking in organisation, though. You want to be able to find ideas later. A variety of formats have proved to be effective for organising the project log. You should select one that works for you. You may like the idea of a standardised form that prompts entries under the points discussed above. An example of how this might be filled in is given in Figure 11.2. The blank form may be photocopied when needed. This approach is good because it disciplines thinking about the project. A loose-leaf binder allows pages to be inserted as they are required. It also allows other pieces of information such as notes from meetings to be included. You can add pages if you need more room for later reflection.

However, you may feel that the standardised format is restrictive. You might prefer the latitude to create entries as and when they are necessary in the way you think fit. In this case a bound notebook is best. It is permanent and pages cannot be lost. Notes from meetings can be added as the meetings happen. Leave some room for later reflection though. Odd pages can always be glued in between the bound leaves. Increasingly, some people like the idea of using an electronic notebook for the project log. These are good for generating presentable versions of the log. However, they may tempt one to revise and refine notes to produce a polished document rather than let them stand as honest and immediate reflection on experienced events (which is what they are meant to be). Electronic notebooks can also prove to be slow and may be quite invasive as a way of making notes in a meeting. Whatever format you choose, remember the function of the log is to aid active learning, not to be a history of the project.

Team discussion points

1 Modern word-processing technology means that the final report need not be written at one sitting. It can be evolved as the project progresses. An outline contents list can be laid down and the details can be filled in as information is gathered and ideas develop. Using the team roles discussed in Section 11.1, discuss how each role can contribute to the overall development of the report. How might the logistics of this be managed? What will be the time management responsibilities of each role?

2 In private, consider the formats available for a project log. Decide on one which you think will work for you. Present your format to the rest of the group. Say what you think are its strong points. Invite (positive!) criticism to identify what might be its weak points. After each group member has done this, consider your choice of format. Can it be improved by making some modification? Does another format look better? Select the format you will use for the project. Don't forget, it is an individual choice. It is not necessary that every member of the group use the same format.

Summary of key ideas

- A few simple planning rules can make the consulting project more rewarding and more successful.
- The consulting project will be managed around the key tasks of collecting information, performing analysis, communicating with the client and the overall coordination of the team.
- The team can take on individual roles based on these key tasks.
- Time is one of the manager's most precious assets.
- An ability to manage time makes the manager more effective, in terms of both productivity and, potentially, leadership.
- A number of simple systems can be used to support time management.
- The project log provides the basis for a good time management system.
- The log should include details on the stages of the project, events and communications that take place. It should consider these in relation to the objectives set and the outcomes achieved. It is also a place where information important for the project may be noted and analysis undertaken.
- Critically, the log is a place where reflection on outcomes, both positive and negative, may be made. The log is a private document. It need not be polished for presentation. Experiment with formats and find one that works for you.

Key reading

Blanchard, K. and Johnson, S. (2000) *One Minute Manager*. London: HarperCollins Business.
Nokes, S., Major, I., Greenwood, A. and Goodman, M. (2003) *The Definitive Guide to Project Management*. Harlow, Essex: FT Prentice Hall (Chapters 4 to 7).

Further reading

Applegarth, M. and Posner, K. (1998) *The Project Management Pocketbook*. Alresford, Hampshire: Management Pocketbooks.
Godefroy, C. (1996) *The Complete Time Management System*. London: Piatkus Books.
Newton, R. (2005) *Project Manager: Mastering the Art of Delivery in Project Management*. Harlow, Essex: FT Prentice Hall.
Porter, M.E. (1985) *Competitive Advantage: Creating and Sustaining Superior Performance*. New York: Free Press.
Tracy, B. (2004) *Eat That Frog! 21 Great Ways to Stop Procrastinating and Get More Done in Less Time*. London: Hodder & Stoughton.

Case exercise

Manor House restaurant

The Manor House restaurant is a small but well-regarded restaurant in the south-east of England. It has seating for 30 people and has four bedrooms. The restaurant's manager, Linda Morgan, has invited in a consulting team. The main issue, she explains, is that the restaurant is very busy at the weekend but is empty during the week. Profits and cash flow would be much better if people used the restaurant outside of weekends. Linda has a 'database' of customers (a collection of visitors' books going back five years). She has asked the consulting team if they will go through the book to analyse how often people are using the restaurant. She wants regular customers to be identified. She plans to offer them a special rate if they will use the restaurant during the week. After the meeting, the team agree that the project is not particularly exciting. (They were expecting something more challenging than just going through old visitors' books!)

Q1 How would you approach this situation?

Q2 Develop a strategy to negotiate with Linda and open up the project. You might consider the following:

What are Linda's desired outcomes and how do these relate to the details of the project she has suggested?

Q3 Can the project be broadened in a way that will work for Linda and make it a more rewarding educational and managerial experience?

Robinson Mason case study: Part 3

The best-laid plans are no guarantee of success. Almost as soon as the programme began, tensions were felt within the Ganymede team. The change management consultants (with some exceptions) had a style that immediately rankled with the Robinson Mason members of the team. They used a relentless alien jargon, insisted on carrying out meetings to their prescribed, even regimented, format, and were entirely inflexible in approach. They appeared personally disorganised, required long hours to be worked for no good reason other than to make an impression on local management, disappeared to their own London offices without informing other team members, and spent inordinate periods of time listening to voice mail not necessarily related to the Ganymede programme.

Robinson Mason staff were also unimpressed by the extravagant behaviour of some of the change management consultants, their fondness for expensive restaurants, and their cavalier attitude to air travel. Further, many of the consultants assigned to Ganymede appeared to have been chosen for their own personal development rather than for the skills and knowledge of external benchmarking or current best practice that they might have been expected to bring.

During the in-country visits, the change management consultants invariably took the lead, decreeing the modus operandi, deciding the meeting timetables, and engaging with the local RM staff in a manner that was considered abrupt and at times offensive. They were obsessive about detecting resistance within the team, and would 'gatecrash' meetings that RM members of the Ganymede team had called to discuss their own particular concerns. It later transpired that the autocratic, programmed style adopted by the change management consultants was deliberate. In an unguarded comment, one of them admitted that this approach was essential in order to ensure compliance and control.

The information systems consultants within the Ganymede team, though in essence software salesmen, shared the RM managers' critical view of the change management consultants' behaviour and were seen as allies, fellow human beings, by the RM members in their daily struggle to live and work with their overbearing colleagues. What made matters no easier was the near-impossibility of contacting, let alone meeting, the European business transformation director. He, together with senior members from within the consultants, comprised the Steering Committee – but quite what they were steering, and where they all were, was a mystery to the Ganymede team. Many of the RM members felt they had not had a proper introduction to the programme, that they were being patronised, that their opinions were not sought and their value not recognised.

As the programme moved forwards, it experienced a body blow. Following a reorganisation of the RM board of directors, the European regional director realised that he was no longer to enjoy board status, and resigned abruptly. The Ganymede programme was therefore without its original sponsor and driving force, and simply drifted along without obvious direction. The new European regional director was something of a surprise. An American, he was relatively new to the RM corporation, having briefly run one of its subsidiaries in Latin America. His background was in finance and general management. However, importantly, he did not carry any of the historical baggage, personal friendships and compromises of his predecessor, and could be expected to view the European operation from a detached and unbiased standpoint.

His immediate priority was to deliver the financial numbers inherited from his predecessor. To achieve this, he would require the cooperation and support of his country general managers. Accordingly, he called them all together to a two-day meeting at Gatwick airport, to define a collective vision for Europe, to go through the details of their operating plans, to identify problem areas, and to agree priorities and solutions. Thus the Ganymede programme was by inference deemed secondary to hitting the prescribed targets.

This gave the opportunity they craved to the RM country general managers and others (such as local marketing directors) who had felt so threatened by the Ganymede programme. They stepped up their resistance and stayed wedded to their existing operating styles. Rather than the thorough overhaul of the Robinson Mason European organisation that it purported to be, Ganymede was now presented by them as an extravagant programme intended merely to define common operating procedures so that the integrated software could be installed across Europe. Ironically, they were indirectly assisted in their resistance by the European business transformation director: with an eye to his own future in the organisation, and coveting the likely position of European finance director, he set about making himself an indispensable ally to the new regional director, only too willing to assist him in identifying cost-saving opportunities and distancing himself from the perceived extravagance of Ganymede.

Just at the time that it should have been validating and finalising its proposals, therefore, Ganymede found itself without a champion, but with a new and sceptical regional director, an absentee programme director, a spirit of emboldened resistance within the RM European general managers, escalating costs, dysfunctional behaviour within the team, and the software implementation timetable beginning to recede. Unsurprisingly, the RM full-time team members who had been told that joining the Ganymede programme was a career-enhancing step began actively to seek positions in other parts of the business.

Discussion questions

1 Mutually supportive personal chemistry is vital for effective teamwork. How might the Ganymede team have developed a more positive and purposeful operating style?

2 What are the project management issues implied by the way in which the Ganymede programme moved forward?

3 Do you think the new European regional director either understood or shared the objectives of the Ganymede programme?

4 Critically evaluate the incoming European regional director's initial approach, decisions and leadership style.

PART FOUR

Delivering the product to the client

Communication skills and presenting your ideas

The key learning outcomes from this chapter are to:

- recognise the importance of effective communication to consulting success;
- understand the process of communication;
- be able to establish objectives for communication;
- recognise that communication has rational and emotional aspects;
- appreciate the advantages and disadvantages of verbal, written and visual mediums for communication;
- recognise the importance of delivering your findings to the client;
- understand the means by which those findings can be delivered;
- appreciate some rules which will make the communication of findings more effective.

12.1 The nature of business communication

Communication is a fundamental aspect of our lives. The facility to communicate subtle and complex messages is what enables us to organise tasks: to decide what needs to be done, to allocate different jobs to different people, to discuss how they should be undertaken and to agree how the rewards of that cooperation are to be shared. In brief, communication allows us to build organisations and use them to create value – to manage and undertake business. It is not surprising that understanding communication and being an effective communicator are critical to success as a consultant.

A consultant aims to develop and promote a new course of action for a business. If the business is to take the consultant's advice, the consultant must communicate his or her ideas effectively. But communication is not just about informing people. It is also about motivating them to act in a particular way. Successful management is not just about understanding the business one is in, or even about being able to make the right decisions. It is also about inspiring people, motivating them, developing the power to push ideas forward and taking a leadership role. These skills may seem elusive, but a major part of them is understanding how to be a proficient communicator. To be effective as a communicator one needs to understand communication at several levels. Communication is not just about transferring information: it is about influence as well. Good consultants not only relate their ideas but also actively *advocate* a course and *motivate* others to follow it. People are social beings and when they communicate they interact at many levels. People act as a result of the information they are given and their actions are coloured by the nature, tone and context of the communication as well as its content. Consultants must understand the *how* of communication as well as *what* is to be communicated. As we will see later, effective communication is an integral part of leadership.

Communication can be thought of as a process. As is often the case when relating ideas it is helpful to create a model that can describe and be used to explore them. A general model of communication has been developed which highlights some of the important features of the process. In this model there is a distinction between the sender of the message and its receiver. The first stage involves the decision by the sender on what they wish to include in the message that has to be sent, that is, what information they wish to send. The next stage involves encoding the message in some form, that is, expressing it in some way using a symbolic system – a language of some sort. The third stage involves transmitting the message through some medium. It is possible that the message may be confused by 'noise' interfering in the communication medium at this stage. The fourth stage involves the receiver of the message actually receiving it and decoding it. The fifth stage involves the receiver interpreting and acting on the message. The whole process is governed by a feedback mechanism. The act of communicating is modified in response to the reactions of the receiver. We may illustrate this process in the form of the diagram in Figure 12.1.

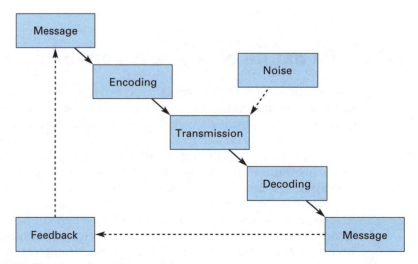

Figure 12.1 The communication process

This model, though quite simple, actually tells us a lot about the nature of communication and how we can go about managing it. In particular it highlights:

- the fact that we never send information directly; it must first be encoded in some way;

- that communication can occur only if both the sender and receiver understand and share the rules of encoding/decoding the message – the language used;

- that the message may be interfered with by noise in the medium through which it is being transmitted – the message may be misunderstood;

- that receiving a message is an active part of the communication process, not a passive one;

- that actions are taken as a result of communication.

These are important points that we will need to keep in mind when we start to consider the management of the communication process.

12.2   Communication as a business tool

Communication is a fundamental aspect of business life. Business communication is not something that is undertaken for its own benefit. Communication is effective only if it leads to the right decisions made and, as a result, the correct courses of action followed. People cannot make the right decisions unless they have the right information to hand. Communication is the means by which people obtain and transmit information and indicate what information they need in order to make decisions. Actions are a result of the decisions that people make. Communication can encourage them to take one particular course of action over others. It is a process governed by feedback. Once initiated, communication leads to further communication. We judge other people's perceptions of our actions by the feedback (response communication) we get. In general, positive feedback encourages or reinforces particular actions. Negative feedback discourages them. Communication, information, decision-making and action-taking are then linked in a loop. Managing communication effectively, using it as a business tool, is about managing this loop in its entirety.

Communication is not simply a passive, background aspect of organisational life; it is the very thing that makes organisations happen. It is therefore important that communication is looked upon as an active part of business activity. And, as with any business activity, the objectives of communication need to be considered. Of course, the extent to which formal and explicit objectives are set will depend on the nature of the communication. A major presentation to the client will demand a formal consideration of objectives. A telephone call to check on some facts will have objectives that are implicit and will not need much explicit consideration. Nonetheless, all communication should be undertaken with some objective in mind. The following is a quite general framework for setting communication objectives. They apply to any communication: not just those between the consultant and client but those between members of the consulting team.

The critical objective is:

- What do I want to happen as a result of this communication?

In other words, the question to be answered is not, 'What do I want to say?' but 'What do I want to happen as a result of saying it?'

Once this objective has been resolved the following questions need to be asked:

- Who will be the recipients of the communication?
- What information needs to be conveyed?
- What actions should the recipient(s) take as a result of the communication?

One of the key actions that the recipient might take is to provide you with some information, so it is also important to consider:

- What information should they give as part of their response? (In other words, 'What do I want them to tell me?')

People act on emotional as well as rational grounds. They emerge from communication encounters feeling motivated or demotivated. So consider:

- How should the recipient *feel* as a result of the communication?

A further question that should be asked is:

- What information do the recipients need in order to act in the way desired?

Don't flood the listener(s) with information. Consider what is the minimum information the audience will need to complete the actions required. Consider whether it will be a hindrance if the recipients have to come back for more information. Or will this in fact help? This question is related to a further one that must be asked:

- What level should the information be at?

How deep is the audience's understanding (and desire to understand) specific details? Do they want a broad picture or a highly detailed account? How technically competent are the audience? How much technical detail do they need? Don't forget that communication is a continuous process, not a one-off exercise. Consider what follow-up actions will be needed as a result of the communication to ensure the desired actions occur. The consultant is engaged in a continual process of communication with the client. This process does more than just transfer information – it is the basis on which an effective and rewarding working relationship is built.

We can integrate these questions into the model of business communication illustrated in Figure 12.1.

12.3   Verbal and non-verbal communication

If the written word is the skeleton of organisational communication then the spoken word is its flesh. Oral communication is so pervasive that we often forget that it constitutes a distinct aspect of organisational life. The types of spoken communication vary enormously and the situations in which it occurs are diverse. Oral communication can occur between just two people, within a small group (the consulting team) or to a large audience. The communication can be one-way or interactive. The forum in which the communication takes place can be either formal or informal. It can occur with the communicators located together, or with the assistance of modern communication technology, separated by enormous distances. Teleconferencing allows long-distance group communication to occur. The spoken word can be 'stored', although this requires the use of sound recording technology.

The advantages of oral communication are:

1 it is flexible: communications can be generated quickly;

2 it is of relatively low cost;

3 the communication can be supported by personal contact: persuasion may be easier;

4 the meaning of messages can be complemented and modified by paralanguage and non-verbal communication (*see* below);

5 it allows instant feedback.

There are, however, a number of disadvantages:

1 It does not (usually) leave a permanent record.

2 It can be difficult to control and direct (especially when large groups are involved).

3 Responses are expected quickly: there may be little time to plan and think ahead.

4 It can easily be dominated, especially where there are strong-willed people with opposing views.

The fact that verbal communication is 'instantaneous' and 'inexpensive' leads to such communication often occurring on an *ad hoc* rather than a planned basis. We can be called upon to respond to an oral communication (say, to give an immediate answer to a question via a telephone call) in a way that we are not with a written communication. We can have time to think before responding to a memo or email. Indeed, as social beings, we are required to indulge in oral communications to a much higher degree than in other forms of communication. Note that every human society has access to a spoken language though, historically, only a minority has found the need to develop written versions of that language.

This insistence that we engage, almost instantaneously, in verbal exchanges means there is a particular challenge in planning for oral communication. However, there is still a great deal to be gained from planning and a little time dedicated to this can reap enormous benefits in terms of its effectiveness. Some situations, particularly those that are formal and those that involve communication to larger groups – presenting the final report, for example – are relatively easy to prepare for. With a presentation or a speech, the planning has a great deal in common with that of written communication. Indeed, the words spoken may be from a written script. With less formal communications, or those to small groups where the oral interaction is highly iterative and built on feedback, the planning may have to occur while the conversation is unfolding.

Planning for oral communication falls into two types: *prior* planning, where what is to be said is decided before the conversation occurs, and *ongoing* planning, which occurs while the conversation is taking place. This second form of planning is, in a sense, more natural in that – to some extent or other – we all do it anyway. Yet, because we are not being given much time to think, it is perhaps the more difficult. It can be made much easier by a little prior thinking about the conversation that is to take place. Oral communication has the same objective as other forms of communication and the same questions, such as the following, should be considered:

- What actions do I wish the recipient of the conversation to take?
- What information should be given?
- What should be the tone?
- How should the recipient feel?

Additionally, however, some consideration should be given to the kind of response the recipients might make:

- What kind of questions are they likely to ask?
- What additional information will be requested?
- What kind of problems and objections might be encountered?

Considering these questions before the communication starts will aid ongoing planning during the communication. It will greatly enhance the effectiveness of that communication. The meaning transferred through verbal communication is not just encoded in the words used, it is also related by how the words are used. The impact of a verbal communication is governed at several levels. The meaning encoded in verbal communications must be considered in terms of *paralanguage* as well as formal language. Speech carries information through the sounds that are made (language). But it also carries important information in the way in which that language is used. Those aspects of spoken language that are not related to the actual content of what is being said are collectively known as *paralanguage*. As an old saying goes: 'It's not what you say but the way you say it.' Paralanguage includes aspects of spoken language such as:

- Tone of voice – indicating emotions, for example anger, expectation, etc.: *They sounded very positive about the idea!*
- Timbre of voice – indicating attitude, for example trembling with apprehension, sneering with condescension, etc.: *It's a complicated idea. I don't understand it. It certainly doesn't help when experts talk down to you about it!*
- Timing – particularly important for indicating degree of consideration and conviction, for example: *The client has finally agreed. Mind you she took some convincing. She paused for ages before she said yes to the budget we proposed.*

Paralanguage is particularly important in communicating the emotional context of what is being said. Consider how flat and unemotional a voice synthesised by a computer can sound. This is because such a voice contains no paralanguage signals. A challenge in planning oral communication that is not encountered in planning written communication is the consideration of non-verbal and paralanguage aspects of the communication. We do, of course, deal with these aspects constantly without really thinking about them. We are, to a great extent, instinctive communicators. If, however, we wish to effectively manage communication and its effects, the ability to consciously control these aspects of our communication is a powerful tool. The fact that there are rational and emotional aspects to all communications means that the effectiveness of communication is an intimate mixture of content and context; of what is said and how it is said. With verbal communications, paralanguage and body language are particularly important signifiers of context. Non-verbal communication includes such aspects of communication as the following.

Facial expression

Particularly expressive elements of the face, changes in which constitute forms of non-verbal communication, are the eyes, eyebrows and mouth. Consider:

> *It was a radical idea – he raised his eyebrows at the thought of it.*
> *She was a bit critical – but with a smile.*

Body language

Body movements add to and extend spoken communication. It is easy to send both positive and negative messages with body language. Most body language signals are sent and received subconsciously.

Posture

The positioning of the whole body with respect to what is being communicated can be a form of expression. An open posture (arms relaxed by the side of the body) is more inviting than a closed, defensive posture (arms folded across the chest).

Gestures

Specific movements may add emphasis, for example pointing, arm opening (indicating welcome), looking at the watch (indicating boredom) or bringing the hand to the chin (indicating consideration). Gesture can mirror meaning. Relaxed body postures are more inviting than tense ones. Facial gestures can indicate whether something is an enquiry or a statement. Open body postures are an indication that the debate is still 'open', closed body postures that it is 'closed'. As discussed above, the objective of business communication is not so much one of delivering information but one of eliciting action. The management of communication can then be considered in two interrelated parts: first, making people receptive to the communication – that is, building rapport – and, second, encouraging them to act on the message – that is, motivating action.

12.4 Written and visual communication

Written communications are the backbone of organisational communication systems. The consultant's report, whether backed up with a presentation or not, is often seen by the client as the 'product' of the consulting exercise – the thing that is actually being paid for. The use of a written medium has a number of advantages in a business context:

1 With the written medium there is time to plan the communication before it is delivered.
2 Written communication is permanent; it can be stored.
3 It is unambiguous: what's written is written!
4 Written communications are easily copied.
5 The receiver has time to analyse the content of the communication at leisure.
6 It can be supplemented with visual communications (e.g. diagrams, graphs, etc.).

There are, however, a number of disadvantages to written communication:

1 It is slow compared with verbal communication.
2 There is little opportunity to modify the communication with paralanguage.
3 Feedback is restricted: there is a limited opportunity for the receiver to explore the communication with the sender (unless verbal communication is used as a supplement). Modern communication technology such as email makes feedback easier. However, it is still slower than verbal communication.

The most important pieces of written communication the consultant makes are the initial project proposal and the final report.

The visual image is a fundamental form of communication. It has a number of advantages:

1 The visual image can be very powerful.
2 It can be used to simplify complex ideas and relationships. (This is an idea discussed earlier, in Section 9.4.)
3 It can be used to support and add impact to other forms of communication.
4 Images are remembered (more so than words).

There are, however, a number of disadvantages:

1 Without supporting explanation the image may be ambiguous.
2 It may require special interpretation skills.
3 Production may be costly.

Visual images used in communication are diverse: diagrams, graphs, photographs, sketches or drawings. Some techniques for visualising information so that patterns and relationships become clear were discussed in Section 9.3. Visual stimuli can be three-dimensional, for example models. The visual image can be used in a variety of communication scenarios:

■ when the subject of the communication is primarily visual;
■ when complicated ideas need to be simplified;
■ when complex relationships need to be demonstrated;
■ when the communication requires emotional impact;
■ when the message needs to be remembered: we remember information in the form of images much better than in a verbal form.

Given its strengths and weaknesses, visual communication really comes into its own when it is used in conjunction with other forms of communication. Some particularly important forms are:

- with written text:
  - diagrams, graphs and charts in reports;
  - images and pictures in product guides;
  - images and pictures in printed advertisements;
- with the spoken word:
  - slides and overheads used in presentations;
  - images in sales presentation materials;
  - images in television and print advertising;
  - models used with small group forums. Particularly important here are stimuli for brainstorming, focus group and other creative sessions.

The visual medium is very effective at representing information in a way that is memorable, draws attention to relationships and has impact. Take it as a rule of thumb that people will remember five to seven pieces of information from a visual image. Try to organise the information that you wish to communicate so that each image has around this number of key points. Key points include not only facts but also relationships between facts; so not only that this year's sales are £2 million but also that they are larger than last year's and smaller than is hoped for next year. Be creative with visual images. Graphs are a good way of illustrating facts and the relationship between them but their impact can be made greater by customising them with bespoke images. Complex arguments can be made clearer by the use of flow diagrams that indicate how different aspects of the argument are logically interrelated. Images can also indicate the way the audience is expected to feel about the information. Imagine a graph of a company's sales performance to which has been added the illustration of a rocket soaring away in flight – or the illustration of a sinking ship!

As a test for a visual image, ask the following questions:

1 If the audience were asked to summarise the image, what five facts would they indicate?

2 How would they feel about those facts? (That is, would they react positively or negatively?)

These points will be developed later in this chapter, when we consider the formal presentation of findings.

12.5 Planning the communication

The communication of the findings of the consulting exercise to the client is an event of great importance. The client is likely to see this as what he or she has 'paid for'. If the consulting exercise was an information-gathering exercise then the communication is the means by which the information is delivered. If the project is offering advice on a business development strategy then the final communication is the means by which that advice is made known. Even if the consulting has taken a process approach and the outcomes delivered are a result of the consultant–client interaction, the final report provides a tangible 'capstone' to the project.

The consulting project will have generated a lot of information and ideas. The main challenge in producing the communication is organising that material so that the message you want to send is delivered in a coherent and convincing way. Barbara Minto, a consultant for McKinsey & Company who went on to specialise in communication, describes one very effective approach in her book *The Pyramid Principle*. The basis is to organise ideas into a hierarchy (a pyramid) so that they are sorted and interrelated. Minto lays down three rules for connecting ideas:

1 Ideas at any level in the pyramid must be summaries of the ideas below them; conversely, ideas at any level may be expanded upon at a lower level.

2 Ideas in each grouping (pathway in the pyramid) must be ideas of the same kind – that is, they must relate in some way and can be grouped together.

3 Ideas in a grouping must be ordered according to some internal logic.

Minto's ideas apply to business communications in general. There are a number of ways in which they might be applied to the challenge of producing a consulting report. The following is my own approach. You may interpret directly Barbara Minto's ideas to devise your own. I use four levels. These are illustrated in Figure 12.2.

The 'big idea'

The 'big idea' is what the whole consulting exercise is about. It is the central theme that unifies the exercise. It should be related to the original aims and objectives of the project. So, the 'big idea' might be 'to expand the business' or 'to improve profit margins' or 'to enter an international market' and so on.

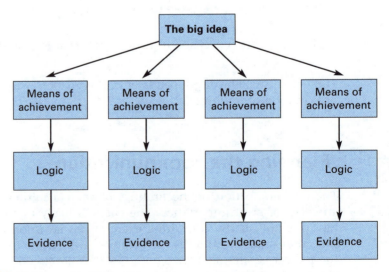

Figure 12.2 The pyramid of ideas for relating consulting findings

Means of achievement

How can the big idea be achieved? Expanding on this is where the consultant adds value. So, if the big idea is to expand the business, this level must expound on the options for expanding the business. It might include increasing market share in existing markets, developing new products or entering new markets. If the big idea is to increase profit margins, the means of achievement level might consider increasing prices, altering the portfolio mix or reducing costs. This level may also be used to close off options which it is felt will not deliver the big idea.

Logic

This third level connects the means of achievement to the big idea. It provides the explanation of why the big idea will be achieved by the means described in the second level. In some cases the logic will be 'obvious' (to you at least). In others it will rely on subtle interpretations. If in doubt, assume your audience would like to have the idea explained.

Evidence

This final level contains any evidence that is available to justify the logic. It might include internal data on sales or costs. It might be data obtained through market research on the market, its potential and the opportunity it presents. It can include discoveries made through creative sessions and explorations of the type reviewed in Chapter 9. Any of these levels can be expanded into sublevels if this helps clarify communication of findings. The pyramid of ideas can be developed as a team exercise through a brainstorming session. An example is shown in Figure 12.3.

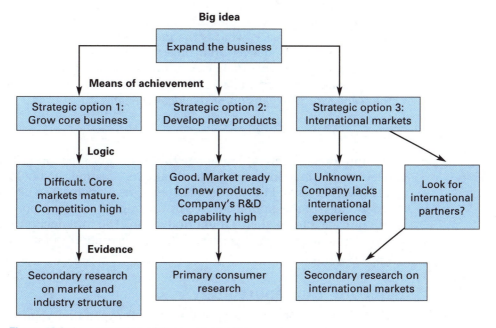

Figure 12.3 An application of the pyramid of ideas

Don't forget, this expansion should be undertaken with a clear view of the objective of the communication. As discussed in earlier in this chapter, a communication objective relates to what you want the recipient to do, not just what you want him or her to know. Presumably, you will want the client to be impressed by your ideas, recognise their value to his or her business and make an effort to implement them. No good consultant would want less.

12.6   The consulting report

A report provides a tangible, accessible and permanent communication of the findings of the consulting exercise. It need not be a long document. In fact, it is a safe assumption that managers do not like to read long reports. What it should be is a succinct and impactful presentation of the opportunity you have discovered for the business. Remember your objectives: it should be a call to action. For an example of a consulting report, please see the Appendix (Marketing plan for Supergelato Ice Cream Ltd).

The report may comprise the following sections.

Executive summary

This is a summary of the findings of the consulting project. But it must be more than *just* a summary. The executive summary is the gateway to the report. It must be short but inviting. A good rule is a one-page maximum. Use bullet points to isolate and summarise your ideas and recommendations. Use an active language style. Be positive. Talk about what the business might achieve if the ideas in the report are implemented. Ask two questions about the executive summary. First, does it invite the reader in? On reading the executive summary will the reader be motivated to delve further into the report? Second, if the reader reads only the executive summary, what is the message he or she will get? Briefly, will the executive summary deliver your objectives for the communication? These two questions may seem contradictory but they are not. If the executive summary is both complete in itself and an invitation to go further it will have impact and set the scene for the expansion of the ideas it relates.

Introduction

The introduction should illuminate the context of the report. It should give any relevant information on the business and its situation. It should also specify the goals, objectives and outcomes that were agreed originally. The introduction will repeat much of the ground covered by the original project proposal. This proposal will provide a template for the introduction. The introduction might be used to give a flavour of what is to come: a further invitation to move into the body of the report.

Body of the report

This is the part of the report where you can expand on your ideas and develop your case. The body of the report can be given a suitable title. It may be broken down into subsections if appropriate. Don't forget, it is generally better to have a lot of short, well-defined and titled subsections than long sections. They make reading and later accessing easier. The pyramid discussed in the previous section can be used to organise the material for the body of the report. It is better to work your way across the levels rather than down the groups. You don't need to provide logic and evidence upfront for every idea. Lay out the skeleton of your overall case first, then flesh out the details later. Be explicit. Tell the reader what your case will be and promise to support it later. Layer your ideas. The written page must be linear. But our thinking is not: it is hierarchical. Expand your themes in a hierarchical manner. Use internal references to signpost where your ideas are going. If the reader feels tempted to jump from one section to another, fine. You may also want to use visual representations of ideas and information. Some techniques are discussed in Section 9.4. A picture really is worth a thousand words!

Summary and recommendations

Remember your objectives. You should close your report with a final call to action. A good way to do this is with a succinct summary of findings and the recommendations listed as bullet points. This format not only repeats the message but also makes the recommendations accessible. We value originality. Some people feel uncomfortable with this approach to report writing. They feel that they are repeating themselves by saying the same thing in the executive summary, the body of the report and then again in the summary of recommendations. So what? It has been observed that a good business communication tells the reader what it will say, says it and then tells the reader what has been said! If the message is a good one, don't be afraid of getting it across.

Appendices

The trick with appendices is to be cynical. Assume they won't be read! They are a good place to put any information that you have used to make your case and that might be of interest to the reader in the future. If the information is valuable to your case then a summary of it (perhaps using a visual representation) should be in the body of the report. Information that will be of use in the implementation of recommendations (say a list of potential customers) should not be hidden away in appendices, it should be highlighted and accessible in the body of the report.

Clearly, the report will speak for you. It will be a representation of your efforts. You should be proud of it. Make time for its planning and preparation. Check the copy and make sure that typographical, spelling and grammatical errors have been removed. Be warned. Many people find it difficult to check their own copy. It is better to have someone other than the report writer to do the copyediting. Modern word-processing technology makes report writing easy. Sections can be added, revised and moved with ease. Spellcheckers take the strain out of copy checking. Impressive visuals can be edited in. A variety of graphics can be used to decorate the report. But ultimately, it is the substance of the report that matters. A simple, well-written, well-laid-out report relating ideas that will have a real impact on the performance of the business is much better than a report rich with graphics but lacking substance.

12.7   Formal presentations

A formal presentation is a very effective means of getting your message across. It allows the message to be fine-tuned using both verbal and visual communications, to get instant feedback from the client and to respond immediately to points and questions. Formal presentations are being used increasingly as a means of inter- and intra-organisational communication. The formal presentation is, however, a challenging mode of communication. To be effective it must be well organised and delivered with confidence. This confidence comes through preparation and practice. It is worthwhile to take time to plan the visual aids to be used. The images need careful consideration if they are to have an impact. They can be relatively expensive and take time to produce and copy, so plan ahead. Some useful points to remember are as follows.

- Analyse the audience. What images will they find relevant and will have impact? What interpretative skills do they have?
- Don't make the images too complicated. Clear, simple images have much more impact.
- Consider the relationships you need to communicate. Use images that emphasise the relevant relationships.
- Don't forget you can use a sequence of images to build up ideas.
- Use the pyramid principle to organise your message.

The images in the presentation should be used to support the presentation. They are *aides-mémoire* for the presenter and add impact to what the presenter says. There are a number of technologies for producing visual material. The oldest and simplest is just a pen and paper. With a little care and attention, quite professional diagrams and graphs can be produced. Word-processing and desktop publishing systems and drawing packages are readily available and with a little practice they can be used to produce sophisticated and professional visual material. Colour is an effective stimulus in visual communication and can be used to differentiate relationships (say, by the use of different coloured lines on graphs). Primary colours have most impact. Desktop publishing packages usually have colour facilities. Colour is reproduced well on overhead acetates and in electronic presentations. Beware, however, if it is intended to photocopy the overheads for later distribution – colour information is lost in black and white copies. A good deal of information can still be represented in black and white by using broken and dotted lines and different cross-hatching styles for areas. The most common devices for visuals are the overhead projector that uses A4-sized acetates and, more commonly now, laptops with electronic presentations, e.g. PowerPoint (these are better for large audiences and more formal presentations). The following are a few points for producing effective visual support of the presentation:

- Remember that the visual material is supporting the presentation not making it! Don't put text on the screen and read from it.
- Keep the images simple. They should add impact to the presentation, not distract from it.
- Put up bullet points to indicate to your audience the key issues you are identifying. These will also act as *aides-mémoire* if you are presenting without notes.

- Use lower-case text. Upper case is austere and can be difficult to read.

- Use a pointer (either a traditional stick or one of the laser type).

- Consider your positioning relative to the projector. You wish to face the audience, not the screen, so position yourself so that you can see the screen with a slight turn of the head. Avoid blocking the audience's view and don't block the image by standing in the light path.

The audience may find it useful to retain copies of the slides you have used, so photocopies may be provided. You must decide whether you wish to give out the copies at the beginning or at the end of the presentation. Giving them out beforehand allows the audience to annotate them during the presentation. However, the audience will inevitably flip through them. They may feel that all they need is in the handouts and so they don't need to follow the presentation in detail. Also you will lose control of when the audience sees particular images for the first time. For these reasons the presentation may lose some of its impact if handouts are distributed first.

The formal presentation can be quite nerve-racking for the inexperienced, but planning, preparation and practice are great builders of confidence. The rules for a presentation are the same as for any other communication. Think about what you want to achieve from it. Be sure of what you want people to do as a result of the communication. Analyse the audience. Some simple rules for an effective presentation are as follows.

- Rehearse and practise the presentation. This is best done as a team. Not everybody need be involved in the actual delivery, but all can add to it.

- Use notes as *aides-mémoire* but try not to read from a script. It is better to consider the points you wish to make and learn them using the visual stimuli as a prompt.

- Time your presentation. Make sure it is the right length for the time available. Make mental notes of some time-points to enable you to time the presentation and make sure it is on track. Place a watch or clock where you can see it discreetly (say, beside the laptop). Avoid looking at a watch on your wrist. It sends a bad message to the audience.

- On the day, dress appropriately, but comfortably. You'll feel much more confident.

- Before the presentation check that the equipment (e.g. overhead projectors, laptops, beamers, microphones, etc.) is working. It is stressful to have to sort out equipment in front of the audience before the presentation can begin.

- Make sure that the slides you intend to use are in the right order.

- When making the presentation use confident body language: make open gestures and avoid the temptation to cross your arms in a protective gesture. Try to make eye contact with the audience. Smile!

- Pace your speech. Take regular deep breaths. This will help control nervousness.

Try not to be anxious about the presentation. The audience are not out to get you! They are interested in what you have to say. With a little practice effective presenting becomes second nature – then you can concentrate on what you want to say! Increasingly, being able to give an effective presentation is a key skill in the modern business world.

12.8   Making a case: persuading with information

Information is needed for making decisions but decisions are not made on the basis of information alone. How it is presented and the context in which it is presented is also important in influencing decision-making. In business, information is usually presented with the intention of encouraging the recipient to take a particular course of action (the 'what do you want the audience to do as a result of receiving the information?' objective). Being influential with information is a matter not only of identifying that information which makes your case but also of delivering it sympathetically to the audience.

Information will be more influential if it:

- is relevant to the decisions the recipient needs to make;
- is pitched at the right level of understanding;
- is presented in a form which makes it easy to understand and digest;
- is supported by impactful visual stimuli;
- is placed in appropriate opinion and feeling contexts;
- is delivered in a situation of good rapport (*see* Chapter 7);
- is part of an interactive process where the recipient is encouraged and supported to explore the information;
- has key points signposted and highlighted.

Don't forget, if you need to organise the information before presenting it, use the pyramid principle described in Barbara Minto's book.

12.9   Answering questions and meeting objections in presentations

Formal presentations usually end with an invitation for questions to be asked. It is useful to develop some skills in dealing with the questions – and their close relative: objections. After having invited questions, look around the audience for signs of someone wishing to ask one. As the presenter you are in control. Even after you have invited questions potential questioners may still be looking for a sign from you that they have a right to speak. Eye contact and a 'yes' will usually be sufficient to elicit the question. When the questioner speaks, really listen to the question being asked. Use active listening. Consider the nature of the question being asked as well as the question itself. Is it a 'head' question, a rational seeking of further information, or a 'heart' question, a more emotionally rooted seeking of reassurance?

Some useful points to remember in answering questions are as follows.

- Summarise the question being asked before attempting an answer. This will ensure that you have understood the question and that the rest of the audience have understood it. It will also give you some thinking time.

- If the question is complex and, in fact, contains more than one question, break it down into individual questions. Indicate that you will answer each in turn.

- Answer the question to the best of your ability. You can do no more! If you do not have the necessary information to hand, say so. Take the questioner's details and offer to get back to him or her with the information. But don't forget to do so!

- After answering a question don't just move on to the next questioner. Close the answer by asking the questioner whether the answer is satisfactory: 'Is that OK?' 'Does that answer your question?' 'I hope that's a little clearer' etc.

Objections are a little more difficult to deal with but there are a few good points to remember. Objections may be more heart than head. They may be individual or may summarise what might be the concerns of the entire audience. Meeting objections may require more than fighting fact with fact. If you come up against an objection, try the following.

- Start by recognising (and even welcoming) the objection: 'Thank you. I'm glad you raised that'; 'Right. I can understand your concerns there'; 'An interesting point. Let me see if I can deal with it.'

- Consider the speaker's feelings when meeting objections (even if he or she doesn't seem to be considering yours). If he or she is seeking reassurance rather than information, give reassurance.

- If the objection is clearly emotional or no answer is obvious, ask a question back. 'This is obviously a major concern for you. Why is that?' 'Have you encountered this kind of problem before?' etc. This will get the objector to explore his or her objection (forcing him or her to put it on a rational footing). It will also give you some thinking time!

It may sound difficult, but learn to regard objections as an opportunity to make positive points.

<table>
<tr>
<td>**Team discussion points**</td>
<td>

1 Go back to the project proposal you have made to the client. Analyse it as a piece of communication. Ask the following questions:

(a) What was the objective of the communication?
(b) Does this objective meet the criteria set for objectives discussed in Chapter 5?
(c) What actions did you want the client to take as a result of reading the proposal?
(d) What is the mix of 'rational' and 'emotional' elements in the communication?
(e) Did you talk the client through the proposal on a one-to-one basis? If not, do you think this might have added to the impact of the proposal?

Discuss these issues in your team.

2 Prepare a short formal presentation (of five minutes with one or two slides) on the theme of what you feel you have gained from the consulting project experience in terms of learning outcomes, transferable skills and enhanced career prospects. Each member of the team should give this presentation and invite (positive) criticism from the other members of the team.

</td>
</tr>
</table>

Summary of key ideas

- An ability to communicate effectively is a critical skill for a consultant.
- Communication is not just about passing information; it is about getting the recipient of that information to act in a particular way.
- Communication has an impact at a rational and emotional level.
- Objectives should be set for communication.
- Communication can take place through verbal, written and visual mediums. Each has its own advantages and disadvantages.
- Verbal communication is influenced by more than just content: paralanguage and body language are also important.
- The final communication of the consulting findings is the 'product' the client is 'paying for'.
- The communication may take the form of a report, a personal presentation or a combination of the two.
- The communication should be planned with the objective of positively influencing the client and getting him or her to implement the ideas presented.
- Using the pyramid principle, organise your message into four levels: the big idea, means of achievement, logic and evidence.
- The most important part of the report is the executive summary: this sells the report to the reader and invites him or her in.
- A presentation should be planned in advance. Impact will be gained if the presentation is pitched to the audience, their level of understanding and interests.
- Visual materials should support the presentation, have an impact and reinforce the key ideas.

Key reading

Zelazny, G. (2006) *Say It With Presentations: How to Design and Deliver Successful Business Presentations*. Maidenhead, Berkshire: McGraw-Hill Publishing.
Minto, B. (2001) *The Pyramid Principle* (3rd edn). Harlow, Essex: FT Prentice Hall.

Further reading

Bowden, R. (2004) *Writing a Report: How to Prepare, Write and Present Effective Reports*. Oxford: How to Books Ltd.
Bradbury, A. (2000) *Successful Presentation Skills* (2nd edn). London: Kogan Page.
DiResta, D. (1998) *Knockout Presentations*. Worcester, MA: Chandler House Press.
Hansen, M.T. and Haas, M.R. (2001) 'Competing for attention in knowledge markets: Electronic document dissemination in a management consulting company', *Administrative Science Quarterly*, 46 (1), 1–17.
Hargie, O. (2006) *The Handbook of Communication Skills*. London: Routledge.

Laborde, G.Z. (1995) *Influencing with Integrity: Management Skills for Communication and Negotiation*. Carmarthen, Dyfed: Crown House Publishing.

Thompson, N. (2002) *People Skills*. London: Palgrave Macmillan (Part II).

Weissman, J. (2006) *Presenting to Win: The Art of Telling Your Story*. Harlow, Essex: FT Prentice Hall.

Case exercise

Holroyd Engineering

Holroyd Engineering is a private company founded some 20 years ago by David Holroyd. The main line of business is machining parts for the automotive industry. The company has 20 employees. David is now 63. He is in the process of passing over control of the business to his son, Donald. However, he still comes in most days. Donald is in his early forties. He heads the management team that consists of four directors. The others are Graham Sullivan, the marketing director, Philip King, the production director, and Tony Milligan, the finance director. Graham, 36, is new to the firm. He joined from a firm of consultants after undertaking a project for the firm. Donald recruited him. David Holroyd recruited Philip, 59, and Tony, 61, shortly after the firm was founded.

Donald Holroyd has called in a consulting team to undertake a full strategic review of the business. He is convinced that it has growth potential that his father has missed. He has asked Graham to lead the project. The team visited the site. Graham had arranged a short presentation on the company and its market. Graham then moved on to show them around. While on the tour they met David. David rather took over and insisted on showing them the latest machine tools. He asked them about the project they were undertaking. When they mentioned looking at the marketing strategy, he grabbed a gear wheel that had just been cut. He held it up. 'Don't worry about marketing,' he said, 'a good product sells itself!'

The consultants have now concluded their work and are due to report to the business at a meeting where all the key players will be there.

Q1 Given the sensitivities outlined above, if you were the project leader for the consultants how would you prepare for the meeting?

Q2 In the meeting itself, what steps would you take as consulting team leader to ensure that the presentation runs smoothly?

Q3 What would be your definition of a successful outcome for this consulting project?

13 Learning from success

Learning outcomes

The key learning outcomes from this chapter are to:

■ learn how to effectively hand over ownership of the project;

■ complete a post-project summary and review;

■ undertake follow-up projects and key client management;

■ use the consulting project as a case study;

■ recognise your success in the consulting exercise;

■ recognise how these successes provide evidence of transferable learning;

■ be able to document these successes on a curriculum vitae and use them to support career development.

13.1 Handing over ownership of the project

In Section 5.5 we discussed the importance of the 'control' phase where the ownership of the project is handed over to the client. The handing over of the project to client management is an important step. It represents the final delivery of the project. It is at this stage that the client receives what he or she feels has been paid for. Hence it is the stage at which expectations are met or, better, exceeded. If this is to happen satisfactorily, it must have been clear from the outset the degree to which the responsibility of the project is about making recommendations or about *implementing* those recommendations. Even if the project is primarily concerned with making recommendations, it is important that these recommendations are presented in an actionable way, so that the client has a clear plan of action to put them into effect and is motivated to do so.

Many consulting exercises often 'fail' at this point because the client does not follow through with the consultants' recommendations. Although the consultant is not exactly at fault because they cannot manage the client after they have left, they do bear some responsibility for not ensuring the implementation phase is not adhered to. It would seem illogical that, having paid for the consultants' time, a client would not implement effectively; but any organisation is a group of individuals, not a homogeneous being. The main reasons why the implementation phase goes wrong are:

- The individuals in the client organisation who are supposed to carry out the implementation of the project are given other priorities.
- The leadership of the organisation is faced with different challenges to those addressed in the consulting project, for example a major new competitor comes on the scene.
- The sponsors of the project leave the organisation or are assigned different roles.
- The funds required to complete the implementation phase are diverted elsewhere.
- The initial momentum is not sustained once the external consultant has left.

Although it is not always possible, a follow-up meeting three to six months after the end of the project is a useful aid to see whether a project is still on track. It can also serve a number of other purposes including providing an opportunity for additional work for the consultant and an opportunity to add to the information in the case study (see Section 13.4).

13.2   Post-project summary and review

The leading consulting firms recognise that their most profitable business comes from a loyal group of clients. This is because the cost of sales is lower than for new clients as less work and fewer meetings are needed to achieve a sale. This only works when the client is continually satisfied with the work done by the consulting company. The way to find this out is first for the consultants involved to complete a post-project summary and for an independent review of the project to be undertaken by a senior member of the consulting company. The latter usually involves a meeting with key members of the client company to discuss the project.

The post-project summary needs to include the following:

- The original aims and objectives of the project.
- The project charter.
- The time plan – predicted and actual.
- Key successes – what went well.
- Key issues – what did not go well or caused problems for the project.
- The end result, i.e. the final outcome of the project.

The project review should be in the form of an interview, as mentioned above. Key areas for discussion should be the overall capabilities of the consultants, where the consultants performed well and areas where they could have done better. Finally, there should be a conclusion as to how successful the project was in the end and whether the client was satisfied with the work and would use the consultants again. In this way, there should be an objective view as to how well the project was undertaken and an assurance that the client remains committed to the consulting company.

13.3   Follow-up projects and key client management

While some consulting business is gained through previous projects not being completed properly, this is a 'distress purchase' and not really beneficial for a long-term relationship with the client. It may also mean that the follow-up project is harder to undertake as a result, with greater resistance from the client. In short, this type of consulting work should really be kept to a minimum. Instead, consultants should 'build' on their previous work in a positive way, hopefully using the goodwill generated from the previous project.

Follow-up projects can be identified either by the consultants themselves, by the senior managers of the consulting firm or by the client. The key is to maintain momentum. There is little point conducting post-project reviews a year after a project has been completed as the client probably would have forgotten about it: it should be done as soon as possible. In addition, it would also be advisable for the same consultants to work on the follow-up to eliminate time and effort wasted on bringing new people 'up to speed'.

For the larger consulting firms, their preferred mode of operation is to have 'key clients'. These are large organisations that are regular users of consultants. Often the consultancies appoint senior managers to also be 'key client managers' for a particular company and their role is to ensure that there is a steady flow of business from their client. A key tool that they use for planning is the 'sales funnel' developed by Miller and Heiman. In order to keep a regular flow of projects, it is important to have potential and actual projects at every stage of the funnel (Figure 13.1).

As the likelihood of conversion increases as you move further down the funnel, the number of projects needed decreases. Similarly, as projects move through the funnel, it is vital to introduce new ones at the top to 'feed it'. Managing this funnel successfully is perhaps one of the hardest tasks for a professional consultant but failure to do so means an unstable business with a 'feast to famine' existence. Using the framework developed in Chapter 2, we can match the sales process against the sections of the funnel (Table 13.1)

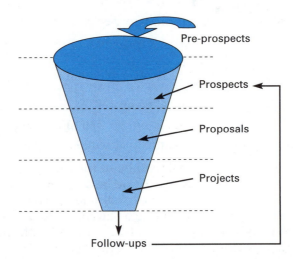

Figure 13.1 The sales funnel

Source: After Miller and Heiman, in Heiman, S.E., *et al.* (2004) *The New Strategic Selling*, London: Kogan Page.

Table 13.1 The project flow

Sales process		Funnel stage
Step 1	Identify potential targets	Pre-prospects
Step 2	Product offering	Pre-prospects
Step 3	Competitive review	Pre-prospects
Step 4	Promotion of services	Prospects
Step 5	Sales enquiries	Prospects
Step 6	Meeting potential clients	Prospects
Step 7	Project proposal	Proposal

13.4   Using consulting projects as case studies

One of the most important marketing tools for a consultant is past experience. Many new clients want the reassurance that the consultant has been involved in similar work. The best way for a consultant to demonstrate this is via case studies of previous consulting projects. They can be very brief, perhaps just a couple of lines such as 'helped a leading food and drink company with their international marketing strategy that doubled their exports'. However, for the case study to be most useful, the more information the better, although prospective clients do not want to read a huge tome! It is ideal if the information can fit comfortably on one side of A4.

However long you make the case study, there are some key elements that need to be included.

Description of client

Although the client may not usually be named for confidentiality reasons, you need to give a clear description including their line of business, their size and possibly their position in their marketplace. You also need to give a little bit of background as to why the client needed your expertise.

Objectives of the consulting project

These should be the key objectives that were defined at the start of the project and included in the proposal. However tempting it might be, do not change these to make the project look more successful as this is a public document.

Work undertaken

This should be brief bullet points giving the reader an indication of the work undertaken in order to complete the project. This is important as it demonstrates your capabilities in certain areas that may be relevant for a future client.

Achievements of the project

Wherever possible these should be tangible, i.e. relate to hard facts such as sales, profits, outputs, number of products remaining in the case of rationalisation. The figures given should be realistic, that is, reflecting the situation before the project started and a reasonable time after, as effects are not often immediate. Again, do not be overambitious with what this project has achieved and refer back to the original objectives.

13.5 Recognising the successes

If undertaken with enthusiasm and with the application of the approaches described in this book, a consulting exercise will provide a positive experience. Value will be created at several levels. It will be an opportunity to develop valuable and transferable skills. It will provide a chance to gain evidence of those skills. A high-level contribution will be made to the progression of a business venture. The consulting experience offers an insight into key senior management responsibilities: decision-making at a strategic level and influencing the course of the business.

A successful consulting exercise – indeed, any successful managerial experience – has three aspects. First is the *experience* itself – the actual activities engaged in. These will include elements of the three skill areas essential to effective consulting: analysis, project management and relationship building. Second is the *learning* that is gained as a result of that experience. This is best achieved through the experiential learning cycle: the application of ideas gained through analysis and then active reflection on the outcomes. Such learning is valuable because it is *transferable*. The third aspect of the exercise is the *evidence* that that learning has been used to create value and that it can be used to create new value in the future.

13.6 Success and transferable skills

The successes achieved in the consulting exercise will provide positive and motivating memories. Yet they have meaning beyond this. They are evidence of having developed valuable and transferable skills. Some experiences that will be of value in the future are as follows.

Objective definition

Managers are directed towards objectives. Objectives will be of value only if they are good ones. Indeed, bad objectives will lead the venture down the wrong path and reduce value. The consulting exercise will have provided practice in creating objectives that are relevant, well defined, achievable and signposted.

Problem analysis

Usually a business's managers will wish to see it grow. This presents a challenge. Businesses are limited by both external and internal factors. The external ones arise from market and competitive conditions. There is a ceiling on the economic value that can be created, given the business's assets. Internal limitations stem from the way in which managers use those assets. It is rare that a little more value cannot be squeezed out of them by working them harder. The things that limit a business will be recognised by managers as 'problems'. Yet problems do not present themselves. If they are to be managed, problems need to be highlighted, defined and rationalised.

Strategy development

A strategy is, at one level at least, just a way of using assets. In particular, a strategy is a way of creating value out of those assets. The development of an effective strategy is one of the great challenges of management. It demands consideration of the internal competencies of the business and the potential of the environment it is operating in.

Project planning

A strategy will create value only if it is put into practice through the right plans. Plans are recipes for action. The project leader or, better, its champion must drive plans. Planning has formal aspects that assist in resource allocation and budgetary management.

External relationship management

Firms prosper only if they can attract external resources. This demands that relationships be built with the external parties who control those resources: customers and investors. Clearly, the ability to manage such relationships is very valuable. A consulting project will be successful only if a good relationship is built and maintained with the client. It presents an opportunity to develop such skills and gain evidence of their possession.

Teamworking

When employers are asked what they consider to be the most essential managerial skill, the answer they give most often is the ability to work as part of a team. The growth in teamworking is one of the most prominent features in the development of management practice in recent times. Teamworking demands an ability both to integrate with and to motivate fellow team members.

Leadership

Leadership is perhaps the most precious managerial skill. It is certainly in demand and there are good rewards for managers who possess it. Leadership is a skill. It is not a fixed aspect of personality. Leadership is about behaviour: it is what leaders *do*. It can be learned. But like any valuable skill it takes practice. The consulting project offers an opportunity both to recognise your own leadership style and to put it into practice.

Any manager who can combine these skills is offering a great deal to any organisation he or she works for.

13.7   Recording successes on your CV and relating them in job interviews

The curriculum vitae (CV) is a particularly important piece of communication. It communicates you and what you have to offer to potential employers and clients. A CV should be thought of as an advertisement. It records your experience and achievements; but its *function* is to get you a job – or at least an interview. The important information to include is as follows.

Personal information

Include your name, age, date of birth, nationality, contact address(es), telephone number(s) and email address.

Education

Give details of formal qualifications (date, subject, grade, awarding institution).

Experience

Outline details of any employment undertaken. This should include the employer, the position and a brief summary of key responsibilities. Avoid verbosity. Use bullet points. This is also the place to refer to the consulting project.

Achievements

A potential employer is interested not so much in what you have done as in what you might do. Past achievements are evidence of what might be achieved in the future. Achievements should be documented in a positive manner. If possible, quantify the achievement. To illustrate, the following are examples of achievements of a consulting project that might be included:

Key achievements of the consulting project were:

- the development of a strategy which increased sales by 20 per cent;
- a plan which enabled the business to enter an international market worth over £100 million;
- an increase in productivity of 30 per cent;
- a sales brief that was instrumental in gaining new customers worth over £100,000.

Referees

A referee is someone who has experience of your work and who is willing to make a positive statement about it. A satisfied client makes a good referee. Include details of the person's title, name, position, employer and contact details.

13.8   Learning from failure

Not everything goes right. A consulting exercise is a complex experience. It presents a rich tapestry of intellectual and human engagements. Many experiences will be positive. But some, inevitably, will be negative. Mistakes and errors of judgement will be made. Information will be misinterpreted. Not all relationships will be good ones. Some people never seem to develop a rapport with each other. There will be disagreements between members of the team over objectives and courses of action. There may even be disagreements with the client.

Such experiences are part of managerial life. They cannot be avoided. But they can be managed. And they can be learned from. Errors that result from the misinterpretation of information or poor judgement present opportunities to challenge the conceptual models and frameworks being used. Some of these will be explicit. These are easy to revise. Others will be locked into the cognitive strategy being used. These must be reflected on and actively revealed. A good consultant is active in revealing his or her own cognitive approach and recognising how it might be developed.

Errors that result in misunderstandings and conflicts with other people must also be used as learning experiences (although they may be more painful than simple interpretive mistakes). Again the challenge is to analyse the experience and see what it says about how the person should be approached in the future and what it says about how people in general should be dealt with. Consider the message sent. How was it interpreted? How might it have been misinterpreted? Don't forget, a message has paralanguage aspects as well as a formal meaning. Also consider the other party's motivation. What did he or she want out of the situation? What did he or she get out of it? The key thing when interpreting a personal exchange is to avoid the temptation to allocate blame – either towards oneself or the other party. It doesn't help. Analyse dispassionately.

Team discussion points

1 For the consulting exercise that you have completed, do a post-project summary and a case study, interviewing the client if you can.

2 What career options have you considered? What skills are going to be valuable to success in these careers? How has the consulting experience given you an insight into these skills? What evidence of their possession have you gained? How might you document this in a CV?

Draft a CV and review each other's as a team.

 ## Summary of key ideas

- Handing over ownership of the project is a critical step. Recommendations should be motivational and action orientated.

- At the end of a project, it is important to do a post-project summary and review to learn from the experience yourself and to help you gain further business with the client.

- Follow-up projects can be a cost-effective means of gaining additional business.
- Management of regular clients is called 'key client management' and the use of a 'sales funnel' is a valuable tool to ensure continuity of business.
- A case study is also a useful tool for you to reflect on the project and use to gain new business.
- A consulting project is a great opportunity to gain things that will be valuable in your future career: managerial experience, active learning, achievements and evidence of achievements.
- Use the consulting experience to sell yourself: document (quantified) achievements on your CV.
- Not all experiences on the consulting exercise will be positive. Accept the negatives as a proper part of managerial life – but learn from them.

Key reading

Cope, M. (2003) *The Seven Cs of Consulting: The definitive guide to the consulting process.* Harlow, Essex: Prentice Hall (Chapters 8, 9 and 10).

Heiman, S.E., *et al.* (2004) *The New Strategic Selling.* London: Kogan Page (Chapters 17 and 18).

Further reading

Bright, J. (2005) *Brilliant CV: What Employers Want to See and How to Say It.* Harlow, Essex: Prentice Hall.

Colb, D.A. (1999) *A Learning Style Inventory: Technical Manual* (revised edn). Boston, MA: McBer & Co.

Eggert, M. (2003) *Perfect CV (Perfect).* London: Random House Business Books.

Jay, R. (2005) *Brilliant Interview: What Employers Want to Hear and How to Say It.* Harlow, Essex: Prentice Hall.

Markham, C. (2004) *The Top Consultant: Developing your skills for greater effectiveness.* London: Kogan Page.

Case exercise

Beta Venture Capital

Beta Venture Capital Partners were looking at an investment in a small technology company, GoFindNow Ltd (GFN) that had been started by the two directors three years ago. The company had grown fast and was now profitable, thanks mainly to its key product which helped Internet search engines work better. The directors of GFN had had several meetings with Beta and had explained the technology, but Beta were nervous in making an investment in something they felt they did not really understand.

So Beta decided to commission a commercial due diligence to help them assess GFN for investment and looked at three consulting companies whom they asked to make a proposal. Two of these, Alpha Consulting and McSlade, they had used before on other similar projects. The third was a new company, John Brown Associates, which had just recruited senior partners from both Alpha and McSlade. Each was asked to provide case studies of similar work in their proposal.

A couple of weeks later, the three proposals were received by Beta and its directors called a meeting to discuss them and make a decision to appoint one of the consulting firms. They examined each of the proposals and all were proposing to do similar work at a rate that was acceptable. The only difference in the firms were the case studies that they offered. Alpha had provided over twenty relating to other commercial due diligences they had completed but none were in the industry that GFN operated in. McSlade offered ten case studies and of these five were commercial due diligences in the software industry. John Brown gave only one but this was for a direct competitor to GFN.

Q1 If you were Beta, which of the companies would you choose and why?

Q2 What do you think are the advantages and disadvantages of breadth of experience versus depth of experience?

Q3 For each of the consulting companies, put together a case as to why Beta should choose them.

Robinson Mason case study: Part 4

In the following 18–24 months, Robinson Mason's European business continued to labour on. Within the RM corporation, the European business was seen as complex, failing, unable to reach its targets, with a director obsessed with balance sheet minutiae rather than strategy, and a cohort of maverick general managers primarily concerned with safeguarding their personal interests.

Some attempts were made at coordinating activity on a pan-European basis. The category director role previously carried out part-time by country general managers was assigned to full-time professional marketers with their own staff. They were expected to plan and coordinate category strategies across the continent, while the local country marketing director and his/her team were expected to input to the strategy development process and to implement what had been agreed. Yet because there was still considerable turnover in categories specific to particular countries, this local business had also to be coordinated effectively. Some progress, albeit grudging, was made in harmonisation of pack sizes and designs, but the initiative was left very much up to the individual category director. In a category where consumer demand was still far from satisfied, with a consequent need for innovation, mundane subjects such as range harmonisation took a back seat to the excitement of bringing new products to market. 'Those kids should be told to tidy up their bedrooms before playing with any more new toys,' commented one exasperated factory manager confronted with an inordinately long list of component SKUs.

In the area of customer management, the Ganymede team, which had developed a handbook for effective retail customer/category management, had done great work. It was launched to the European sales managers who took to it as a useful, unthreatening tool that would assist them in their dealings with the trade. Its implementation, however, was hampered by the excitable and idiosyncratic behaviour of the new European sales director, who could not appreciate that his role was to support the RM sales teams rather than to negotiate with trade partners. The European regional director also came to the conclusion that having a dozen country general managers reporting to him direct was somewhat inefficient. As a result he reorganised the reporting structure into four regional groupings, the heads of which would report to him; their former general manger colleagues retained their positions, but would in future report to the head of grouping. Some saw this as a slight.

But many of the key recommendations of Ganymede were lost or ignored. Very firm recommendations had been given over portfolio strategy and prioritisation, but no action was taken. A very well considered approach to innovation had been developed, and subsequently sidelined. A brand management handbook had been created, but was not used. A blueprint for a streamlined organisation had been outlined, but rejected as too radical. A means of overhauling the strategic planning and budgetary processes so that 'tough decisions are taken early' was compromised by operating units' insistence on protecting their particular vested interests and controlling their own financial numbers. In general, the regional director appeared to believe that consensus rather than radical change or even confrontation was the best route forward, and he appointed additional HQ staff to manage the complexity of the organisation, rather than to attack it.

One of the more positive aspects of Ganymede was with the supply chain. Perhaps because the previous regional director had been able to take the tough decisions, close down some factories, and move production to centralised locations before Ganymede had started, the team were more able to address refinements of implementation. Thus a first-class planning, sourcing and logistics function run by genuine experts was able to operate, leading to considerable improvement in customer service and satisfaction. By contrast, implementation of the integrated software system was something of a disaster. Despite RM having some highly competent business analysts and IS experts, the system itself was unfriendly and unwieldy. Go-live deadlines were not met, costs overran, and service suffered. It was nearly six months before a country general manager could log in and see the previous day's sales performance – something previously taken for granted. Similarly, credit control was hampered by the inability of the finance director to have ready sight of aged debt reports. Operatives learned to manage despite the system, rather than because of it, and a 'blame the consultant' attitude developed. By implication Ganymede was seen as an expensive failure.

Yet despite the regional director's laudable attempt to manage the complexity of his organisation, the same dilemma remained. The products offered to the consuming public were tired, unexciting, without significant innovation and badly under-supported. So much cost was still taken up by the complex organisational structure that it was not possible to communicate a motivating consumer value proposition for the various brands to anything approaching a competitive level. Share therefore continued to be eroded, sales targets proved illusory, trade partners and competitors continued to take advantage and the business suffered.

By this time much of the same malaise affected the RM organisation as a whole. Profit warnings were given, the Chief Executive resigned, the share price crashed, and Robinson Mason was saved from oblivion by a very convenient reverse takeover by Wessel GmbH, a company with a quite different and much more determined management style.

Discussion questions

1 Critically appraise the leadership style of the European regional director.

2 What is your assessment of the Ganymede programme and the roles played by the various parties involved?

3 If you were one of the change management consultants, required to deliver a review of Ganymede in order to pitch for business from other clients, what points would you make?

4 If you were the CEO of Wessel GmbH, what actions would you take to address the complexity and poor sales performance of the Robinson Mason European business?

Consulting as a career

The learning outcomes from this chapter are to:

■ appreciate the structure and dynamics of the global consulting industry today;

■ know who are the key players in the consulting world;

■ understand the common career structures in consulting companies;

■ gain an insight into becoming a consultant;

■ recognise the opportunity to develop an internal consultant managerial style;

■ understand the value consultancy skills offer for non-consulting jobs.

14.1 The consulting industry today

The consulting industry is large. Just how large depends on definitions of what is or is not a consultancy project. Most definitions would include the following: information technology (IT) consulting and system integration, corporate strategy, operations management, human resources management and outsourcing. In Europe, the split of business between these sectors in 2004 is outlined in Table 14.1. In addition, some estimates also include *business advisory services* that include all mergers and acquisitions and public flotations work done by accountants, merchant banks and other financial institutions. Revenue from these services worldwide was estimated to be $63 billion in 2005 and is set to rise to an estimated $85 billion by 2008 (*source*: Kennedy Information, Business Advisory Services: *Delivering Financial and Business Consulting Capabilities Report 2006*).

It is estimated that $255 billion was spent globally on consultancy in 2005 (including business advisory services) and that this is set to grow at an annual rate of just under 8 per cent to 2009 (*source*: Kennedy Information, *The Global Consulting Marketplace 2006*). The market had been very buoyant until 2001, growing in excess of 10 per cent per annum. However, in 2002, for the first time in three decades, the market *fell* by 6 per cent (*source*: Kennedy Information, *The Global Consulting Marketplace 2003*) due to a tougher IT market and an increased scepticism

Table 14.1 The consulting industry's share of business in Europe, 2004

Type of consulting	% share of business
IT consulting/system integration	26
Operations management	27
Corporate strategy	17
Outsourcing	19
Human resources management	11

Source: http://feaco.mayflowerserver.de/images/downloads/Anlagen/FeacoSurvey_2004_FINAL.pdf, p. 5 (consulted 21 August 2007).

among consultancy buyers following the Enron/Andersen scandals. The net result was a reduction in the number of consultants employed (an estimated 15 per cent of consultants left the profession in 2002) and also a reduction in the average fee rate. This proved to be a short-term setback as the industry continued to grow after a flat year in 2003 due to three main factors. The first was the increase in core demand from 'laggard' industries as trends such as globalisation and information technology increased the complexity and competitiveness of the environments in which businesses operated. Managers recognised the importance of knowledge rather than simply products or price as a basis for competing. Businesses now wanted to stick to their core expertise and so they wanted to bring in specialists to manage non-core activities when they are needed. The continued strong growth in outsourcing is a testament to this (see Section 2.3).

The second factor was the continued demand for IT spending as the use of technology became more critical to effective modern businesses. The Internet has a major impact on the way many established industries operate. For example, the airline industry, spurred on by the low-cost carriers, has used e-ticketing to significantly drive down operating costs. The third factor in the growth of consulting has been the increasing demand from governmental and associated organisations (see Section 2.4). In recent years the boundary between the private sector and the state has been pushed back and become blurred. This is a worldwide phenomenon. Increasingly, it is accepted that government has a role only where the market cannot operate but would still like to exercise some degree of influence. As a result, government departments are outsourcing work and offering tenders to private firms for capital projects.

The outlook for the consulting market looks very promising, not only due to the demand for business advisory services but the other sectors will also show growth due to the following trends (*source*: Kennedy Information, *The Global Consulting Marketplace 2006*):

- **Strategy** – 'classic' strategy work is in vogue again, driven in part to the increase in mergers and acquisitions.

- **Operations management** – demand continues for standard OM to improve efficiency, with projects focusing on the two ends of the chain, i.e. research and development, and customer relationship management.

- **Human resources** – demand for benefits consulting is slowly increasing, as is services for talent management but this sector remains the slowest in growth terms.

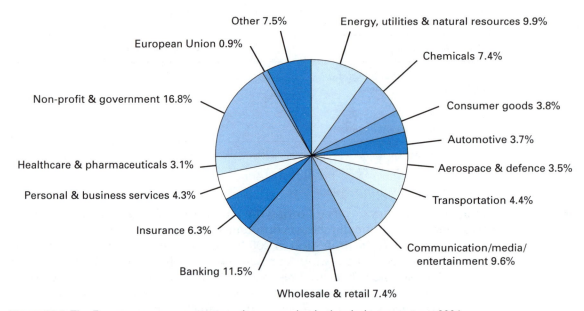

Figure 14.1 The European management consultancy market by key industry sectors, 2004

Source: http://feaco.mayflowerserver.de/images/downloads/Anlagen/FeacoSurvey_2004_FINAL.pdf. Figure 6, p. 10 (consulted 21 August 2007).

- **IT** – general improvement in business environment has led to more spending on IT projects.
- **Business advisory services** – changes in company law in 2002, when there had to be a division between auditors and business advisers and further regulations, has provided the growth in this sector. This, coupled with increased merger and acquisition activity, will continue to provide opportunities for consultants.

All types of business call on the services of consultants. Figure 14.1 gives details of the breakdown of consultancy sales into key industry sectors in Europe for 2004.

The sectors showing the significant growth in the last few years are: non-profit and government (for reasons, see above); personal and business services, which reflects the growth in the leisure and 'do it for me' sectors; banking, where consolidation and increased competition has driven a search for improved processes; and transportation, due again to the booming leisure industry. The areas of consulting experiencing negative growth are the European Union, due to pressure on budgets; aerospace and defence, as demand for military spending declines; and the wholesale and retail sectors, which are experiencing tough conditions due to competition, particularly from the Internet players.

14.2 Key players in the consulting world

The consulting industry has a relatively low concentration. It is fragmented and includes a number of sectors. In general, the trend is for players to be large with a global reach or small and offering a specialised service. The main types of consultant firm are as follows.

IT firms

As the cost of their traditional products (hardware and software) become more competitive and profits are driven down, the IT companies have increasingly looked towards consulting as a means of increasing revenue. At first, they tried to achieve this organically but often did not have the credibility or the critical mass. So the recent trend has been to buy consulting businesses, particularly those from the accounting firms, for example IBM's purchase of PWC Consulting. However, the sale of AT Kearney by the company EDS to its management team in January 2006 may indicate that the fit between mainstream consulting and IT consulting may not have been that profitable. Table 14.2 gives the main IT firms that have significant consulting operations.

Accountancy firms offering consultancy

There has been a major change here following Andersen's woes. In response to criticisms, many of the accountancy firms have sold off their mainstream consulting operations either to the management or to other consultancies (particularly IT). 'Consulting services' are still offered but they tend to have a narrow focus around financial and transaction (mergers and acquisitions) services. These, though, are becoming quite a significant part of their business. For instance, the advisory services of PriceWaterhouseCoopers earned revenues of $4.38 billion in the year to 30 June 2006, 21 per cent of their total revenues (*source*: Company report 2006). It was also their fastest growing segment, increasing by nearly 20 per cent on the previous year (*source*: ibid).

Major consulting-only firms

These are large firms with a global reach. Their core business has always been in consulting and they offer a wide range of services. Table 14.3 gives the most recent revenues and the number of consultants they employ. These firms account for nearly 22 per cent of all revenues earned by consultants (excluding business advisory services).

Small specialist 'boutiques'

These are firms which are (relatively) small and which offer a specialist service in, for example, human resources consulting or strategy development. They have

Table 14.2 IT firms with large consulting operations

Company	Consulting firm acquired	2005 consulting revenues	% total business
IBM	PWC Consulting	$14.19bn	15%
CSC	Numerous small companies	$7.59bn*	52%
Cap Gemini	Ernst & Young Consulting	$1.11bn	13%
Atos Origin	KPMG Consulting	$0.98bn	14%

Note: * All IT and professional services revenues.
Source: Company reports.

Table 14.3 Number of employees and revenues in major consulting firms

Company	No. of employees	Revenue	Period
Accenture	140,000	$18bn	Yr to 31 August 2006
Deloitte Consulting	33,000	$7.8bn	Yr to May 2005
Mercer Consulting	18,900	$3.8bn	2005
Booz-Allen & Hamilton	17,000	$3bn (est)	2005
Altran Technologies*	16,150	$1.7bn	2005
McKinsey	12,900	$3.8bn (est)	2005
Boston Consulting	5,500	$1.5bn (est)	2005
Bain & Company	3,200	$1.1bn	2005
PA Consulting	3,000	$0.6bn	2004
ATKearney	2,500	$0.8bn	2005

Note: * Acquired Arthur D. Little in 2002.
Source: Company reports and www.hoovers.com (consulted 4 December 2006).

remained niche players in order to capitalise on their reputation in the area. Some important players in the strategic consultancy area are OC&C Strategy Consultants, LEK Consulting, Roland Berger and Spectrum Strategy Consultants.

'Gurus' and independents

'Gurus' are academics who have created a name for themselves by researching and developing ideas on how business might be approached. The term guru is taken from Sanskrit, the language of ancient India. It refers to a religious teacher. Gurus often promulgate their ideas through popular books. They may combine active consulting with teaching and seminar work. Well-known and influential management gurus include Tom Peters in the USA, Charles Handy in the UK and Kenichi Ohmae in Japan.

Many individuals run their own consulting services as sole traders, as small limited companies or together as partnerships. Independent consultants offer a range of services, often quite specialised. Professional bodies such as the Chartered Institute of Marketing and the Institute of Human Resource Management in the UK often support them. These bodies offer professional training and accreditation and provide a forum for all-important networking.

A number of leading consultancy firms issue magazines or journals (see Table 14.4). These provide a medium for communicating new ideas on themes in management

Table 14.4 Journals produced by leading consultancy firms

Journal	Consultancy
McKinsey Quarterly	McKinsey & Co.
Strategy & Business	Booz-Allen & Hamilton
Executive Agenda	A.T. Kearney
Mercer Management Journal	Mercer Consulting Group
Outlook	Accenture
Perspectives	Boston Consulting Group
Best of Bain	Bain & Company

Table 14.5 Major consultancies' Internet websites

Consultancy	Website
A.T. Kearney	atkearney.com
Accenture	accenture.com
Arthur D. Little (Altran)	adlittle.com
Atos Origin	atosorigin.com
Bain & Company	bain.com
Booz-Allen & Hamilton	boozallen.com
Boston Consulting Group	bcg.com
Cap Gemini	capgemini.com
Deloitte Consulting	deloitte.com
IBM Business Consulting Services	ibm.com
LEK Consulting	lek.com
LogicaCMG	logicacmg.com
McKinsey & Co.	mckinsey.com
Mercer Consulting Group	mercermc.com
OC&C Strategy Consultants	occstrategy.com
Roland Berger Strategy Consultants	rolandberger.com
PA Consulting	paconsulting.com
Spectrum Strategy Consultants	spectrumstrategy.com

and are promotional devices. They are often available via the Internet and are worth reviewing, both to keep track of development in management thinking and as a good source of information on individual consultancies, particularly their specialisms and style of working. All major consultancy firms now have informative pages on the Internet. A list of websites is given in Table 14.5.

14.3 Career structure in consulting firms

All management consultancies organise themselves in their own way. But they can be quite hierarchical in their structures, especially the larger firms. This provides a definite ladder for gaining experience, building expertise and developing a career. In practice, teams that cut across levels of responsibility undertake most consulting projects. Being team based, most consultancies operate with a professional, informal culture. Job titles vary, but some of the common roles (in ascending order of seniority) include the following.

Analysts

Analysts are responsible for gathering information and processing it for the consulting team. They would probably have little contact with the client, until they gained more business experience. While they would be placed within an industry (e.g. consumer goods) or practice group (e.g. strategy), they would not be expected to have detailed knowledge of either. Most graduates would start here straight from university or business school. Only the large firms offer these positions.

Consultants

Consultants undertake the evaluation of the client business and make recommendations on its behalf. They have the most direct contact with the client and would increasingly be given more exposure to the management of consulting projects as they become more experienced. It is at this point that they would start to specialise in a particular area to build up expertise. These are either analysts who have been promoted after a couple of years or those who have been in industry and have moved to consulting as a career change.

Senior consultants or managers

More experienced consultants have responsibility for leading a consulting team undertaking a project on behalf of a client. In addition they would be expected to have in-depth knowledge of their specialist area, be it an industry or a practice. They would typically have 3–5 years of consulting experience and have already demonstrated their ability to take on the responsibility of running small consulting projects. They would also be more involved in dealing with members of the client team and building key relationships to gain repeat business.

Business development managers

Business development managers within the consulting business are responsible for developing the firm's products and building its relationship with clients. They will also be involved in some large, complex consulting projects at a strategic level. Most at this level would have 5–10 years of consulting experience.

Directors (or partners)

Directors (or partners if a private firm) are the most experienced consultants, who take on responsibility for the development of the organisation as a whole and who lead its strategic development. They will also maintain contacts with senior personnel in the client companies and will have overall responsibility for projects. As the most senior in the organisation, it would be expected that they would have 10+ years of experience in this field.

14.4 Becoming a consultant

As has been discussed above, new graduates can join the larger consulting companies as an analyst straightaway. Otherwise the normal entry into consulting is after a period working in 'client companies'. Many join after completing an MBA from one of the prestigious business schools such as Harvard or Insead that require candidates to have at least five years' working experience. Both routes have their merits and any individual needs to think carefully about the route they follow that would be best suited to them and the area in which they want to have a career. If one wants to be a 'career consultant', then starting as an analyst makes the most sense. If, however, the long-term goal is to use a period as a consultant to hone general business skills, then an individual may be better to start as a graduate in industry, possibly complete an MBA, then apply to be a consultant.

Whatever route is followed, some key questions need to be addressed before a candidate identifies which consulting firms they will apply to:

1 Does the firm offer positions at the level that is appropriate to me?

2 Is their area of consulting of interest to me?

3 Do I have the right skills (and experience) for this firm?

4 What is the balance of work at office versus on client site (an indication of how much one would travel)?

5 What is the experience of previous new employees (i.e. does this sound like a firm I would like to work for)?

6 What is the remunerations package – not only salary but other perks such as pension, private healthcare, car allowance and holiday entitlement?

7 What is their training programme?

In the previous chapter, we discussed putting together a good CV, which is vital. However, a lot of consulting firms also use the 'case question' technique as a means of recruitment. This is in addition to the normal questions about a CV that candidates normally face and typically it can be over half the time spent at the interview. The types and examples of case questions are detailed in Biswas and Twitchell's book *Management Consulting: A Complete Guide to the Industry*. They have defined 10 broad types, together with examples, which are given below:

- **Brain teaser** – Why are manhole covers round?
- **Business strategy** – Should a food retailer offer other services, such as insurance?
- **Human resource management** – What should banks do with their counter staff as ATM networks expand?
- **Market entry** – How should a gourmet coffee chain locate its stores?
- **Market sizing** – How many people surf the web in a single weekday?
- **Mergers and acquisitions** – Should a gin distillery buy a beer company or a snack company?
- **New product introduction** – Should a food company offer olives with stones, or without?
- **Opportunity assessment** – Should a soda bottler backward integrate into the manufacturing of syrup?
- **Pricing** – How does the post office price a first-class stamp?
- **Profitability loss** – A pharmaceutical company is losing money; what should it do?

From the above, we can see that the question can be varied and it is important not to think that there is a 'right' answer. Instead the interviewer is trying to establish how good are your consulting skills in tackling the question. So they will be looking for good analytical, project management and relationship skills of the type that have been detailed in this book. As with all things, practice here is key and the more of these 'case questions' you tackle, the better you will be at doing them. Biswas and Twitchell have a good section on examples for a candidate to work through, including some sample answers. Another good source of information is the website vault.com (there are separate sites for Europe and Asia via links on the home page).

14.5 The internal consultant

The changes that are driving the demand for consultancy services are also changing the way in which internal managers work. The old way in which businesses operated, with fixed structures defining hierarchies in which people worked, are no longer appropriate. In today's fast-changing and unpredictable environments businesses need to be flexible and responsive to developing customer needs. Old structures must be flattened. Multifunctional teams with open membership must replace monolithic closed departments. Managers must forget about the jobs they are *supposed* to do and look towards the tasks they *must* do in order to make their businesses more competitive. Today's manager cannot simply look to a historical (and therefore out-of-date) job description. William Bridges has suggested in his book *Jobshift* (1995) that managers must learn to thrive in a workplace without jobs, or at least jobs as they were understood. This presents both an opportunity and a challenge. The strategies and skills of the effective consultant allow those challenges to be met and those opportunities to be exploited. The internal consultant is simply a manager who develops the role and approach of a consultant while employed in a permanent capacity. Some managers have always taken advantage of this opportunity, whatever their official job title. Many organisations now recognise the role, though. The following characterises the approach of the internal consultant.

Awareness of the resources needed by the organisation

All organisations need external resources if they are to survive and prosper. These include the goodwill (and hence spending) of customers, investors' valuable capital, the support of suppliers and distributors, human expertise and information. As discussed in Chapter 1, attracting these resources is the way in which the consultant creates value for the client. The internal consultant is as keenly aware as the external consultant of the resources he or she is obtaining for the organisation, the value of those resources and the management of the relationships critical to obtaining them.

Constant redefinition of job

No two consulting projects are the same. The role of the consultant changes with the challenges he or she meets. For the internal consultant, the job he or she does undergoes constant evolution. This means a constant redefinition of role, responsibilities and relationships, both internal and external. External relationships are managed to maintain resource flows; internal ones so that the whole organisation recognises the developing role.

Demand for change

Change is not always easy. But it is easy to resist. A different future offers uncertainty. To seek solace in what is known is a natural reaction. Yet change is a necessary facet of organisational life. The environment changes, competitors change, and the business must change in response. The internal consultant will not only accept change positively, he or she will actively demand it. Indeed, the internal consultant will be in the vanguard leading that change. This is not to say that change for change's sake is good, but that well-thought-out and well-managed relevant change is.

Constant development of skill profile

Active learning demands that skills are seen not as something we have but as something we are in the process of gaining. Internal consultants must evaluate the skill demands of the tasks they face, assess personal competencies, identify any skill gaps and source a means of developing those skills.

Intrapreneurial planning

All managers create change. Entrepreneurs are managers who drive *significant* change. An *intrapreneur* is simply a manager who behaves entrepreneurially within an established firm. The intrapreneur is a manager who leads the organisation so that it can change to exploit significant new opportunities. Effective entrepreneurship demands planning. An opportunity must be identified and its value evaluated. A strategy to exploit that opportunity must be devised. That strategy must be put into effect. It is in this area perhaps above all others that the internal consultant comes into his or her own.

14.6   The value of the consulting experience in non-consulting careers

This book describes a set of skills that makes consulting effective and is the basis for success as a consultant. These skills are not exclusive to consulting: they are general management skills. An ability to use information and analyse it, to identify valuable options, to make plans that use resources efficiently to exploit those options and to build relationships so that people follow skills that will make any managerial career successful. This will be so in technical, specialist or general management roles. The skills of the consultant will be particularly evident when leadership and teamworking are called for. It is for this reason that successful consultants frequently move into high-profile permanent managerial positions, often on the invitation of satisfied clients.

Team discussion points

1   Each person in the group should seek out one or more of the websites of the major consultancies. Imagine that you have been taken on to undertake a recruitment drive for that firm at the analyst and consultant level. What would you look for in prospective candidates? Give a short presentation (of five minutes with two overheads) of your findings to the rest of the group. Give them a one-page summary advising them how to approach that firm to discuss career prospects.

2   Taking one of the case questions outlined in Section 14.4, work in a team to come up with a solution, not forgetting to use the key skills required of a consultant.

Summary of key ideas

- Consultancy is a large and evolving sector.
- The growth drivers are set to continue, albeit at a slower level than seen previously.
- Becoming a consultant can take place at any stage in one's career but the key consulting skills need to be demonstrated in successful interviews.
- Changes in established organisations mean that the internal consultant will have an ever more important managerial role.
- Consultancy skills are general management skills. A person with consulting skills can look forward to success in a wide variety of roles and organisations.
- Consultancy skills will be of increasing relevance to managers in not-for-profit organisations.

Good luck in developing a successful consulting career, whomever you work for!

Key reading

Biswas, S. and Twitchell, D. (2002) *Management Consulting: A Complete Guide to the Industry*. New York: John Wiley and Sons (Chapters 5, 7 and Appendices).

Fombrun, C.J. and Nevins, M.D. (2003) *The Advice Business: Essential Tools and Models for Management Consulting*. Upper Saddle River, NJ: Pearson Prentice Hall (Chapters 1, 25, 27 and 28).

Further reading

Armbruester, T. and Kipping, M. (2001) 'Strategic change in top management consulting: Market evolution and current challenges in a knowledge-based perspective', *Academy of Management Proceedings*, A1–A16.

Bellman, G. (2001) *The Consultant Calling*. Chichester, West Sussex: Jossey-Bass Wiley.

Bridges, W. (1995) *Jobshift: How to Prosper in a Workplace Without Jobs*. London: Nicholas Brealey.

Cosetino, M.P. (2005) *Case in Point: Complete Case Interview Preparation* (4th edn). Needham, MA: Burgee Press.

Harris, C. (2005) *Consult Yourself: The NLP Guide to Being a Management Consultant*. Carmarthen, Dyfed: Crown House Publishing.

IMC (2006) *The Inside Careers Guide to Management Consultants 06/07*. London: Cambridge Market Intelligence Limited.

Nippa, M.C. and Petzold, K. (2002) 'Economic functions of management consulting firms – An integrative theoretical framework', *Academy of Management Proceedings*, B1–B16.

Vieira, W.E. (1995) 'Management consulting in the 21st century', *Journal of Management Consulting*, 8 (4), 2–3.

Case exercise

AB Consulting

AB Consulting is a successful firm founded 10 years ago that has grown into a medium-sized operation with 1,000 employees. The directors of ABC now feel that it is the right time to start recruiting new graduates to fill the post of analysts. Hitherto they had only recruited experienced business people either from other consulting firms or from industry. They intend to offer five posts this year and, if successful, they will start an active recruiting programme at the leading universities the following year. The directors have decided to adopt the common practice of using 'case questions' to try to get the best candidates. One key question on business strategy is to be asked to all interviewees: 'How does a medium-sized consulting firm like ABC become one of the leading players, competing with the likes of McKinsey and Accenture?'

They have looked at the CVs of all those who have applied and have narrowed down the list to 25 whom they invite for an interview. All the candidates are able to answer questions about their CV well but when it comes to the key case question, the results are as follows:

■ All of the candidates saw the growth of the firm merely as an exercise in increasing the number of consultants.

■ The majority of ABC's business comes from the UK and Northern Europe which only three of the prospective employees noticed but did not see as an issue.

■ Five of the candidates did recognise that ABC was known primarily for its consulting work in the public sector but did not factor this in when making their recommendations.

The Directors have therefore been unable to make a definite decision on which of the candidates, if any, they wish to appoint. They decide to invite back ten of the most promising interviewees for a further session and this time they want to get it right.

Q1 If you were the directors of ABC, how would you approach this second interview?

Q2 If you were the interviewees, what would you do to prepare for the second time?

Q3 Given the case question above, what facts do you think are important in determining your answer?

Example of a consulting report: Supergelato Ice Cream Ltd

Background

Supergelato Ice Cream Ltd ('SIC Ltd') has been making premium quality ice creams for over 50 years from their base in Leeds, West Yorkshire. Started by the father of the current managing director, Tony Bellagio, this is a small, privately owned business. Tony, together with five other members of his family, own and run the total operation including manufacture, distribution, sales and marketing. From their base, they supply catering establishments such as cafes and restaurants and small retail outlets throughout West Yorkshire. They also own and operate an ice cream parlour in Leeds city centre where new products are trialled.

Their brand 'Supergelato' is well known and regarded in their home area but has little presence outside West Yorkshire. The firm's sales and profits are around £30 million and £5 million respectively but Tony has ambitious plans to increase sales to £100 million and profits to £20 million in three years' time. To do this, he needs to significantly expand his operation without sacrificing the quality of the product. He also believes that the growth can come organically, rather than buying other operations. Tony has called you in to advise on how he may achieve his plans for growth; specifically, he requires a detailed marketing plan from you.

Marketing plan

Executive summary

SIC Ltd's strategic aim is to be the leading premium ice cream manufacturer in the North of England with sales of £100m and profits of £20m by 2010.

- The market for premium products is very strong and SIC Ltd is well placed to take advantage of this.
- The product range needs to be rationalised and costs reduced to achieve profit targets.
- The pricing policy needs to be reviewed and a premium maintained to competitors.

- A new promotional strategy should be implemented for both catering and retail customers and direct consumers.
- A revised distribution strategy needs to include larger retail outlets and catering establishments outside West Yorkshire.

Market review and potential

The market for premium products is very strong and SIC Ltd is well placed to take advantage of this.

- The market for premium ice creams is growing by 20 per cent per annum in the UK versus 5 per cent for standard ice creams.
- This is an 'adult' market where unit prices and margins are higher than the general market which is aimed at children.
- Although an 'indulgence' product, consumers still want to know what the product contains and SIC Ltd's products are known for being additive-free.
- There are few niche upmarket businesses producing ice cream in the North and so SIC Ltd can create a position of being a leading 'local' supplier using local ingredients, which is increasingly popular with discerning consumers.
- This is a highly seasonal product with large, rapid fluctuations in demand but SIC Ltd's flexible production can take advantage of this.

Product strategy

The product range needs to be rationalised and costs reduced to achieve profit targets.

- SIC Ltd currently produce over 100 different flavours of ice cream and around 50 different flavours of sorbet; however, 80 per cent of their sales and 90 per cent of their profits come from 20 products.
- Further analysis reveals that the catering customers tend to only order the basic five flavours on a regular basis and only in the key summer months of July and August will they order any others.
- Retail outlets will only take a maximum of four lines excluding vanilla at any one time but these need to change to encourage repeat purchase.
- Production is mainly done in small batches, so the cost of producing lots of different flavours currently is not a problem but will be when production is tripled.
- Therefore, it is recommended to reduce the ongoing product range to around 10 lines and produce in larger batches to reduce costs: 'special' products will be produced but at a higher price.

Pricing strategy

The pricing policy needs to be reviewed and a premium maintained to competitors.

- The price to the catering or retail customer is currently the same irrespective of the quantity ordered: there needs to be a reward for customers ordering in larger quantities.

- Following on from the product review, only the 'standard' products will be on the price list; any 'special orders' will be quoted separately and attract at least a 10 per cent premium.
- Pricing to the national supermarkets should reflect their buying power but should not be detrimental to the overall profit target.
- The recommended retail price should be between 10 per cent and 20 per cent above the competitors to reinforce the premium nature of the product.

Promotional strategy

A new promotional strategy should be implemented for both catering and retail customers and direct consumers.

- With the expansion of the distribution base, the product needs to be promoted directly to the end consumer for the first time to ensure the product sells.
- The brand 'Supergelato' is recognised for its almost hand-made quality and this will be the main message to the consumers.
- Advertising will be as targeted as possible, using region-specific media and point of sale material.
- Following the successful trial with a current catering customer, boards will be offered to customers promoting Supergelato outside their establishments.

Distribution strategy

A revised distribution strategy needs to include larger retail outlets and catering establishments outside West Yorkshire.

- Given the retail strength of the large supermarkets, an approach needs to be made to get Supergelato stocked in their premium Northern stores.
- The other retail chains in the North that are currently not customers will also be targeted as long as they can offer a minimum purchase to ensure deliveries are as efficient as possible.
- Currently the Bellagio family sell and distribute the product themselves; in the future they need outside support to do this, so they can concentrate on manufacture and marketing.
- The proposal is to recruit a salesperson whose remuneration is largely commission based to ensure the maximum possible sales.
- Distribution of the product should be outsourced to a specialist contractor covering the North of England.

Index